PETER KUPER: CONVERSATIONS

Conversations with Comic Artists
M. Thomas Inge, General Editor

Peter Kuper: Conversations

Edited by Kent Worcester

University Press of Mississippi • Jackson

www.upress.state.ms.us

The University Press of Mississippi is a member of the Association of American
    University Presses.

First printing 2016
∞
Library of Congress Cataloging-in-Publication Data

Names: Kuper, Peter, 1958– interviewee. | Worcester, Kent, 1959– editor.
Title: Peter Kuper : conversations / edited by Kent Worcester.
Description: Jackson : University Press of Mississippi, 2016. | Series:
    Conversations with comic artists | Includes index.
Identifiers: LCCN 2016007470 | ISBN 9781496808370 (cloth : alk. paper)
Subjects: LCSH: Kuper, Peter, 1958––Interviews. | Cartoonists—United
    States—Interviews.
Classification: LCC PN6727.K85 Z46 2016 | DDC 741.5/973—dc23 LC record avail-
    able at http://lccn.loc.gov/2016007470

British Library Cataloging-in-Publication Data available

Books by Peter Kuper

Stations of the Nightmare. New York: Tor, 1982. Illustrations for a story by Philip José Farmer.

The Last Cat Book (with Robert E. Howard). New York: Dodd Mead, 1984.

New York, New York. Seattle: Fantagraphics, 1987.

It's Only a Matter of Life and Death. Seattle: Fantagraphics, 1988.

World War 3 Illustrated: 1980-1989 (coedited with Seth Tobocman). Seattle: Fantagraphics, 1989.

The Jungle (an adaptation of Upton Sinclair's novel). Evanston: First/Classics Illustrated, 1991. Hardcover reissue by NBM in 2004; reissued by Papercutz in 2010. French, Italian, and Spanish editions follow.

ComicsTrips: A Journal of Travels through Africa and Southeast Asia. Northampton, MA: Tundra, 1992.

Stripped, An Unauthorized Autobiography. Seattle: Fantagraphics, 1995.

Give it Up! New York: NBM, 1995. French, German, Italian, Spanish, and Swedish-language editions follow.

World War 3: Confrontational Comics (coedited with Scott Cunningham, Sabrina Jones, and Seth Tobocman). New York: Four Walls/Eight Windows, 1995.

Eye of the Beholder: A Collection of Visual Puzzles. New York: NBM, 1996. *Ponts du vue*, a French-language edition, was published by Cá et Lá in 2005.

The System. New York: DC/Vertigo, 1997. French, Greek, Italian, and Spanish-language editions follow. Reissued in hardcover by PM Press in 2014.

Mind's Eye. New York: NBM, 2000.

Topsy Turvy. New York: Eye Press, 2000. Distributed by Top Shelf.

Speechless. Marietta, GA: Top Shelf, 2001.

The Metamorphosis. New York: Crown, 2003. Czech, French, Hebrew, Italian, Portuguese, Spanish, and Turkish-language editions follow.

Sticks and Stones. New York: Three Rivers Press, 2004.

Theo and the Blue Note. New York: Viking, 2006. *Teo Y la Nota Azul*, a Spanish-language edition, is published by Sexto Piso in 2012.

Spy vs. Spy 2: The Joke and Dagger Files. New York: Watson-Guptill Publications, 2007.

Stop Forgetting to Remember: The Autobiography of Walter Kurtz. New York: Crown, 2007. French and Spanish-language editions follow.

Diario De Oaxaca: A Sketchbook Journal of Two Years in Mexico. USA and Mexico/Spain: PM Press/Sexto Piso, 2009. *Journal de Oaxaca*, a French-language edition, was published by Rackham in 2011.

A Través del Esperjo y lo que Alicia Encontro alli (illustrated Spanish-language edition of *Alice Through the Looking-Glass and What She Found There*). Madrid: Sexto Piso, 2010.

MAD Presents: Spy vs. Spy—The Top Secret Files! New York: MAD, 2011.

Drawn to New York: An Illustrated Chronicle of Three Decades in New York City. Oakland, CA: PM Press, 2013. A Spanish-language edition, *Diario de Nueva York*, was published by Sexto Piso in 2011; a French-language edition, *Les Carnets d'un New-Yorkais*, was published by Cá et Lá in 2012.

Self-Evident. New York: Eye Press, 2012.

Spy vs. Spy: Fight to the Finish! New York: MAD, 2013. A Spanish-language edition, *¡Pelea Hasta El Final!*, is published in Mexico City by Televisa in 2015.

Tercer Oje (an all-new, Spanish-language Eye of the Beholder collection). Colombia: Editorial Robot, 2013.

World War 3 Illustrated: 1979–2014 (coedited with Seth Tobocman). Oakland, CA: PM Press, 2014.

Ruins. London: SelfMadeHero, 2015. A French-language edition, *Ruines*, is published by Cá et Lá, and a Spanish-language edition, *Ruinas*, is published by Sexto Piso.

CONTENTS

INTRODUCTION

Peter Kuper is one of the country's leading cartoonists. A New York City-based illustrator, artist, editor, and educator, Kuper is the first cartoonist to have published an ongoing comic strip in the *New York Times*. His artwork has graced the covers of *Time*, *Newsweek*, *Business Week*, the *Village Voice*, the *Nation*, and the *Progressive*, among many others. His illustrations and comics have appeared in *Mother Jones*, *Details*, *Rolling Stone*, *Harper's*, *Esquire*, the *New Yorker*, *Heavy Metal*, and virtually every other mainstream magazine and newspaper in the United States as well as publications internationally. His political graphics and cartoons have won industry awards and have been widely reprinted in book collections, as well as displayed in museums and galleries.

Kuper's reach extends far beyond the news media, however, and his contributions to the cartoon arts have taken many forms. His early travelogues, wordless comics, and comic book series *Bleeding Heart* (1991–1993), for example, were all part of a *fin d'siecle* alternative comics arts scene that has enjoyed a lasting impact on North American comics. He has been writing and drawing the popular feature *Spy vs. Spy* for *Mad* magazine for nearly two decades, and he served as an expert witness for the defense in the famous Mike Diana obscenity trial.[1] His graphic books include *The System*, *Sticks and Stones*, *Speechless*, *Theo and the Blue Note*, *Drawn to New York*, *Diario De Oaxaca*, *Ruins*, and adaptations of Franz Kafka's *The Metamorphosis* and Upton Sinclair's *The Jungle*. A seasoned public speaker and educator, Kuper has taught classes for nearly thirty years at the School of Visual Arts. He has also taught at the Pratt Institute, Parsons School of Design, the Fashion Institute of Technology, and, most recently, Harvard University. In a career that arguably began when he first started contributing to and editing comics fanzines as a teenager, Peter Kuper has fashioned an accomplished, thoughtful, and eclectic body of work that encompasses illustration, editorial cartooning, comic strips, comic books, graphic novels, graphic journalism, personal essays, artist's books, children's books, book design, fine art, travelogues, adaptations of literary classics, and animation.

Even as he has pursued solo projects, Peter Kuper has been an integral member of the circle of artists associated with the magazine *World War 3 Illustrated* (*WW3*). Founded at the tail end of the 1970s by Kuper and his childhood friend and longtime collaborator Seth Tobocman, *WW3* is a collectively produced, irregularly published, not-for-profit anthology of political graphic art that continues to provide a beacon and a rallying cry for the cause of nonfiction comics. In his Top Shelf collection *Speechless*, Kuper recalled that he and Tobocman were both "frustrated by the lack of outlets for political graphics and comics . . . with the hostage crisis in Iran, the threat of nuclear conflict, and Ronald Reagan running for president, *World War 3 Illustrated* seemed like an appropriate title."[2] They had already worked together on offset publications in middle school and high school. In 1970 they launched *Phanzine*,[3] and between 1971 and 1973 coedited three issues of *G.A.S. Lite*, the official magazine of the Cleveland Graphic Arts Society, which made room for mainstream and underground comics alike.[4] By the end of the 1970s they were both living in Manhattan. Kuper was taking classes at Pratt and the Art Students League, and Tobocman was in the process of extricating himself from NYU.[5] In collaboration with Christof Kohlhofer, and with production assistance provided by Ben Katchor, they set out to create a home for serious-minded, real-world cartooning.

The result was a magazine that looked and felt markedly different from the usual comics fare. As Ryder Windham noted in his 1992 *Comics Journal* interview with Kuper, "From the start, *WW3* has embraced a realistic, emotional, and direct approach in both content and form. Like the other creators whose work has appeared in *WW3*, Kuper has used the magazine as a personal forum for documenting his real-life experiences as a world traveler, his responses to political matters at home and abroad, and his desire to create what he calls 'world comics'—making his artform as universally understood as possible."[6] Since then, the magazine has showcased work by established figures, but has at the same time nurtured the talents of younger and less-known artists. It has incubated numerous individual projects and inspired a bookshelf's worth of edited volumes.[7] Having recently celebrated its thirty-fifth anniversary, *WW3* has spun-off no fewer than three best-of anthologies, each coedited by Kuper and Tobocman. While *WW3* did not of course invent the political cartoon genre, it has become a *de facto* school within the ambit of socially engaged nonfiction cartooning. Certainly the number of self-published, small press magazines that were launched during the Carter administration, and that have continued to thrive and flourish in the present era, is vanishingly small.

Many cartoonists are identified with a specific character, ongoing series, or graphic novel, or are known for the work they've undertaken within a single genre. The same cannot be said of Peter Kuper. A fan of *Spy vs. Spy* may well have never heard of *World War 3 Illustrated*, or recognize that the same artist responsible for their favorite *Mad* feature also, say, created *The Metamorphosis* graphic adaptation that was assigned in their English class. The sheer diversity of Kuper's output, whether measured in terms of format, technique, or subject matter, is striking. Yet Kuper's imagery tends to be readily identifiable. Over the years he has developed a distinctive visual style that combines compositional elegance with a keen sense of political urgency. His work has a self-assured and meticulous quality that has only become more disciplined and refined over the years. He can craft a gripping story using words and pictures in sequence, but he also knows how to compose an arresting image. Whether the theme is the latest corporate scandal, or a glorious natural vista, his images are witty, carefully arranged, and sometimes painfully blunt. He can also create landscapes and sketches from real life that are achingly beautiful. Over the years his pencils, brushwork, and stencils have become tighter as his familiarity with and mastery over a range of tools and technologies has expanded and intensified. Although he started out mainly creating black-and-white images, he is adept with color, and has over time developed a distinctive palette. In many respects he is the consummate professional, but his artwork has a delightfully quirky aspect that is only occasionally foregrounded.

Peter Alan Kuper (1958-) was born in New Jersey and grew up in Cleveland Heights, Ohio. He has two sisters and is the youngest of three siblings. For many years his father taught physics at Case Western Reserve University, and his parents were both very active in environmental causes, via the Sierra Club and other local and national nonprofits. From all accounts Alan and Virginia Kuper provided their children with a warm and loving home environment, and the family strongly encouraged Peter's artistic, cultural, and political interests. They spent a year in Israel at the end of the 1960s, followed by a trip across Western Europe in a Volkswagen van, which helped instill a love of foreign travel in Peter and his sisters.[8] Peter Kuper also reports that a family trip to New York City to see his uncle perform in *Fiddler on the Roof* on Broadway played a critical role in terms of kindling his interest in both the arts and the Big Apple. After spending an unhappy year at Kent State University, he relocated from Ohio to New York in 1977, where he has resided ever since— with the important exception of extended travels to Africa, Asia, Europe, and the Middle East, and he and his family's two-year sojourn in Oaxaca, Mexico in 2006–2008. He met his future wife, Betty Russell, in Spain on a solo trip around Europe in 1984, and they were married in New York City three years later. Their daughter Emily Russell Kuper was born in 1996, and affectionate depictions of Betty, and Emily, can be found in several of his stories and books, most notably *The System* (1996), *Stop Forgetting to Remember* (2007), *Diario De Oaxaca: A Sketchbook Journal of Two Years in Mexico* (2009), and *Drawn to New York* (2013).

As this suggests, many of Peter Kuper's comics and cartoons are concerned with his experiences in and responses to the big city. He's also written and drawn extensively about his travels outside the United States. He's sketched, told stories, cracked jokes, revealed intimacies, conjured up street scenes, celebrated nature, revived historical figures, and tackled political issues big and small. Some of his comics are autobiographical, some are quasi-autobiographical, and some are completely disconnected from anything he has ever directly experienced. As of this writing he is the author and editor of nearly 30 books, from graphic memoirs, graphic novels, and comic strip collections, to anthologies, sketchbooks, and his best-selling adaptation of *The Metamorphosis*. His literary output comes to approximately one book per year, not counting freelance illustrations, short stories, and other smaller-scale pieces. Few of his generational peers are as hard working, and fewer still are as peripatetic from the vantage point of theme, genre, and technique. His most recent book, the full-color novel *Ruins* (2015), runs 328 pages in length and is his most ambitious effort yet. His published work is likely to continue to move in several different directions at once, and to embrace the unexpected, even as it retains specific concerns and preoccupations, both visual and political.

As the first full-length study devoted to Kuper's formidable career, *Peter Kuper: Conversations* is organized around ten informative interviews, profiles, and roundtables. In addition, it provides a detailed chronology, a list of additional readings, and twenty-four reprinted images. The conversations date from the period between 1995 to the present. They address such varied topics as the nuts and bolts of his creation of graphic novels, Mexican street murals, Hollywood deal-making, nuclear war, *Spy vs. Spy*, New York City in the 1970s and 1980s, teaching at Harvard, climate change, R. Crumb, Jack Kirby, *Mad* magazine, and *World War 3 Illustrated*. Even as certain themes are revisited and reworked, the interviews differ in tone and emphasis from each other. While four interviews are one-on-one, two are one-on-two (the interviewer plus Kuper and Seth Tobocman). Three of the interviews are based on transcripts of roundtable conversations that include other prominent political cartoonists, and one is a magazine profile that incorporates Kuper's own words. Fully half of the featured interviews and roundtables focus on the genesis and development of *World War 3 Illustrated*, sometimes incorporating the perspectives of key *WW3* contributors, while the other half are mainly or entirely concerned with

Kuper's solo projects. The preponderance of the interviews and roundtables are either previously unpublished or long out of print.

The one name that comes up again and again in this volume, whether in the context of *WW3* or Kuper's solo career, is that of Seth Tobocman. While they are very different people, and have pursued distinct artistic agendas, they have collaborated on one project or another for virtually their entire lives. Even before the Kuper family moved to Cleveland Heights in the early 1960s their parents were friendly, and for many years their fathers both taught in the physics department at Case Western Reserve University. The two boys bonded in first grade and by middle school were attending comic book conventions together, escorted by one or more of their parents. Since that time they have marched together, created graphic art together, served on panels together, sat through interviews together, edited books and magazines together, and displayed their work in group shows. Tobocman is perhaps more of a day-to-day activist, and has arguably embraced a grittier visual style. While he has published fewer books, each has generated their own cultural ripples. A greater percentage of Tobocman's work is directly political, and for one reason or another, his work is less likely to appear in color. He seems less inclined than Kuper to use puns, parody pop culture, or offer up punch lines. But they are almost certainly the single most important artistic influence in each other's lives, and careers, and it makes sense—particularly given the achievement of *WW3*—that of all of Kuper's friends, associates, and generational peers it is Seth Tobocman whose voice and sensibility commands the most space and attention in the book, aside from Kuper himself.

The interview that opens the collection originally appeared in Robert Bhatia's small-circulation zine, *What the Hell?* It reflects a time before the advent of the Internet when irregularly shaped self-published magazines often provided the only outlet for information about nonmainstream cartooning and music. It is perhaps worth noting that this is the only interview in the book in which Kuper is asked about (and then taken to task for) his musical tastes, which is certainly suggestive of the period. Like many zines that came and went in the 1990s, *What the Hell?* was a lively and energetic periodical; the issue that featured the Kuper interview, for example, also included a lengthy interview with Joe Sacco as well as a number of appealing sketches and collages by the zine's editor.

The second interview is an affectionate profile by the writer Douglas Wolk that appeared in a glossy magazine called *World Art: The Magazine of Contemporary Visual Art*. While the *What the Hell?* piece appeared in 1995, Wolk's profile ran in 1996. More so than with Bhatia, Wolk is interested in the materials, methods, and tools that Kuper uses as an artist. The roundtable that follows features no fewer than seven political cartoonists—Fly, Peter Kuper, Mac McGill, Ted Rall, Tom Tomorrow, Seth Tobocman, and Matt Wuerker—most of whom are either associated with or have at least contributed to *WW3*. While the transcript was published in *Comics Forum*, a U.K. comics magazine, in fall 2002, the roundtable itself was held at the NYC Socialist Scholars Conference in the spring of 2001. Here the emphasis is not so much on technique as national politics and the challenges facing freelance illustrators and cartoonists.

What the Hell?, *World Art*, and *Comics Forum* are no longer publishing, and the relevant issues are almost impossible to track down. By contrast, the *Comics Journal* is still going strong, albeit in the form of a web journal along with an annual print volume. "The *World War 3 Illustrated* Roundtable," from 2006, brings together five *WW3* editors and contributors—Sabrina Jones, Peter Kuper, Kevin Pyle, Nicole Schulman, and Seth Tobocman—to talk about the magazine's influences, internal dynamics, and political stances. Christopher Irving's interview took place three years later and provided the source material for a profile that Irving posted on his website, www.nycgraphicnovelists.com,[9] and in *Leaping Tall Buildings: The Origins of American Comics* (2012), with photographs by the late Seth Kushner.

Michael Dooley's 2013 interview touches on several different facets of Kuper's career, including the differences between working and living in New York and Oaxaca, his experiences with non-U.S. publishers, and his affection for print. The three interviews that follow Dooley's are all tied to the thirty-fifth anniversary of *World War 3 Illustrated*. Alex Dueben's conversation with Kuper and Tobocman was originally posted on comicbookresources.com, while Steven Heller's interview with Kuper and Tobocman provided the source material for an *Atlantic* magazine profile that investigated how "the comics zine stays angry, even if it doesn't have Reagan to skewer anymore."[10] For the website adastracomix.com, Nicole Marie Burton interviewed Scott Cunningham, Kevin Pyle, and Seth Tobocman about *WW3* and political cartooning more generally. While Kuper did not participate in this roundtable, his name is referenced more than once and their engaging conversation provides yet another lens on the life and times of the only durable magazine of its type, at least in the English language.

The book's longest interview closes the volume's main section. It is by the editor and is based on lightly edited transcripts of four 60–90 minute conversations that were conducted in the summer of 2015 at Kuper's Upper West Side studio. It addresses topics that are barely canvased elsewhere in the book, from parenting, teaching, and religion, to studying at Kent State, working as a self-publisher, and collaborating with HBO. At the same time, this concluding interview circles around themes that were flagged in earlier conversations. Taken as a whole, the assembled interviews and roundtables provide an in-depth oral history of political and alternative cartooning in New York from the 1970s to the present day. They address the complex legacy of the underground comix movement, the struggle to create viable outlets for political cartooning, and the challenges associated with developing and maintaining a productive career outside the framework of the mainstream comics industry. They tackle questions of technique and style, craft and commerce, print and Internet, and art and politics. They also offer wry observations about daily life, family life, urban life, and the comics subculture. While most of the interviews are concerned with serious political and artistic themes, several include laugh-aloud moments that reflect Kuper's well-developed sense of humor. Anyone with a substantive interest in the history of political and alternative cartooning is likely to find the collection informative as well as entertaining.

As an added bonus, *Peter Kuper: Conversations* features revealing interviews with four comics legends—Vaughn Bodē, Robert Crumb, William (Bill) Gaines, and Jack Kirby. The interviews were jointly conducted by Kuper and Tobocman for the Cleveland fanzine *G.A.S. Lite* when they were teenagers. Harvey Pekar encouraged his famous friend R. Crumb to consent to being interviewed by the two young fans in 1971 and made the necessary introductions. The Vaughn Bodē interview was conducted at a Detroit Triple Fan Fair convention in 1973, while the Gaines and Kirby interviews were conducted at the 1973 Comic Art Convention in New York City. With the sole exception of the Kirby interview, these remarkable conversations have not seen the light of day since they were first published more than forty years ago.[11]

These cultural time capsules evoke a very different world from our own, both in terms of the comics industry and the sociocultural context more generally. This is made abundantly clear from the interview with R. Crumb (1943-), for example, which took place at a time when Crumb was burned out as a counter-cultural celebrity and was for the most part declining interviews. Given that Kuper and Tobocman were on the verge of achieving puberty, the frankness of Crumb's responses to their questions is bracing. "What were or are your goals in life?" they asked. "To draw as many comics as I possibly can without getting in a rut," Crumb scribbled on the questionnaire they gave him, "and to fuck a lot of women and girls, and to listen to a lot of good music, and take a lot of drugs and eat a lot . . ." His answer to their next question—"Has your style changed since you started underground comix?" is equally provocative: "Yes . . . It changed quite radically during the time I was taking a lot of LSD . . .

Through acid I became more immersed in the collective subconscious and less attached to my own ego—which improved my drawing and gave it a richness it lacked before that . . . In fact, I think I'm about due for another trip . . ." The interview with Vaughn Bodē (1941–1975), which was conducted only two years before Bodē's untimely death, exudes a similar vibe. Their talk covers his experiences in the U.S. Army, his adventures in underground comix, and his negotiations with Hollywood. While Bodē doesn't explicitly refer to psychedelics, he jokingly claims to have spent time on other planets, and encourages his youthful interlocutors to "keep on trucking!"

By comparison, the Kuper-Tobocman conversations with Bill Gaines (1922–1992) and Jack Kirby (1917–1994) are fairly sedate, although equally compelling from the standpoint of comics historiography. Gaines offers his thoughts about Alfred E. Newman, the Comics Code, working with artists like Frank Frazetta and Wally Wood, and the economics of publishing comic books, while Kirby explores the storytelling logic behind such characters as the Hulk, Galactus, the Silver Surfer, Orion, Big Barda, and Steve Ditko's Mr. A. At the conclusion of their interview, Kirby extends his thanks to "you guys for your interest. And if you represent a group or club, I thank them for their interest. I'd like to say hello to anyone who reads what we had to say here, and I hope their interest in comics keeps up." It's a little unsettling to think of the contrasting personality types roaming the corridors of a big city comics convention in the late sixties and the early seventies.

Over the past couple of decades, comics and cartooning has generated an outpouring of interest on the part of scholars, publishers, critics, and curators. To a large extent this new wave of comics studies has focused on a select number of creators and genres, such as autobiographical comics, journalistic comics, experimental comics, and, most recently, superheroes. Political cartooning and illustration of the type produced by Peter Kuper and other *WW3* contributors has yet to receive the attention it merits. This book represents an effort to not only affirm Kuper's relentless artistry, but also to call attention to the larger circle of political and alternative cartoonists that Kuper has been an integral part of for the past several decades. The paucity of secondary scholarship on Kuper, *World War 3 Illustrated*, and politically minded cartooning more generally is conspicuous.

Working on this book has deepened my admiration for Peter Kuper's visual artistry and range. It has also confirmed my suspicion that he is a *mensch*. I would like to close by expressing my heartfelt gratitude to Peter, not only for putting up with my innumerable questions, and for providing the artwork that enlivens these pages, but also for his many and varied contributions to the world of comics. I would also like to thank the book's contributors, as well as Karen Green, Charles Hatfield, Sabrina Jones, Gene Kannenberg, Jr., Guy Lawley, Amy Pryor, Kevin Pyle, Betty Russell, Seth Tobocman, and Ryder Windham. This book is dedicated to Bill Restemeyer and Chris Toulouse.

KW

Notes

1. According to Wikipedia, Mike Diana was "the first artist ever to receive a criminal conviction for obscenity in artwork in the United States." Because of hand-drawn images he published in a self-distributed mini-comic titled *Boiled Angel*, Diana was sentenced by the State of Florida to "three years of supervised probation, a $3,000 fine, 1,248 hours of community service," and was ordered to "avoid contact with minors." He was also required to "follow a state-supervised psychiatric evaluation at his own expense, to take an ethics-in-journalism class, and ruled that he was to submit to unannounced, warrantless search of his personal papers by the police and deputized probation officers from the Salvation Army, which would allow them to seize any drawings or writings." See en.wikipedia.org/wiki/Mike_Diana. Accessed on October 14, 2015.

2. Peter Kuper, *Speechless*. Marietta, GA: Top Shelf, 2001, 38. In his 2001 *Comics Journal* interview, Seth Tobocman supplied further details: "We sort of ran into the Iran hostage crisis and the enormous amount of patriotic propaganda that was part of the culture at the time. I remember these big buttons that said, *Fuck Iran* on them. They were sold in grocery stores by very respectable people. So we wanted to do an antiwar comic book." See Kent Worcester, "Waxing Politick with Seth Tobocman," *The Comics Journal* 233 (May 2001), 78.

3. In their *Phanzine* Editorial, the two twelve-year-olds emphasized the immense challenges facing comics fandom: "Perhaps you have noticed that most people do not recognize comic books as a fine art (and if you haven't, you've been in hibernation for a long while!). Comic books will never attain their ultimate glory as long as their main market rests with the 'bubble gum brigade.' It should be the duty of all fandom to educate the public on the subject of graphic arts."

4. Kuper also self-published issues of *Melotoons*, in 1972 and 1976, and in 1981 founded *Ubiquitous*, a college arts magazine at Pratt Institute that is still being published. See ubiquitouspratt.tumblr.com/.

5. See http://www.sethtobocman.com/bio.html. Accessed on October 15, 2015.

6. Ryder Windham, introduction to "Peter Kuper," *The Comics Journal* #150 (May 1992), 69. We were unable to secure permission to reprint Windham's interview.

7. In addition to the three *WW3* edited collections, see, inter alia, Lois Ahrens, ed. *The Real Cost of Prisons Comix* (2008); Steve Brodner, ed. *Artists Against the War* (2011); Paul Buhle and Nicole Schulman, eds. *Wobblies!: A Graphic History of the Industrial Workers of the World* (2005); and Harvey Pekar and Paul Buhle, eds. *The Beats: A Graphic History* (2010). The Additional Resources section provides bibliographic information on these and other examples of the *WW3* book genre.

8. Seth Tobocman painted a vivid portrait of the Kuper family in his online review of *Ruins*: "Peter Kuper grew up in a very unusual 1970s suburban household. His mom, Ginger Kuper, was a very artsy lady. She had a desk job at the Cleveland Orchestra and was an amateur potter. The house was full of clay sculpture along with Native American textiles, block prints, plants, and nature photographs. One of Peter's uncles was an illustrator and his work decorated the walls. Another uncle was a Broadway actor. His older sisters were a dancer and a photographer . . . Peter's father was a scientist, but not the kind who is lost in abstract thought. Alan Kuper (known as "Buzz") liked to take walks in the woods. The family went on regular camping trips. Buzz had a subscription to *National Geographic* and would eventually become president of the local Sierra Club. Alan Kuper was also outspoken in opposition to the Vietnam War, took his kids to peace demonstrations, allowed his son to become the first boy I knew to grow his hair long. My sister and I, along with most of our schoolmates, envied the Kuper kids for having 'such nice parents.'" See Seth Tobocman, "Beautiful *Ruins*," adastracomix.com/2015/10/25/beautifulruins/. Posted on October 25, 2015.

9. See graphicnyc.blogspot.com/2009/11/diario-de-peter-kuper-from-world-war-3.html. Accessed October 14, 2015.

10. See Steven Heller, "*World War 3* Has Raged for 35 Years." Posted July 3, 2014.

11. The Kuper/Tobocman interview with Jack Kirby was reprinted in *The Jack Kirby Collector* 47 (Fall 2006) under the title "Cleveland Rocks!"—even though the interview took place at a comics convention in New York City. The complete interview has never been posted online, and the print edition is out of print.

Works Cited

Kuper, Peter, and Seth Tobocman. "Cleveland Rocks!" *The Jack Kirby Collector* 47 (Fall 2006): 4–5.

Tobocman, Seth. "Beautiful *Ruins*." Adastracomix.com/2015/10/25/beautifulruins/. Posted on October 25, 2015.

Windham, Ryder. "Peter Kuper." *The Comics Journal* 150 (May 1992): 68–101.

Worcester, Kent. "Waxing Politick with Seth Tobocman." *The Comics Journal* 233 (May 2001): 78–102.

CHRONOLOGY

1958	Peter Kuper is born on September 22, 1958 in Summit, New Jersey. His parents are Alan "Buzz" Birk Kuper (1924–2008) and Virginia "Ginger" Apolsky Kuper (1925–2009). They are married in 1949 and raise three children: Holly, Katherine, and Peter.
1964	The Kuper family moves to Cleveland Heights, Ohio, where Alan Kuper joins the science faculty at Case Western Reserve University (1964–1978). He retires early to devote himself to environmental causes. Peter Kuper becomes friends with his future collaborator Seth Tobocman.
1965	Kuper purchases his first comic book—*Thor*, by Stan Lee and Jack Kirby.
1968	The Kuper family visits New York City to see Ginger Kuper's brother, Boris Aplon, perform in *Fiddler on the Roof* on Broadway.
1969–1970	The Kuper family lives in Israel for a year, where his father works as a researcher at the Technion in Haifa. They spend several months in both summers traveling through Europe in a VW camper van.
1970	Kuper and Tobocman copublish *Phanzine*, a comics fanzine, and attend a comics convention, the Detroit Triple Fan-fair in Detroit, Michigan.
1971–1973	Kuper and Tobocman coedit three issues of *G.A.S. Lite*, the official magazine of the Cleveland Graphic Arts Society. The inaugural issue includes an interview with Robert Crumb; subsequent interview subjects include Neal Adams, Vaughn Bodē, William Gaines, Isaac Asimov, and Jack Kirby.
1971	Kuper trades 78 rpm records for original art with Robert Crumb. Kuper is introduced to Crumb by Harvey Pekar.
1972	Kuper self-publishes *Melotoons* #1, which includes pages photocopied from a Crumb sketchbook. As part of his school's "Humanistic Curriculum," he teaches a one-credit course on comics

	that mainly focuses on underground artists like Vaughn Bodē and Robert Crumb.
1976	Kuper provides illustrations for his high school yearbook and graduates from Cleveland Heights High School. A second issue of *Melotoons* is published, with cover art by Crumb and interior pages from Crumb's sketchbook.
1976–1977	Kuper attends Kent State University for two semesters, intending to major in Fine Art.
1977	Kuper visits New York during spring break and is verbally offered a job working at Zander Animation. In June he moves to NYC and attends night classes at the Art Students League. The promised job never materializes.
1978–1980	Works part-time at Harvey Comics, inking *Richie Rich*.
1978–1981	Kuper studies Fine Art at the Pratt Institute.
1978	Contributes illustrations to *Close Encounters* magazine, and travels to England, France, and Israel, where he works on a kibbutz for two months as a banana picker.
1979–1982	Works as an assistant to the comic book artist Howard Chaykin at the Upstarts Studio.
1979	Peter Kuper, Seth Tobocman, and Christof Kohlhofer coedit the first issue of *World War 3 Illustrated*, with production assistance provided by Ben Katchor. Kuper also contributes "A Space Story" to *Heavy Metal* (August).
1980	Writes and draws a short story, "Shiver and Twitch," for *Commies from Mars* #3.
1981	Founds, edits, and publishes *Ubiquitous*, an arts magazine aimed at the Pratt Institute community. Contributes interior art to Philip José Farmer's *Stations of the Nightmare* (Pinnacle), and a short story to *Heavy Metal* (November). Contributes pencils, inks, and lettering to a story by Seth Tobocman ("When Dinosaurs Ruled the Earth") in *WW3 Illustrated* #2.
1982	Edits the second issue of *Ubiquitous* and contributes first illustration to the *New York Times Book Review*, art directed by Steven Heller. Continues illustrating for the *New York Times* until present. Contributes short stories to *Commies From Mars* #4 ("True Martian Romance"), *Crazy* #91, *Eclipse* #6, and *Heavy Metal Magazine* (October).
1983-present	Begins contributing illustrations to INX, a syndicate of New York-based illustrators that provides freelance editorial cartoons. He becomes INX's co-art director in 1988.

1983   Contributes to *Crazy* magazine #94 (April), *Epic Illustrated* #18 (June), and *Heavy Metal* (August).

1984   Travels to England, France, Israel, Scotland, and Spain, where he meets his future wife in Madrid. Co-creates a piece for *Heavy Metal* (August) written by Anthony Stonier, and contributes a short story ("Mr. Cruise") to the same magazine a month later. *The Last Cat Book*, with Robert E. Howard, is published by Dodd Mead. Contributes three stories to *WW3 Illustrated* #3.

1985   Travels to England and Scotland. Contributes numerous illustrations and two short stories to *WW3 Illustrated* #4.

1986   Illustrates Janice Prager and Arlene Lepoff's *Why Be Different? A Look into Judaism* (Behrman House). Travels to France and the Netherlands. *WW3 Illustrated* has its busiest year: in this one twelve-month period Kuper coedits and provides cover art and two short graphic stories to *WW3 Illustrated* #5 ("Religion Issue"), contributes two stories to *WW3 Illustrated* #6, and coedits and provides cover art and two stories to *WW3 Illustrated* #7.

1987-present Teaches comics and illustration at the School of Visual Arts in New York City.

1987   *New York, New York*, a collection of Kuper's comics, is published by Fantagraphics. Travels to Greece and Mexico. In collaboration with Seth Tobocman, Josh Whalen, and Chuck Sperry, he coedits *WW3 Illustrated* #8, to which he contributes a short story ("Color Blind"). Co-writes with Charles Santino and illustrates the comic ("Free Press") that appears in *Commies from Mars* #6.

1988–2006   Serves as Art Director of INX, a syndicated editorial illustration service.

1988   Kuper marries Betty Russell. Fantagraphics publishes a collection of Kuper's stories titled *It's Only a Matter of Life and Death*. He contributes a short story titled "One Dollar" to *Heavy Metal* (v. 12 #1) and a short story titled "Red Tape" to *Heavy Metal* (v. 12 #3). Also contributes to *Arcane Comix* #2 ("Fly in My Eye") and *Heavy Metal*—"Mr. Cruise" v. 8 #6. Contributes illustrations and the cover art to T.E.D. Klein's *Raising Goosebumps for Fun and Profit: A Brief Guide, for Beginners, to the How's and Why's of Horror* (Footsteps Press). With Tobocman, Drooker, and Aki Fujiyoshi, he coedits *WW3 Illustrated* #9 (for which he provides the cover art and a five-page story, "Disinformed"), and, with Drooker and Tobocman, he coedits *WW3 Illustrated* #10, to which he contributes two short stories, "Train to Berlin" and

"Promised Land." He also contributes stories to *Itchy Planet* #3 and *Prime Cuts* #8.

1989   Fantagraphics publishes *World War 3 Illustrated: 1980–1989*, which includes three of Kuper's stories. With Seth Tobocman and Eric Drooker, Kuper coedits *WW3 Illustrated* #11 ("The Riot Issue"). Contributes a seven-page story ("Mystery") to *Heavy Metal* (May) that is subsequently republished in *WW3 Illustrated* #12. Travels with Betty for eight months through Egypt, India, Israel, Kenya, Rwanda, Tanzania, Malaysia, Thailand, and Indonesia. His work is featured in a group show at the Society of Illustrators in New York.

1990–1993   *Heavy Metal* publishes Kuper's sardonic black-and-white comic strip "The Adventures of Wormboy." The magazine also publishes Kuper's politically minded feature "Modern World" (November 1990 - September 1992), as well as various one-off illustrations and short stories.

1990   Travels to Czechoslovakia, Germany, Hungary, the Netherlands, and Poland. *World War 3 Illustrated* receives a grant from the National Endowment for the Arts for a *WW3* retrospective show at the ATA Gallery in San Francisco, California. With Sabrina Jones and Seth Tobocman he coedits *WW3 Illustrated* #13, to which he provides two short stories, "Baby Dream" and "Black Market."

1991–1993   Fantagraphics publishes five issues of Kuper's *Bleeding Heart*, a comic book series.

1991   Kuper and Emily Russell's graphic adaptation of Upton Sinclair's *The Jungle* is published by First Publishing. Spanish, French, and Italian-language editions are published in 2006. He pencils and inks "The Wasp and the Snake," and the cover illustration, for *Aesop's Fables* #1; pencils and inks "The Ape and the Fisherman" for *Aesop's Fables* #2; and pencils and inks "Mercury and the Sculpter" for *Aesop's Fables* #3 (Fantagraphics). With Scott Cunningham, Sabrina Jones, and Seth Tobocman, he coedits *WW3 Illustrated* #14, to which he contributes cover art and two stories, "Bombs Away" and "Dreams of Reason." With Cunningham, Jones, Tobocman, and Villa Piazza, he coedited *WW3 Illustrated* #15, to which he contributes two stories, "The Jungle" and "The Insult That Made a Man Out of George." He also provides the cover art to the *Dallas Observer* (April and June) and interior illustrations for *2 Live Crew Comics* #1 (Fantagraphics), and contributes a one-page story to *Born to be Wild*, a benefit book for the People for the Ethical Treatment of Animals. *The New Comics Anthology* reprints Kuper's short story "Mr. Cruise." His work is featured in a group show at the New School in New York.

1992 — Kuper's *Comics Trips: A Journal of Travels through Africa and Southeast Asia* is published by Tundra. The book is later reissued by NBM. Kuper and Tobocman's "Crack House/White House" is reprinted in Karrie Jacobs and Steven Heller, eds. *Angry Graphics: Protest Posters of the Reagan/Bush Era* (Peregrine Smith Books). Kuper contributes illustrations and graphic short stories to *New York Mix*, the *New York Times*, *Rock the Vote*, and the *Village Voice*, as well as graphic short stories to *Drawn and Quarterly* #9, *Heavy Metal* #140, *Nozone* #4, *Realgirl* #4, and *WW3 Illustrated* #17. With Martin Kozlowski, he organizes a retrospective show of INX artists at the Parsons School of Design that travels to Paris the following year. Travels to Belize, Guatemala, and Honduras, and contributes a short story to *Big Mouth* #1 (Fantagraphics). With Cunningham, Jones, Tobocman, Piazza, Isabella Bannerman, and Sandy Jimenez, he coedits *WW3 Illustrated* #16, to which he contributes a seven-page story, "Bangkok." With Cunningham and Tobocman, he coedits *WW3 Illustrated* #17, to which he contributes an eleven-page story, "TKO."

1993–2002 — Self-syndicates "Eye of the Beholder," first to the *New York Times* and subsequently to *Funny Times*, *San Diego Reader*, *Tucson Weekly*, *Liberation*, and other publications. "Eye of the Beholder" has the distinction of being the first regularly published comic strip to ever appear in the pages of the *New York Times*.

1993 — Kuper creates the cover art for Dennis Eichhorn's *Real Stuff* #12 (Fantagraphics), and for *WW3 Illustrated* #20, and contributes illustrations and short stories to *The New Yorker* the *Comics Journal*, *Details*, the *Eastside Week*, *Heavy Metal*, the *New York Times*, the *Progressive*, and *Pulse!* Contributes two stories to *WW3 Illustrated* #18, "Fuck the Fucking Fuckers" and "In God We Trust." With Scott Cunningham and Kevin C. Pyle Kuper coedits *WW3 Illustrated* #20 ("Television"). Creates the official poster for Oporto, Portugal's largest comics convention. Contributes a short story to *Nozone* #5, a small press comics anthology, as well as to *Duplex Planet* #4. Travels to Ecuador and the

Galapagos Islands. His work is featured in group shows at Exit Art and the California College of Arts and Crafts in San Francisco, California.

1994   Kuper contributes illustrations and graphic short stories to the *Boston Globe Magazine*, *Business Week*, the *Comics Journal*, *Details*, the *New Yorker*, *Poz*, *Print Magazine*, *Pulse!*, the *Village Voice*, and *Worth*, as well as the cover art for *Duplex Planet #6*. Fantagraphics publishes two issues of *Peter Kuper's Wildlife*. Testifies as an expert defense witness for the Comic Book Legal Defense Fund in the obscenity trial of cartoonist Mike Diana in Florida. Contributes the cover art to *Hands Off!*, a black-and-white comic published to benefit Washington Citizens for Fairness to Fight Hate and Discrimination. Travels to Portugal. Contributes short stories to *Different Beat Comics #1* (Fantagraphics) and *Bob Marley—Tale of the Tuff Gong, Volume 1* (Marvel Music). His work is featured in group shows at the Lambiek Gallery in Amsterdam, Holland, the Vox Populi Gallery in Seattle, Washington, the Design Center College in Los Angeles, California, and the Ward-Nasse, Exit Art, and Charas galleries in New York City.

1995   *Rolling Stone* names Kuper Hot Comic Artist of the Year, and his story "The Virgin," from *Wild Life #1*, is nominated for an Eisner Award in the Best Short Story category. Kuper's *Kafka: Give It Up! And Other Short Stories* is published by NBM; the book is later translated into German, Portuguese, Spanish, French, and Swedish. Fantagraphics publishes *Stripped: An Unauthorized Autobiography*. Provides cover illustrations to *The Baffler #7*, *Boston Globe Magazine*, *Newsweek*, *Business Week* and *The Stranger*, and interior illustrations for *Men's Journal* and *Time*. Contributes a short story ("The Beaten Path") to *Blab! # 8*. Co-organizes a *World War 3 Illustrated* retrospective show at the Parsons School of Design. In collaboration with Scott Cunningham, Sabrina Jones and Seth Tobocman he co-edits *World War 3: Confrontational Comics* (Four Walls/Eight Windows). Travels to Indonesia and New Guinea. *Comics Lit* magazine #1. *Last Gasp Comics and Stories #2*. Contributes to *The Vertigo Gallery #1* and *Nozone #6*, and cover art to *Animal Man #78* and *#79*. His work is featured in a solo show at De Banda Desenhada, Oporto, Portugal, and at a group show at the Parsons School of Design.

1996   Daughter Emily Russell Kuper is born. Kuper's *Eye of the Beholder* is published by NBM; an expanded version, titled *Mind's Eye: An Eye of the Beholder* is published by NBM in 2000, while a French-language edition appears in 2005. Three issues of Kuper's mini-series *The System* are published by DC/Vertigo; DC's collected edition appears the following year. Brazilian, Greek, and Italian editions of *The System* are published in 1998, while a Spanish and French-language editions appear in 2010. Contributes illustrations to *Smart Money*, *Indy Magazine*, and *World Art* #14, and stories to *ComicsLit* magazine #11 and #12. Nancy Folbre and Randy Albelda's *The War on the Poor* (New Press) includes images by Kuper and other *WW3* contributors. Nominated for an Eisner Award, for Talent Deserving of Wider Recognition.

1997–1999 Develops an animated show for HBO based on *Stripped, An Unauthorized Autobiography.*

1997-present Kuper illustrates "Spy vs. Spy" for *MAD* magazine, starting with issue #356. He also provides numerous one-off illustrations and cover concepts for *MAD*.

1997   Kuper provides cover art and a short autobiographical story to *Mind Riot: Coming of Age in Comix* (Aladdin). He contributes "Exorcise" to *Blab!* #9 and "Spine" to *Blab!* #11, and "Dreams of the Rarebit Fiend" to *Blab!* #12. He also contributes stories to *Weird War Tales* #2 and *World War 3 Illustrated* #24. In addition, he contributes illustrations and graphic short stories to the *Cleveland Plain Dealer*, the *Comics Journal*, *Details*, the *New York Times*, *Out Magazine*, and the *Washington City Paper*, and cover art for the *Village Voice*. Nominated for an Eisner Award for Best Limited Series. His work is featured in group shows at Exit Art, and at a gallery in Coimbra, Portugal, as well as in a solo show at the Curcio Spector Gallery in New York. Publishes limited edition hand-colored prints of "Riot," from his adaptation of *The Jungle* and *The System*.

1998–2000 Political cartoonist for the *New York Daily News* with the weekly strip *"New York Minute."*

1998   Kuper's story "Chains" appears in *Gangland* #1 (DC), and is reprinted two years later in the collection *Gangland* (DC). Interlink publishes a CD ROM version of *Peter Kuper's ComicsTrips:*

A Journey of Travels through Africa and Southeast Asia, with additional animation, writing, photos, art, sound recordings, and original music. His story "Porn Again" appears in *Blab!* #10. Contributes cover art to *New City*, *Philadelphia Weekly*, and *Time* magazine. Contributes to *The Life and Times of Robert Crumb: Comments from Contemporaries*, *Mother Jones*, and *WW3 Illustrated* #26. His work is featured in group shows at the Words and Pictures Museum in Northampton, Massachusetts, the Storyopolis gallery in Los Angeles, California, and the New Museum of Contemporary Art in New York. *The System* is nominated for an Eisner Award, in the Best Graphic Album-Reprint category. After HBO closes its animation department, actor Forrest Whitaker's production company options *Stripped, An Unauthorized Autobiography*. Working with director Frederic Duchau, Kuper again develops *Stripped* for animation.

1999   Contributes illustrations and short stories to *Forbes*, *Isthmus*, *Mother Jones*, *New Times*, the *New York Daily News*, *New York Magazine*, the *New York Times*, the *Oklahoma Gazette*, and *Time*, as well as *Blab!* #10. Designs a t-shirt for the Comic Book Legal Defense Fund, and provides the cover art for *Busted! The Newsletter of the CBLDF*. His work is shown as part of an exhibit of political art, titled Urban Encounters, at the New Museum of Contemporary Art in New York.

2000   *Topsy Turvy: A Collection of Political Comic Strips* is published by Eye Press, and *Mind's Eye: An Eye of the Beholder Collection* is published by NBM. Contributes illustrations to *Free Times*, the *New York Daily News*, and *Time*, and a short story ("Metamorph-Simpsons") to *Treehouse of Horror* #6. His work is featured in a group show at Exit Art.

2001   Kuper receives a journalism award from the Society of Newspaper Designers, and *Speechless* is published by Top Shelf. With Jordan Worley and Seth Tobocman he coedits *World War 3 Illustrated* #32, for which he provides the cover art and two short stories, "War of the Worlds" and "The Indomitable Human Spirit." He contributes short stories to *Treehouse of Horror* #2, *Blab!* #11, *Blab!* #12, and *Legal Action Comics* #1, as well as illustrations to *Time* and the *Cleveland Plain Dealer*. His work is the subject of a solo show at the Parsons School of Design in New York and is featured in a *WW3* group show at Parsons. Chuck Sperry of

Firehouse Press publishes "*World War 3* Show Poster" and "Peter Kuper INX Show Poster," two limited edition silk screen prints with art by Kuper.

2002   Kuper's four-page story "Deep Blue" appears in *Blab!* #13, while his short story "Bombed" is published in *New and Used Blab!* (Chronicle Books). He contributes to *9–11: Emergency Relief* (Alternative Comics), *Dark Horse Maverick: Happy Endings*, and *Too Much Coffee Man* #14, as well as a two-page story and back cover art to *Captain America: Red, White and Blue* (Marvel). Kuper's work is featured in group shows at the Library of Congress in Washington, D.C., the Yerba Buena Center for the Arts in San Francisco, California, the Society of Illustrators, and Exit Art.

2003–2005   Teaches illustration at the Parsons School of Design.

2003   Kuper's "Dead Sea Stroll" appears in *Blab!* #14, and is subsequently reprinted in Paul Buhle, ed., *Jews and American Comics: An Illustrated History of an American Art Form* (New Press). Contributes to *The Comics Journal* Special Edition Volume 3: Cartoonists on Patriotism! His adaptation of *The Metamorphosis* is published by Crown; Spanish, French, Czech, Italian, Portuguese, Turkish and Hebrew-language versions are subsequently published. With Kevin C. Pyle and Susan Willmarth, he coedits *WW3 Illustrated* #34 ("Taking Liberties"), to which he contributes a short story. His work is featured in a group show at the University of North Texas as well as a solo show at the Museum of Comic and Cartoon Art. With Mac McGill, Christopher Cardinale, and Seth Tobocman, Kuper is invited to participate in exhibitions in Milan, Italy and to create murals at COX18, a squatted community center in Milan. "Blue Planet," a limited edition offset poster is created for Cox18 exhibition. The transcript of a panel that he takes part in, which addresses "Early Creative Responses to 9/11 by Comic Artists," is published in the *International Journal of Comic Art* 5.1 (Spring).

2004   Kuper receives the 2004 Gold Medal in the Sequential Arts category from the Society of Illustrators. He contributes "Dream Machines" to *Blab!* #15, cover art for an issue of *Delosk Op*, and "Ceci N'est Pas Une Comic" to Mack White and Gary Groth, eds. *The Bush Junta: Twenty-five Cartoonists on the Mayberry Machiavelli and the Abuse of Power* (Fantagraphics). His book *Sticks and Stones* is published by Three Rivers Press. *World War 3 Illustrated*

#35 includes his story "Richie Bush," while Ragged Edge Press publishes *Richie Bush —The Poor Little Oligarch*. Contributes the cover illustration to *Rosetta: A Comics Anthology* vol. 2. (Alternative Comics), and the artwork for a short story written by Alan Moore for *Tom Strong's Terrific Tales* #10. His work is featured in group shows at Exit Art, the Society of Illustrators, and the Maryland Institute of Art in Baltimore. U.S. Customs officials seize copies of a Slovenian magazine, *Stripburger*, which includes a reprint of "Richie Bush," on the grounds that Kuper's story constitutes piracy. The Comic Book Legal Defense Fund intervenes and successfully makes the case that Kuper's work is parody rather than piracy. Creates two limited edition prints during an artist residency at the Maryland Institute College Art (MICA): "Sticks and Stones" and "A Little Fable."

2005   Kuper's "A New Yorker," appears in Pete Friedrich, ed. *Roadstrips: A Graphic Journey Across America* (Chronicle Books); his story "Solidarity" appears in Paul Buhle and Nicole Schulman, eds. *Wobblies: A Graphic History of the Industrial Workers of the World* (Verso). Creates a cover illustration for the *New York Press* and contributes to *The Comics Journal* Special Edition Volume 5: Manga Masters, to *Blab!* #16, and to the *Cleveland Plain Dealer*. Kuper's essay "Launching *World War 3*" appears in Steven Heller and Michael Dooley's *The Education of a Comic Book Artist* (Allworth). His work is featured at group shows at the CoproNason Gallery in Santa Monica, California and the American Museum of Illustration in New York, as well as in a solo show at the Heights Art Gallery in Cleveland, Ohio. With Ryan Inzana, Kuper coedits *WW3 Illustrated* #36 ("Neo-Cons").

2006–2008   Peter and his family live in Oaxaca, Mexico. During this period, Eye Press publishes twelve limited edition Giclée prints of Kuper's drawings. They are eventually reprinted in his 2009 book *Diario De Oaxaca*: Oaxaca Stain (2006), Chinkultic (2008), Fuera Ratas (2008), Lancondona (2008), Monarchas (2008), November 25th (2008), Palenque (2008), Perros del Calle (2008), San Augustinillo (2008), San Cristóbal (2008), Yaxchilán (2008), and Zocalo Blues (2008).

2006   *Theo and the Blue Note* is published by Viking; *Teo y la nota azul*, a Spanish-language version appears in 2010 from Sexto Piso. Contributes short stories to *Graphic Classics: Jack London* (Eureka

Productions) and *Blab!* #17, and illustrations to *Royal Flush Magazine*. Harry Katz's *Cartoon America: Comic Art in the Library of Congress* (Abrams) includes an example of Kuper's work that is part of the Library of Congress's permanent collection.

2007   *Stop Forgetting to Remember* is published by Crown, while *Spy vs Spy 2: The Joke and Dagger Files* is published by Watson-Guptill Publications. His story "Bully for You!" appears in *Blab!* #18. He contributes the introduction to *Army@Love* (Vertigo) illustrations to *Time* magazine, the *Virginia Quarterly Review*, the *Cleveland Plain Dealer* and the *Cleveland Free Press*, and cover art and an eleven-page story ("Oaxaca, Oaxaca") to *WW3 Illustrated* #38. His work is featured in a group show at the Norman Rockwell museum in Stockbridge, Massachusetts, and he serves as the keynote speaker for the opening event. His work is also featured at a group show at Curtiduria in Oaxaca, Mexico.

2008   Kuper writes the introduction to David A. Berona's *Wordless Books: The Original Graphic Novels*, published by Abrams. Spanish publisher, Astiberri Ediciones, publishes *Stop Forgetting to Remember* (*No Te Olvides de Recordar*.) His work is featured in group shows at the Puffin Foundation Gallery in Teaneck, New Jersey, the Art Students League gallery, and the Society of Illustrators. Serves as a featured guest at the University of North Dakota Writers Conference (along with Salman Rushdie, Junot Díaz and Alexandra Fuller, among others), and at a lecture series on comics sponsored by the Jewish Community Center of San Francisco. Sundog Press publishes "Give It Up!," a limited edition, silk screen on paper portfolio, and "The Helmsman," a limited edition artist book. Both stories are adaptations of Franz Kafka short stories. Sundog Press also publishes "Ceci N'est Pas Une Comic" and "Lucha Libre," two limited edition prints. "This is Not a Comic" a two-page comic commenting on the U.S. elections, appears in *Virginia Quarterly Review*, Libération(France), Internazionale (Italy) as well as newspapers in Spain and Brazil.

2009   Kuper's "This is Not a Comic" receives a Silver Medal in the Sequential Arts category from the Society of Illustrators. Kuper collaborates with Harvey Pekar on "Gary Snyder," a biographical comic that appears in Paul Buhle, ed. *The Beats: A Graphic History* (Hill and Wang). He also contributes "Bill Talcott: Organizer" to Harvey Pekar and Paul Buhle, eds. *Stud Terkel's Working: A*

Graphic Adaptation (New Press). With Kevin C. Pyle he edits *WW3 Illustrated* #39 ("Wordless Worlds"). The Museum of Comic and Cartoon Art (MoCCA) hosts a solo show of Kuper's work in conjunction with the publication of *Diario de Oaxaca: A Sketchbook Journal of Two Years in Mexico* (PM Press and Sexto Piso); a French-language version appears in 2011. Receives an arts grant from the Puffin Foundation, and coedits *WW3 Illustrated* #39. His work is the subject of a solo show at the Museum of Comic and Cartoon Art, and is featured in group shows at the Toledo Museum in Toledo, Ohio, the Andy Warhol Museum in Pittsburgh, Pennsylvania, and the Society of Illustrators and Exit Art galleries. Sundog Press publishes "The Bridge," a limited edition accordion book. "Zocolo Tank," a limited edition hand-colored serigraph is published in Ravenna, Italy.

2010   Kuper receives a Gold Medal in the Sequential Arts category from the Society of Illustrators. Contributes short stories to *Simpsons Comics Presents Bart Simpson* #54 ("Bart on the Fourth of July") and #56 ("Ri¢hie impon"), as well as *Treehouse of Horror* #16 ("Tell-Tale Bart"). Kuper's "This is not a Comic" is reprinted in *The Best American Comics 2010*. Illustrates a Spanish translation of Lewis Carroll's *Alice in Wonderland* published by Sexto Piso. Pens the foreword to Fredrik Stromberg's *Comic Art Propaganda: A Graphic History*, published by St. Martin's Griffin. Teaches illustration at the Fashion Institute of Technology. Co-curates a retrospective of *World War 3 Illustrated* at Exit Art. His art is featured at group shows and at the School of Visual Arts gallery, as well as at solo shows at the Objecto A gallery in Buenos Aires, Argentina and at La Jicara gallery in Oaxaco, Mexico.

2011-present Visiting Lecturer in the Visual and Environmental Studies department at Harvard University. Teaches Harvard's first class on graphic novels.

2011   Illustrates Spanish edition of Lewis Carroll's *Through the Looking-Glass and What Alice Found There*, published by Sexto Piso. *Diario de Nueva York* is also published by Sexto Piso in Mexico; a French-language version appears in 2012. Kuper contributes two full-color illustrations ("Coney Island Summer" and "Yiddish Summer Camps") as well as coauthors and draws a six-page black-and-white graphic story ("Abraham Lincoln Polonsky") to

Harvey Pekar and Paul Buhle, eds. *Yiddishkeit: Jewish Vernacular and the New Land* (Abrams). *MAD* publishes *MAD Presents Spy vs. Spy—The Top Secret Files!* Kuper's humorous story "Bart on the Fourth of July" is nominated for an Eisner Award for Best Short Story. Receives a Silver Medal from the Society of Illustrators in the Sequential Art category, and an Inkpot Award from Comic-Con International. Steve Brodner's edited collection *Artists Against the War* (Underwood) includes work by Kuper. His art is featured in a group show of *World War 3 Illustrated* at the University of North Dakota, and on 1 of 24 trading cards issued as a fundraiser by the Comic Book Legal Defense Fund. He contributes a short story to *Bart Simpson Comics* #64 ("¡Viva La Bart!"), and a short essay on 9/11 for *Aperture* #204 (Fall), as well as the 2011 MoCCA Festival poster. Sundog Press publishes a limited edition "*World War 3* Portfolio" that features the work of eleven *WW3* contributors, including Kuper, along with Kuper's "A Modest Proposal," a limited edition artist book. Sundog Press also publishes "The Metamorphosis" a limited edition silk screens prints print. Buddha Press publishes "Fat Cat," and "Yin Yang Cat," two limited editions silk screens prints. Invited to Sydney, Australia (along with Jim Woodring and Scott McCloud) for presentations of their work at the Sydney Opera House accompanied by live music.

2012–2013   Serves as the art director for weekly political illustration for the French newspaper, *Libération*.

2012   Contributes to *Jack Davis: Drawing American Pop Culture*, to *Simpsons Comics Presents Bart Simpson* #72 ("Rock 'n' Roll") and #76 ("Southern Fried Simpsons"), and to Russ Kick's *The Graphic Canon* vol. 1 (Seven Stories Press). Kuper's "Eye Press" publishes a limited edition of 100 copies of *Self-Evident*, a small notebook sized book of 100 self-portraits. His work is the subject of a solo show at the Institute of Graphic Arts in Oaxaca, Mexico. Sundog Press publishes "The Top," a limited edition accordion book that is adapted from the Franz Kafka short story, as well as "Binary Inventions," a limited edition print.

2013   Contributes a story titled "Mind Over Matter" to *Pure Entertainment* #1 (April). *Drawn to New York: An Illustrated Chronicle of Three Decades in New York City* is published by PM Press. *MAD* publishes *Spy vs. Spy: Fight to the Finish.* He provides a variant cover to *Wonder Woman* #19. With Scott Cunningham he edits, and contributes a story to, *WW3 Illustrated* #45 ("Before and After") with cover art by Kuper. His work is the subject of a solo show at the Society of Illustrators, and at an artspace in Medellin, Colombia. *Third Eye,* an Eye Of the Beholder collection, published by Robot Editions in Medellin, Colombia. Sundog Press publishes "The Trees," a limited edition accordion book that is adapted from the Franz Kafka short story.

2014   Kuper's three-page black-and-white graphic biography of Bernard Wolfe "Limbo" appears in David Berger and Paul Buhle's *Bohemians: A Graphic History* (Verso). A new hardcover edition of *The System,* and *World War 3 Illustrated: 1979–2014,* edited by Kuper and Tobocman, are published by PM Press. He contributes an adaptation of a WWI poem by Isaac Rosenberg in *Above the Dreamless Dead* edited by Chris Duffy (First Second), and a short graphic bio of Harvey Kurtzman ("Corpse on the Imjin!") for Monte Beauchamp's *Masterful Marks: Cartoonists Who Changed the World* (Simon & Schuster). *Print Magazine* reprints Kuper's 1994 one-page graphic story ("It's Obscene!") about the legal battles faced by the underground cartoonist Mike Diana. Sundog Press publishes "The Vulture," a limited edition accordion book that is adapted from the Franz Kafka short story.

2015   *Ruins,* Kuper's 328-page graphic novel, is published by SelfMade-Hero. Reviews appear in the *Times Literary Supplement,* Editions in Spanish; *Ruinas,* and French; *Ruines,* published. In collaboration with a company called Modify Watches, Kuper creates four watch face designs using imagery from *Ruins.* Pens the introduction to Szegedi Szuts' *My War* (Dover Graphic Novels). Nominated for an Eisner Award for Best Short Story ("Corpse on the Imjin!"). Receives an arts grant from the Puffin Foundation, and contributes an eight-page story ("Climate Unchange") to *Vertigo Quarterly SFX* #3, as well as a "Comic Tribute to Jules Feiffer" that is posted on www.observer.com. His art is featured in the Vértigo Galaria 'El Sistema' group show and a one-man show at Museo de la Caricatura in Mexico City.

2016   Pens the afterword to Giacomo Patri's *White Collar* (Dover Graphic Novels). For information about current projects please visit www. peterkuper.com

PETER KUPER: CONVERSATIONS

Peter Kuper Interview

ROBERT BHATIA / 1995

From *What the Hell?* #5. Reprinted by permission.

Robert Bhatia: You're originally from New York?

Peter Kuper: I'm originally from Cleveland Heights, Ohio. I moved to New York in 1977. I've been here for a pretty long time. I came when I was eighteen.

RB: To go to college?

PK: I actually wanted to get into animation. I visited New York on my spring vacation, a year before I moved here. And I went around to different animation houses with my sketchbook. And one guy said, "Oh yeah, sure, we'll give you work. Come back this summer." And so I moved here thinking that I had a job lined up, but I never got a chance to *see* the guy. I couldn't get past his secretary and he never gave me any work. Which, I gather, is fairly typical.

RB: When did you start getting into comics?

PK: When I was pretty young, maybe when I was 7 or so. I was really enthused about Marvel. I didn't read DC's comics at all; I only read Marvel. And when I was about eleven, I got deeply into them. My friend Seth Tobocman and I went to a comic convention in Detroit in 1970. And it was, you know, your basic comic book convention.

RB: Dan Pussey-type people?

PK: Yeah. I was a prime candidate for the Dan Pussey look-a-like competition. And around the same time Seth and I started doing a fanzine. But at that time, back in 1970, there weren't comic shops. You bought your comics from a drugstore. There were no specialty stores. And we were just a bunch of people who were really interested in comics. You could probably count them in your neighborhood. You could probably count them in your *state*! [laughs]

After that I came to New York every year, starting in 1971, for the big New York comic convention. It was like the biggest convention. And I was interested in all aspects of comics. I was a little bit older when I first started to read underground comics. One of my sisters dated a guy who brought over underground comics. And shortly thereafter, you know, when I'd started smoking pot, [laughs] I started actively looking for the stuff that interested me more. I mean, I still read superhero comics up until I was 17 or thereabouts. But at some point it all seemed kind of like, crappy. I had been a serious fan of "mainstream" comics, going so far as to publish zines and so on. But all that faded.

Seth moved to New York, and I moved to New York shortly after. We ended up going to art school together—Pratt. And we were both disenchanted with the state of comics. We were no longer reading superhero comics. There weren't very many mainstream titles that we liked. For whatever reason, the idea of publishing was still in our blood, so we started *World War 3*. This was in 1979. And we're still both working on it, almost fifteen years later.

RB: Were you into the hippie scene?
PK: Well, I was kinda young. The . . .

RB: . . . tail end of it?
PK: Yes, exactly. I mean, it wasn't like I was going to have to go to Vietnam. The war was winding down by the time that I was a junior or senior in high school.

Both of my parents are pretty liberal, and they both marched against the Vietnam War, so I was conscious of that from an early age. And I had older cousins, and even to some extent siblings, who were definitely part of the hippie subculture. Mainly I read underground comics. I like Crumb's stuff, of course, but I also liked Corben's work, and Greg Irons, and the *Fabulous Furry Freak Brothers*. I was pretty much willing to read anything that was a comic. I would even read an issue of *Richie Rich* if it was lying around.

I had older cousins who were definitely threatened by the draft. I just wasn't all that politically informed. I didn't exactly know what the whole deal was.

RB: Yeah.
PK: When I was fourteen.

RB: You had a passing sort of idea.
PK: Yeah, I mean, my parents had me stuffing envelopes for McGovern. [That's a really scary name for a politician—RB] when I was fourteen or so. And I think, pretty early on, it just struck me that I was more interested in comics that had some kind of content, you know? I loved the comics that did that.

Even as I was still reading superhero comics I was beginning to realize that they were aimed at the mentality—and libido—of a fifteen year old. At the time, that was thoroughly true. Now there is a greater range of material coming out of places like DC Comics, such as *Sandman*, aimed a greater range of audiences. Whereas, at the time, somebody like Stan Lee was *definitely* writing for kids. And so I think the shift in my tastes was just a matter of natural evolution. And for the guys I knew who were still interested in superheroes, we just parted ways. I was like, "You're getting a little *old* for this, aren't you?"

There's a reason why it appealed to you then, and there's a reason why it dies for you, too. There was a long period where I just had *zero* interest in superheroes. And yet I ended up working for Howard Chaykin at his studio after I got to New York. His work involved science fiction and superheroes. Frank Miller also used the studio, as did Walt Simonson and a number of other people.

RB: There's a story in *Bleeding Heart* where you were working for a cartoonist who told you, "Don't mess this up, you little shit!"
PK: Yeah, yeah . . .

RB: Was it that place?
PK: Yeah, that was it.

RB: [laughs]
PK: Yeah, that was like, always . . . [phone rings]

RB: Where were we?
PK: Uh . . .

RB: Howard Chaykin.
PK: Yeah, well, anyway, I worked in his studio, and saw a lot of commercial comics. And of course through art school I was seeing a lot of work that wasn't very commercial. At some point, for me, superhero comic art became all too similar, to some extent, partly because it was such an incestuous culture. You know, comic artists looking at other comic artists to do more comic art? And I was guilty of doing the same thing. I was bored, and so I started to look at artists *outside* of comics for inspiration. And just drawing from *life*. And that became what I was interested in, rather than stylistic issues.

RB: Genre things, I guess.
PK: Yeah, just like *flash* and *polish* and all that stuff just became bullshit to me. I mean, it just made me feel really *ill*. Because, you know, it was so *lifeless*. So

I started doing more work that was based on real life experiences. I needed to open the window on that, and get away from generic comics. At this point I didn't even want to *look* at most comics. To some extent, I still feel that way. It's like, if I look at too many comics I find that something deadens in me.

RB: Even if you look at alternative type comics?

PK: It depends. I still read a lot of comics, certainly, but I'm always interested in looking outside of comics. Because I find that it's really easy to just regurgitate the same stuff you see. To some extent alternative comics has become another boys' club. Or maybe it's now a boys' and girls' club. That's a big change. But it still gets boring. And that's like the biggest sin of all—creating boring art. That's why I find, stylistically, I try to keep doing different things and working with different forms, because I am trying to not get bored. I think that's a big fight for any artist. Part of what's so screwed up about comics is that we're all shoved together in one big vat. It's like if somebody held a music convention, and invited classical musicians, and jazz musicians, and death metal musicians, and pop stars, and said, "Oh, you all do music, here, get together. I'm sure you'll all have plenty to talk about!"

You know? That's how it feels We *don't* have a lot to talk about. I mean, there can be some cross-pollination. Our work gets printed on paper, for example. But the association gets thinner from there. And so, I could meet somebody who is a superstar in the world of superhero comics and not have a clue about who they might be. Sometimes somebody will introduce me and say, "This is so-and-so" and they'll look at me like they're expecting me to *know* who they are, and I'll have no idea. I suppose I'm pretty smug about this, but a lot of the time when I look at current superhero work, I'll just say to myself, "Oh, they looked at Jeff Jones, or Bernie Wrightson, or Jack Kirby, or Jim Steranko, or Neal Adams." There's a set of artists that most of them take off from. There's so much style, and so little content. I'm soooo tired of that.

RB: You've said you like Crumb's work, right?

PK: Oh yes, a great deal.

RB: How did you feel about the strip he recently drew for *Weirdo*, "When the Goddamn Jews Take Over America"?

PK: I thought that his intent was one thing, and that the outcome was another. I know that that piece was picked up by, like, skinhead groups and republished in some of their magazines. And I would really like to know if he would have been comfortable knowing that was going to happen. It seemed to me that it follows suit with a lot of what he does. Which is kind of a "fuck you" to his audience. And people go, "Oh, that's great!" You know, he says, "I hate people. I was actually making fun of everyone, and you took it as a compliment." And it seems like he keeps on trying to up the ante. "What can I do that will *piss* you people off, and not make you think of this as wonderful? It's like he's trying to push the envelope. In this case, he was trying to subtly say, "This is all the stereotypical hatred that's in our heads —deal with it." But there's a real problem if it can be published in a very different context and immediately read as being anti-Semitic. It's the best, most beautifully drawn racist and anti-Semitic tract you could put together. And I'd really like to know if Crumb would have been comfortable, knowing that it was going to get republished by neo-Nazis. Because it seems to me that these are people that he would be terrified by.

From what I gathered from his work, I suspect that this wasn't the outcome he was looking for. Let's put it this way—speaking for myself, I'd be really upset and frightened, if I were to put something out there and people completely misunderstood what I was trying to say. I've had pieces picked up and, you know, *bent*. And that makes me think about how, if you can change the context, and make the piece say something completely different from what I was trying to say, that that means that I was doing something *wrong*. I mean, I'd like to not have my work be so easily transformed.

RB: Let's talk about your Pratt years.
PK: Ok.

RB: Barron Storey was one of your teachers, right?
PK: Right.

RB: Do you think he was an influence on your work?
PK: Sure. Well, actually, I just sat in on his classes. But I did start a magazine when I was at Pratt, called *Ubiquitous*. The fact that Barron agreed to do a comic strip for the magazine helped it get off the ground. He'd never done a comic before. I approached him and said, you know, "if I do this magazine . . . you're gonna do a comic, right?" And he was like, "yes." And I was really excited about this idea. Of course, now he does comics all the time. And he's probably one of the bigger influences on many people who work within the superhero genre. Other superhero artists who have influenced by Barron's work include Bill Sienkiewicz, Dave McKean, Kent Williams . . .

RB: I wouldn't consider them superhero artists, necessarily.
PK: Alternative superhero? I mean, Bill Sienkiewicz has done a lot of comics for Marvel . . .

RB: Sure, but Dave McKean . . . have you seen *Cages*? That's hardly superhero comics.

PK: You're right. But he crosses back and forth. He's part of a group of cartoonists who still *toy* with superhero material, but in a more stylistically artful way.

What more can I say about the Pratt years? Well, I started working on *World War 3* when I was there. Actually, Dan Clowes was also at Pratt, pretty much at the same time that I was. And I barely knew him. It was more, after the fact. But I was really glad I went to art school. Because, they get you to look at the wider world art, rather than only comics. And I already had a pretty good idea about what I wanted to do with comics.

RB: You wanted to do a superhero book?

PK: Not quite. It was more in the tradition of *Heavy Metal*. More of a fantasy . . .

RB: Like, dragons and . . . ?

PK: No! Science fiction. I was reading a lot of science fiction back then. And the teachers at Pratt were really resistant to comics. Basically they were saying, "Look at this other work." You know, German expressionism and so on. They also told me to, "Look out the window," and to, "Try drawing from this live model." And they also said, "Try learning *how* to draw." It's often the case that people in comics jump to a stylized version of the human figure, and they don't have a clue as to what's involved with anatomy. And this got me to actually go and dissect cadavers . . .

RB: Really?!

PK: Yeah, my anatomy class went to the Columbia Medical School and we drew from cadavers.

RB: Jesus! [laughs]

PK: Yeah, it was interesting. And I kept a sketchbook at Pratt. It just got me to sort of expand my perspective. The most vital piece of information that any teacher gave me was when someone told me that, "You have to know something in order to forget it." It's like if you start doing abstract work, without going through the progression that leads up to it? To me, what's interesting about Picasso is that he did this *progression*. He didn't just start seeing the world as a cubist or whatever. And then you had people just doing abstract work that didn't go through a process to get there, and it just seemed hollow. So now I teach a class at the School of Visual Arts in comics. And I cough up a lot of these same ideas that I heard from my teachers at Pratt, which just says, "Stop looking at comics to get ideas about doing comics." Get a sketchbook; look at life. And, for that matter, if you want to come up with stories, they don't have to be out-there fantasy stories. Stories can be based on internal experiences. And I always find that every student ends up having all sorts of stories to tell.

RB: When did you start reading Kafka?

PK: I don't know. I read *Metamorphosis* in college, or something like that. And I thought it was just great. But then I got into looking at his short stories. A friend of mine was a huge Kafka fan. We'd be sitting around, having a beer, and he'd whip out a Kafka short story and just read it out loud.

RB: Uh-huh.

PK: And it just struck me that this would translate beautifully into comics. I feel a real sense of kinship to the kinds of stories that Kafka wrote and to the dark humor that's in there.

RB: At what point did you start getting illustration jobs for big magazines?

PK: Pretty early on, actually.

RB: Really?

PK: Well, at the tail end of my last year in school, I suddenly looked at what I was doing and decided that I hated the direction I was going in. Because I was trying to be more realistic, and I just did this big bust out. I started doing linoleum prints, and I had a least politically leaning content. I was interested in making political work, and the kind of work I was starting to do reproduced really well in newspapers. One of the first places I went was the *New York Times*. I got a job right off the bat with the *Times*'s book review section before I graduated from Pratt. And I had done some illustration work while I was in school. I illustrated a science fiction book, for example. All of the illustrations that I created for the book were in the tradition of realism. Sort of a Brad Holland type thing. And for chapter headings I'd done linoleum prints. And when I looked at the book as a whole I decided that these little, tossed-off chapter headings were the things I liked most about the entire project. You know, of the thirty-odd illustrations that I had created for the book, the chapter headings were the things I liked most about it. They seemed to be the most uncontrived.

Part of the reason had to do with the materials I was working with. Linoleum forces you to do things differently. A lot of things that were very clichéd in my linework got thrown out when I worked with linoleum. And once I did some illustrations for money I started to really hustle. Part of the reason was because I worked in the studio with Chaykin. I got to see how hard everyone worked to drum up jobs. Hustling for work just seemed really normal to me by the time that I graduated from Pratt. And, frankly, I had become a bit of a workaholic. I spent a lot of time running around. As a matter of fact, I was a better self-promoter than I was an artist for a good long time. You know, just pushing, going around to magazines, mailing out work, and doing all that stuff. It's a huge headache. And, as time goes by, I hate it more and more. Because it's really just salesmanship. And I often see crappy work that is *pushed*, and sells, and somebody's making a good living. And then I see great work, where the artist is not a good businessman. Basically you shouldn't have to be a businessman to be an artist. But the truth is, you do.

RB: Yeah!
PK: So I guess, fortunately, that I have enough businessman in me to be able to do both. It's scary how fundamental that is to being able to get work.

RB: So what made you decide to do politically oriented comics?
PK: I guess a lot of it had to do with the historical context. Reagan was president, and there was the ongoing threat—especially with Reagan in office—of nuclear war. And it just hung over my head. And I just thought, "If the world is devastated in a nuclear blast, I don't want the last thing I have to hold up be some moronic fluff piece. If I ever have a kid, and if they turn to me and say, "Well, what did you do, while Rome was burning?" [laughs] You know? I would like to be able to say something meaningful. At some point during this period I made a pact with myself that, if I ever got good enough to get my work out there, that I would work on trying to have something that wasn't just self-serving. I wanted to talk about what was *on my mind*, and what was *pissing me off*, and what was scaring me and all that. And those things were obviously tied into political issues. Politics was hard to avoid. What's sort of funny is that I just find that almost everything I want to talk about is political in nature. If I want to talk about sex, for example . . .

RB: Yeah?
PK: There's so many right-wing forces that want to *block* that discussion, so that what seems to be a very private matter, something that is completely non-political, turns out to be *quite* political. You know, I could get up on a soapbox and yell about the president until I was hoarse. But the second I did anything that is about sex, then advertisers will threaten to pull out.

Kuper's stencil art portrait of the 39th president of the United States, Ronald Reagan, circa 1982

RB: [laughs]

PK: The magazine editor will suddenly say, "No, we can't run *this*." It amazes me. So I'm kinda startled to see that everything I have any interest in is connected to politics. Everything we do, on some level, *is* political. You could be going along with the status quo—*that's* a political action, whether you know it or not. It's very often that people will say, "Oh, I'm not interested in politics," or, "I find politics boring." It's like they're viewing it as political science, rather than as a very interactive part of what you're allowed to do and what you're not allowed to do.

RB: Yeah.

PK: The fact that somebody wants to issue a court ruling about whether you can kiss a guy or not, if you're a guy, or whether a woman can kiss another woman. There's just incredible *heat* on so many actions that people want to do naturally.

RB: So was that why you changed *Bleeding Heart* to *Wild Life*?

PK: No, I changed *Bleeding Heart* to *Wild Life* to increase sales. It's pretty simple. The distributors started to slack off on taking it. And I felt like I was on a roll with the last couple of issues. I had finally found what it was that I wanted to do. I started creating all new material. Rather than trying to revive sales over four or five issues I started a new title in hopes that distributors would give it another chance. It doesn't even get as far as the comic shop, you know. Whether it's a good comic or a bad comic, it doesn't matter; if the distributor turns it down then you the comic buyer don't even get to see it. So sales jumped a thousand copies when we gave it a new title. That was the bottom line.

RB: In one of the ads for *Bleeding Heart* there's a quote from Jello Biafra. Were you ever into the whole punk scene?

PK: Barely.

RB: Barely?

PK: Barely. You know, I listen to some of it. That's just about it. The person who put that ad together pulled the quote from somewhere. I didn't have anything to do with it. But I've met Jello Biafra. At one point we did a *World War 3* show in San Francisco, and he came to the opening. In addition, *Maximum Rock 'n' Roll* has interviewed us, and I think that some of my work appeals to the punk sensibility, and that it comes out of the same place.

RB: What kinds of music do you like?

PK: I have really eclectic tastes. I listen to a fair amount of jazz and a fair amount of pop music. I mean, I like Nirvana and I also like the Police. A lot of times, when I'm working on, say, a piece about the 1970s I'll listen to music from that period. It's a really excellent way to get back in touch with that. Let's see . . . I've been listening to Deep Forest; I just got one of their CDs. Some Sting [yuck—RB], some REM. And I listen to a fair amount of rap music. I like Naughty by Nature in particular. I'll just go through a phase where I want to listen to music that is as grating and as irritating as possible. Then I feel like I need to listen to music that's a little more soothing. It just depends on . . .

RB: Your mood?
PK: Yeah. So it's real eclectic.

RB: What *cartoonists* do you like? [laughs]
PK: Uhhh . . .

RB: Let's get into some name-dropping here.
PK: OK. Let's see. [Lorenzo] Mattotti?

RB: Yeah, yeah.
PK: I *love* his work. And I really like what David Mazzucchelli is doing. And [Miguelanxo] Prado? He just did a book called *Streak of Chalk* that NBM published. I like Seth Tobocman's work a lot, and Eric Drooker's. James Romberger. Love his stuff. Some of these people I work with on *World War 3*. I mean, take Eric Drooker's work. It's not like either of us sits and stares at each other's work, but there's obviously a kindred mentality at work. [laughs] It's funny, somebody came up to me and asked me if Eric Drooker was like my pseudonym?

RB: [laughs]
PK: It's just that there's this funny symbiosis between our work. And it's the same with Seth. We grew up drawing together, and we've done collaborations together. And I've gone onto doing stencils because of working with him.

You know, I really enjoy looking at Saul Steinberg's work, along with Ralph Steadman, and George Grosz. When I look at this stuff it strikes me as being very passionate. I generally favor work that has passion in it, where the person is coming from a personal point-of-view, rather than making stuff that's simply stylish. To me, when I look at a lot of contemporary illustration, it's just *sheen*. And I'm much more interested in content.

I read a lot of stuff that Drawn and Quarterly publishes—pretty much across the board. They publish a lot of really good things.

RB: You have to mention Jim Woodring.
PK: Jim Woodring, of course.

RB: Because every cartoonist that I've interviewed has had something to say about Woodring's work, so you have to say something about him.
PK: Oh, okay. Jim who? [laughs] No, I love his stuff. And of course I like Dan Clowes. And there's Peter Bagge's *Hate*. I like guys like Tardi, and I really like

Chris Ware's book. I recently picked up the *Smithsonian Book of Comic Strips*—that has a lot of great material, by people like Lionel Feininger. It's great when you have never heard of an artist and find out that they were doing just a catalogue of great work that nobody's ever heard of. You know, there are a lot of artists outside of comics who are worth looking at. I'm interested in art as an overall form, not as a narrow form. It always blows my mind when you have people who know nothing about comics, or nothing about fine art, or nothing about illustration. To me, it's like, "Do you like art or *don't* you?" If you do, I would imagine it would be interesting to explore art. To sneer at illustration, because it's commercial art, or at comics, because it's some low form, it's just *ignorance*. And there's a lot of ignorance going around.

RB: I wanted to ask you about something. When Joe Matt fantasizes about other women, in his comics, he gets a lot of flak from his girlfriend. You've also drawn stories about your fantasies, so what does your wife have to say about that? [laughs]

PK: Well, I haven't put her in any compromising positions in my comics. And she knows all of my old stories.

RB: Uh-huh.

PK: Our agreement is that she has the final cut on anything that involves *her*. Other than that, it's my life.

RB: You can fantasize all you want? [laughs]

PK: Well, a lot of my strips are not so much about the fantasies themselves, as they are about the fallout. [phone rings] The illustration world never sleeps.

RB: Where were we? Oh yes, I was thinking of your strip, "Beat It."

PK: Right.

RB: And also about the story in *Bleeding Heart* which talks about your homosexual experience.

PK: My homosexual encounter, yes. [laughs] Actually, the funny thing is that it wasn't about the homosexual encounter. It was about a long-running shitty relationship with a girl, and the hilarious turns that, you know, happened during that time with her. And I'd thought of that strip as being about that relationship with *her*; the other thing was a complete side bit.

RB: Yeah.

PK: But because it's rather dramatic, that's what sticks in people's minds. [laughs]

RB: What was it like, testifying for the Mike Diana case?

PK: That was very surreal. It was definitely one of the more surreal experiences I've had in the comics world. It was like talking to a brick wall. It was a scary experience because I got to see that sort of ignorant mentality in action. The prosecutor was basically trying to take me apart on the stand. The thing is, though, that I've spent enough time with comics that I actually *am* an expert. I don't have to pretend. It's not an area that I'm *vague* about. I know the subject well. And no prosecutor is going to know it better than I do. Especially when they rush to put a case together. And they figured that, I don't know, they'd walk into a comic shop, get a rough idea of what it was about, and be able to throw out a bunch of stuff at me. When they did that, all I had to do was give an actual answer to their question, and this made them look foolish. This at least seemed obvious to me, but it was all dismissed. Basically I was a "Jew from New York," a Jewish crack user from New York. And R. Seth Friedman, who publishes *Factsheet 5*, couldn't be more of an expert on zines. Probably the number one expert in the country. And to the prosecution he was just a "Fag Jew from San Francisco."

RB: [laughs]

PK: So that's how the prosecutor portrayed us, as being the other. "Here in Pinellas County, we don't have to listen to those *other* people." You know, "They do what they want up in New York and San Francisco. But *here*, we have a different standard." And the people in the jury said, "That's right! That's right!" And so that's how it ended. I thought I had reached the jury with my testimony, and in fact, so did the defense. They were clapping me on the back, and took me out to a strip club afterwards . . .

RB: [laughs]

PK: . . . and bought me drinks. But I might as well not have bothered, given the way that the trial turned out. On the other hand, in the final analysis, Mike Diana became almost famous, thanks to the prosecutor. They ended up doing exactly what they didn't want to do, which is to help promote his work. Hopefully this will all be behind him at some point and he'll be able to do what he wants.

Kuper recounts his experience on the Mike Diana obscenity trial in 1993

You know, I'm not crazy for what Mike does. He's developing. Let's see what he does in ten years. And if he's doing the same thing as he's doing now, I won't be interested, frankly. But what Mike Diana does, and what I do, is not really that far apart. Certainly, in the eyes of the prosecutor, it could easily have been me. That's one thing I got a really strong sense about. I could see clearly that by doing *World War 3*, I'm like a commie, you know? A Zionist, occupation government, anti-American homo. And people like that would love to see me in jail, basically for just expressing myself through my work. And that wasn't something I was totally unaware of, but it's amazing how New York offers a much more permissive environment. Somebody like Mike Diana would be one of many cartoonists.

RB: He'd probably not do as well as he's doing down in Florida [laughs].
PK: Oh no, absolutely not. And it's not that he's doing that well down there, it's just that, he'd be a blip on the screen here in New York. It just makes you realize that things are pretty fragile. That there's a fine line between what's okay and what's not.

RB: Who is your favorite *Love and Rockets* character?
[Peter looks at me quizzically]

RB: [laughs] I don't know why, I . . .
PK: No comment.

RB: Okay.
PK: Hopey. [laughs]

RB: I just thought I'd add in a silly question like that.
PK: Yeah.

RB: Umm . . .
PK: Why don't you ask me who my favorite X-Men character is?

RB: [laughs]
PK: Wolverine, dude! He rocks!

RB: What was the last movie you saw in a theatre?
PK: The very last one I saw was . . . *Spanking the Monkey*. [laughs] And I saw *The Client*. Fairly forgettable, fast food entertainment. There's not that many good movies out there.

RB: What was the last good movie you saw?

PK: The good movies. Let's see. I liked *Red Rock West* a lot. [laughs] I like the crime/murder mystery genre. And there's about three good movies like that. You know, like *Blood Simple* or something like that. I saw *Strangers on a Train* recently. I just love Hitchcock movies. *Paris is Burning*, that was a very disturbing one. God, it's real easy to draw a blank.

RB: What do you think of Peter Bagge using an inker? [laughs]

PK: It's fine.

RB: Fine?

PK: Fine, yeah.

RB: Okay.

PK: You know, it seems to me that there's a lot of concern over how . . .

RB: That he's selling out or something.

PK: Yeah, something like that. There's a lot of that running around. And I certainly feel that, now and again when I see somebody do something, I just think, "Did you *really* need the money?" Or, "Did you really need to do that?" But for the most part, the truth is that making any kind of living at comics is very hard. It's real easy to believe that people should be held up to various standards. Like, I remember reading in *Destroy All Comics* that Jim Woodring had just written an issue of *Aliens* or whatever.

RB: Uh-huh.

PK: You know, I don't give a *shit* if he did that. He does good work. I like what he does. You know, if somebody's produced a number of really good things . . . I mean, I try to live by a kind of code of my own. For example, I turn down work all the time. Every week I turn down jobs. Because they're dopey, and I don't need the money to do a fluff piece that has nothing to do with politics. Sometimes I'll take an illustration job if it isn't too abhorrent from a political standpoint. I did something for *Entertainment Weekly* this week. The political content is just slightly above zero. The truth is, I fretted about taking that job. I didn't lose a lot of sleep over it, but I just had this creeping feeling. Like, I want people when they look at my work to see consistency to it. But in this case it was like, "Where am I going with this?"

RB: [laughs] You don't have to hold up to anybody's standards, basically.

PK: Yeah, I mean, I'm making up my own rules, and I think most people are trying to do that. It's like, would you say to somebody who's a waitress, "How *dare* you work there slopping that food! I can't believe you're . . ." Well, most people do all kinds of shitty jobs trying to *make ends meet*. I mostly applaud artists who are trying to do good work. You know, I applaud Spike Lee for all the attempts that he makes. He is, in a lot of ways, asking to be held to a higher yardstick. So he's going to get shit for when he misses the mark. You can complain about it, but I don't write him off for it. I applaud him for trying. Because there's definitely intent there. I'm trying to think of who's truly pure on all the markers you could put together.

To bring it back to Peter Bagge, do you want to see more issues of *Hate*? Do you want to be able to read it more regularly? He can only do so much.

RB: Yeah.

PK: I think that Peter's trying to figure out how to do it in a way that he can get it out there. In fact, I think it's a smart move toward trying to get his comic out to a *much* larger audience. And, if he doesn't compromise in terms of tone, and ideas, and the mentality behind it, if having an assistant can help him get it out, then he should go for it.

You know what? I'm *glad* that Matt Groening has managed to get his stuff out with the mentality that's in the work. I wish it wasn't sold as Butterfinger ads, and all the other hype, because I think that cheapens it. But I'm *glad* that it's out there in the mainstream, the way it is. I'd really like to get my work in front of people who don't otherwise see it. I don't want them to *have* to walk into a comic shop to see what I do.

As soon as you start selling anything, you've obviously done something wrong. I think it's worth being suspicious about your own work, especially if it starts getting out there too much. But at the same time it doesn't all have to be four people reading it in order for it to keep its value. There's a lot of contradictions here. I run into contradictions all the time. If I do work for *Time* magazine, I'm doing work for an *evil conglomerate*. So is the *New Yorker*. So is just about any place that's owned by somebody else. You know, I did a record cover for BMG, which turns out to be owned by RCA, which is owned by General Electric, which owns NBC, and GE does nuclear power. It's mindboggling! Every time I get a job I could say, "I'll get back to you in a couple of weeks, after I've tracked down *who* you're evilly connected to." So, what brand of light bulb do you have in your home?

RB: Yeah.
PK: There are contradictions everywhere.

RB: Here's a good one. Do you vote?
PK: Yeah.

RB: Do you think it makes a difference?
PK: I'm totally upset with the choices that I'm given. They've already cheated before you get to the voting booth.

RB: Yeah.
PK: But, yes, I think it does make a difference. Even the difference between George Bush and whatever the schmuck we have now . . .

RB: [laughs]
PK: Presidents are all too often cheerleaders. In Reagan's case, he was an excellent cheerleader for the right. In Clinton's case, he's primarily ineffectual. There's this or that he can do, taking minor steps. But I find that preferable to galloping ahead, into the destruction and all that . . .

RB: Fire and brimstone.
PK: Yeah. I remain stupidly optimistic, probably because I travel so much. That's instilled some optimism in me. Just getting a chance to see the world. I'm *happier* that way. So I try to keep my head up.

It's like, if we're running toward destruction, like a locomotive on the tracks, it feels like I'm throwing a grape on the rail, and hoping that it's going to slow down the train. It's such a juggernaut moving toward bad trouble. But I take solace in the fact that the subways run more or less on schedule. Considering how fragile the system is, it's amazing that the subway system works at all. I find that is a driving force a lot of the time. It makes me say, "Okay, then, I've got to get to work. I have to get these images out there. I only have X amount of time." You're going to die, in a fairly short period of time. So I use these things as a means to keep myself running.

RB: Do you think that makes a nice closing?
PK: Yeah, sort of a precipice kind of a closing.

RB: [laughs]
PK: Like, we're all going to die, but hey, it keeps me drawing. [laughter]

System Failure

DOUGLAS WOLK / 1996

From *World Art: The Magazine of Contemporary Visual Arts* #14. Reprinted by permission.

Peter Kuper's comics, collected in his book *Stripped*, are introduced by his alter ego, "Hef." In a comfortable bathrobe, smoking a pipe, the world-famous, much-loved cartoonist looks back and laughs at his foolish youth. Now he's at the top of the world, flying around his beloved city and looking down at the little people below.

The real Kuper resembles Hef . . . up to a point. It's true that after decades as a struggling cartoonist, Kuper is in a comfortable position. He's an award-winning illustrator who's done covers for *Time*, comics for everyone from the *New York Times* to *Mad*, and book adaptations of Kafka and others. He has a lovely Manhattan apartment and a baby daughter. At the time we spoke, his solo show was about to open at Curcio Spector, a small gallery on the Lower East Side, and he was in final negotiations for an animated TV series based on his autobiographical pieces. But he engages his environment—from the ripped-up streets of New York City to the collective struggles of the art community—with street-level candor. *World War 3 Illustrated*, the magazine he cofounded and still helps edit, continues to present powerfully political material by emerging cartoonists, and Kuper's own provocative, conscience-driven work has made him one of the most important activist comic artists of his generation.

Born in 1958 and raised in Cleveland, Ohio, Kuper came to New York City when he was 18 to work as an animator. Returning to art school shortly thereafter, he met up with and cofounded *World War 3 Illustrated* with his childhood friend Seth Tobocman. *WW3* was conceived as an anthology of political comics, mostly by little-known cartoonists. Seventeen years and 24 issues later, now assembled by a revolving group of editors including Kuper and Tobocman, *World War 3 Illustrated* may be the longest-running zine anywhere. "It's a huge amount of work for nothing," Kuper says—and then corrects himself. "For practically no pay—not for nothing."

At the opposite end of the visibility scale, Kuper also has the distinction of being the first cartoonist to do a regular strip for the *New York Times*. *Eye of the Beholder* was proposed by an art director at the *Times* in the early '90s. "He said that they wanted it to revolve around the city, and that it should have no ongoing characters, but each comic to relate to the next somehow. As I thought about it, I realized, 'If there's text there, it's going to be a real problem, because every week I'm going to be dealing with an editor suggesting I change a word here or there.'" His solution was to draw it as a wordless strip, with four panels of cryptic images of the city or its residents followed by a fifth that showed the perspective uniting the first four, and usually providing some kind of political snap that called attention to social inequality or urban fear. *Eye of the Beholder* ran for five months in the *Times* before moving to a number of alternative weekly papers, where it still appears regularly; a book collection was recently published by NBM.

Eye of the Beholder is drawn in one of two styles Kuper has most used in his mature work, a scratchboard technique that brings to mind woodcut/comics pioneers like Lynd Ward and Frans Masereel, as well as more-recent artists like Eric Drooker [a Drooker calendar hangs above Kuper's drawing board]. It has also appeared in his autobiographical stories and in *Give It Up!*, Kuper's adaptation of several Franz Kafka stories. For Kuper, the scratchboard method has roots in some of his early experimentations with linoleum-print comics: "I was really drawn to that, working with materials as opposed to strict pen-and-ink—something where there was some sort of process there . . . There's a comics style that's fine if it's straight cartooning, but there's that sort of in-between place where it ends up looking pretentious. I found that when I moved into [other materials], that shift broke the shackles of the traditional pen-and-ink."

Another process-based style has dominated Kuper's more recent comics work: an extraordinary stencil technique whose bold shapes and indeterminacy of detail evoke both a universal language of symbols and the sidewalk graffiti of the cities in which most of Kuper's stories are set. The indeterminacy also provides him with a challenge: "I think it's easy for me to get facile with materials, so that I know what the outcome is, and then somewhere in the process it becomes deadened. In dealing with using stencils, it has been a continuous surprise to me. Until I'm putting the last mark down, I really don't know what I've got."

The most extensive and impressive example of Kuper's stencil technique to date is *The System*, a comic-book mini-series, recently collected into a book, that depicts the interrelated stories of a few dozen city dwellers, rich and poor, and the poisonous political and economic system that connects them. Each panel of The System leads into the next by either continuity (a skateboarder in the background of one panel is in the foreground of the next) or transformation (the screaming face of a stabbing victim becomes a subway car in a tunnel). Like *Eye of the Beholder* and various stories Kuper has done in *World War 3 Illustrated* and elsewhere, *The System* is told wordlessly, conveying its story solely through images and implication.

Kuper's interest in wordless comics has recently led to an unexpected assignment: He is the new artist for *Mad* magazine's long-running feature *Spy vs. Spy*, which he has transformed into a boldly, playfully designed strip as visually audacious as George Herriman's *Krazy Kat*. As Kuper says, "At first, I just thought, 'You know, it just wasn't what I do, it's somebody else's characters.' But then I thought . . . 'No harm in doing a sample.' And as soon as I sat down, I realized that I had grown up on *Mad*, that all my wordless comics were influenced by *Spy vs. Spy* and Sergio Aragones, among others. It flew with them, and I thought, 'Well, I think I could really get cozy with this.' It seems like there are some possibilities, you know, for getting politics into it."

It's pretty clear that "getting some politics into it" is a priority for Kuper in nearly all the work he does. He adapted Upton Sinclair's *The Jungle* for Classics Illustrated a few years ago, and a lot of his own writing is in the same vein: fiction that serves the same purpose as investigative journalism, bringing awful truths to light and exposing the mechanisms by which the powerful hoard and abuse their power. His stories take on the horrific disparity between the very rich and the very poor, the fear of nuclear war, the corruption of the legal and political systems. Those have been his concerns since he started drawing comics, he explains: "It's so much work doing a comic strip, and I didn't want to do it about nothing . . . Over the years, I've found that there were so many things going on that I feel really compelled to talk about or respond to. I've found I'm doing more and more personal things as time goes by—stories about losing my virginity, let's say—but I find that there is an innately political content to them—in so many things. It's almost unavoidable to me . . . I'm a very optimistic and enthusiastic person and all that, but nonetheless, every time I look around, I just feel like, 'Wow, we are just spiraling down, and I don't want to be fiddling while Rome burns.' And it's cathartic, too, to talk about these things. Just to get some of this stuff out makes me less crazy."

Besides, Kuper points out, *World War 3 Illustrated*'s existence—and continued survival—is as much a political statement as its contents, and important to its creators as well as to its readers. The magazine has championed the cause of Mike Diana, the first American cartoonist to be imprisoned on obscenity charges (Kuper testified in his defense at his trial), and Mumia Abu Jamal, an American journalist on death row who many believe was framed for political reasons; it's also given them an outlet for their work to be published. "To take action at all, I think you have to start by getting over that feeling that it's hopeless. I think one of the things that can have an impact is seeing work out there, or reading books, or seeing art that you feel has that spirit, that sort of community.

"With something like *World War 3 Illustrated*, in a lot of ways, even though the comics may be talking about this political issue or that, the magazine *itself* is the achievement: bringing together a group of maybe 50 people with different points of view . . . Now there's stuff we are not going to print; we're definitely leftwing. But a lot of the point is to create a place that's like a mini-society, with room for people who have something important to say but don't necessarily have all of their chops together; that has room for a broad group of people under a single umbrella, so that we can all move toward a unified cause of, if nothing else, putting out a magazine. If you're going to talk about changing society, and you can't get together in a room with a group of people and get anything done, then you're truly hopeless. But if you can do that . . ." He gestures toward a studio wall that holds copies of the run of *World War 3 Illustrated*, as well as a book that features highlights from its first 16 years.

The walls of Kuper's studio and apartment are also decorated with some of his more three-dimensional work. He's started doing paintings on old windows that are divided into individual panes—like panels of a comic strip—making use of missing or broken panes as features of the medium. In the course of his extensive travels (his book *ComicsTrips* includes stories and sketchbooks from an eight-month voyage he and his wife made a few years back), he's created a series of designs for "travel masks," which he's had carved by master mask-makers in Bali and elsewhere. All the masks are stylized faces based on travel experiences: "jet lag," "new in town, please rob me," and the like. They all have names, but Kuper doesn't have to explain them—particularly in the context of the iconic vocabulary he's developed in his comics, it's pretty clear what each one represents.

That's the way Kuper intends it to be. "Cliché has a really bad connotation, but the reason why something becomes cliché is because of its associative experience. I try to keep what I'm doing consistent, as opposed to creating icons based on other people's icons that I've seen before. Comics continually reference other comics . . . There's this incestuous dying gene pool that's just regenerating itself based on other stuff. There are these things that go around—no matter where you go in the world, you'll see them. And the artists who use them aren't necessarily connected, but they were connected to the general pool of something that related to it. Certainly, when I feel like I've touched that at all, I feel like that's the greatest achievement."

There are some questions, though, that need to be answered by an artist who conceives of his work as explicitly or implicitly political: is the point to sway people's opinions, and if so, whose? If you're putting political work in a magazine read mostly by people whose opinions are fairly close to your own, in what way is it supposed to work? "As time goes by," Kuper says, "I worry less and less about *trying* to do that, and more and more about just putting out what I feel, and figuring: If nothing else, the converted will have something to read."

Comics: Underground, Adult, Real-Life, and Radical

KENT WORCESTER / 2002

From *Comics Forum* #24. Reprinted by permission.

Kent Worcester: We have assembled an exciting lineup of political cartoonists. I'm going to ask each panelist to talk about what it means to be a political cartoonist today, what kinds of sacrifices are involved, and whether this is a good time to be a political cartoonist.

Mac, could you start by describing what it's like being a political cartoonist in New York today?

Mac McGill: O.K. For me, it's a continuous struggle, economically and everything else. I don't hustle my work out to the mainstream. I work with people and publications that I have respect for and care about. I've been squatting for a while in New York City, so my overhead is low, and I teach part-time, so I don't really market my work a lot. I do a lot of artwork at home, and put it out there to publications and organizations I really care about. A lot of times it's for free, or for very little money. And it's a struggle. It always has been. But it's a struggle that I love, because at the end of the day I'm proud of the work I do. That's what matters. I want to do the work I really care about.

KW: Tell us about your work.

MM: I do illustrations for *Tikkun* and other progressive publications. I like to do socially conscious stories about people, personal stories, and also about broad subjects such as racism. I work in pen and ink a lot, and I provide a lot of detail. I really get off on that, you know. I do a lot of personal stories. I do a lot of work in the neighborhood, and around the area here on the Lower East Side, where I live. Did I answer your question?

KW: Yes, that's good.

Seth Tobocman: I've been doing political comics since the 1980s, and I feel this is a good time to be doing comics on political issues because there's a lot more people getting involved than were in the '80s. In that sense, my work gets used a lot. It's always been really difficult financially. I can't recommend this as a way to make a living, although I have tried to do that, and I do get some money from it, I think in terms of the amount of time that you have to put in, nobody would say that it's a great deal. I'd say that the great thing about doing political illustration has been the way people will pick up a piece of artwork and use it for their own purposes. I'll have done a piece of artwork, and five years later I've seen that it's been used by groups all over the world, in their literature. I think Mac, Fly, and Peter have all had this experience. There's a drawing I did in the 1980s that wound up being used by the African National Congress without my ever knowing that they were going to do that. It's really great to be able to put work out and know that people have some use for it. And the economics of cartooning was never that good. For me, they're probably a little better now than they were a few years ago, but that's because I've been hustling a lot.

Fly: My name is Fly, and I guess I've been doing political comics for a little over ten years now. It wasn't really a decision that I made, like, "Now I will be a political cartoonist." I've drawn incessantly since I was very young. Ever since I can remember I've always had a sketchbook. And when I came to New York City I didn't really have a place to live. I was homeless for a couple of years, but I was in the neighborhood and I met Seth, and the *World War 3* crew, and I went to some of their meetings, and when I was showing Seth my sketchbook he was very encouraging, and was telling me that I should draw comics. So I had been playing around with the comic thing for a while, but when he was encouraging me, I thought, OK, I'll try it. Some of my first comics were in issues of *World War 3*. But I didn't make a decision to become a political cartoonist. It was just the fact that I was drawing my life, basically. And it's definitely not a financial decision, either. I usually don't make any money doing my comics.

A lot of my comics are about situations living in the squats on the Lower East Side. I've been living in a squat for over ten years now, and so a lot of my comics are about the struggle to keep the building open, the struggle to work on the building, like internal dynamics, and I've also done a lot of comics on street punk lifestyles, which is not really a mainstream thing. So a lot of art directors and people who would give you illustration jobs kind of look at it and they see like, you know, punks fighting cops, and they're like, "We'll call you." And so it doesn't get me a lot of jobs. I have to work at other jobs to supplement my income, and a lot of the politics that I'm portraying in my comics are very extreme, and under the radar. As a political cartoonist, most of my stuff is underground; I do a lot of stuff for punk zines, and I have a compilation of stuff published by Autonomedia. I do put out my own self-published zines, but it's definitely not a financially secure situation.

Peter Kuper: When I was in art school, back in the late 1970s, I was doing political illustrations and comics. Particularly in terms of political comics, there weren't very many outlets for this kind of stuff. As it happens, Seth and I were both going to Pratt Institute at the time, and we were having the same general experience. So we decided to self-publish. We founded *World War 3 Illustrated* in 1979, and it's still being published to this day. That was one means of jumping over the hurdle of, "How do you get out there and get published?" because nobody wants to publish you until you get published. And it gave not only the two of us, but also a whole number of people, an opportunity to get their work printed, and it continues to do so. The magazine has created a home for a lot of work, and a lot of images in general—poster art, stencil art—that you might see on the streets. And that we've tried to sort of grab that kind of work and get it into our pages so that it doesn't just become a distant memory, and becomes part of the history of work that was done.

I went through a period of time where I attempted to do political illustration, found it difficult to find outlets for it. I started doing more traditional, boring illustration projects while doing comics for *WW3* and a few other places. Basically I just hit a point where I simply couldn't bring myself to do illustrations on widgets when, say, there was a Gulf War going on, or whatever. It was maddening to try and compartmentalize like that, and so I started to basically narrow what I was doing, and say, well I'm going to do work that will have some social or political commentary in it. And, interestingly, I found that there were a lot of publications, such as the *New York Times* and *Time*, that feature essays, sometimes written by people whose point of view I can't stand, and sometimes whose point of view I agree with. And I've found that I am able to get a lot of the imagery out in publications like that.

SECRETS of THE GRAPHIC NOVELIST*

*BOY'S CLUB VERSION

Formation of a cartoonist: the early years

I probably run into more trouble for using images that have sexual connotations in them, than for political images. I've run into more stumbling blocks where somebody says, "that looks phallic," like, say, a policeman's nightstick, than saying, "I have a policeman with a bloody nightstick." Primarily by doing more and more of the kind of thing I think I do best, and hustling a lot, I have been able to find work in more mainstream venues. Comics is in the midst of a renaissance now, but for the last, say, twenty years, those of us who've been doing it have been struggling with the fact that it's a medium that people look down on and don't consider to be art. But there's a decent group of us. I think that as things are turning out, it's looking brighter for political cartooning now that books like [Joe Sacco's] *Safe Area Gorazda* are being covered in the *New York Times Book Review*. It may have taken me eight years to do a single book, but I find if I'm working on several things at the same time, then one comes out here, and one comes out over there, and they seem to be coming out more often. A lot of it is really just working all the time and having your ear to the ground for what new outlets may come out, finding alternative papers that may not pay much, but if you find a bunch of them, then it starts to translate into something.

Ted Rall: I've been doing this since the 1980s, and it pretty much took me from about 1987 when I got serious about political cartooning. And it really was my mission. I've always wanted to do this, and so I didn't care if I got paid or not—I was willing to do it because I had to do it. I think that's pretty much the case for most artists. They don't have any choice.

I blundered into syndication in 1991 when the *San Francisco Chronicle* lost a deal that they were looking for with a well-known cartoonist, and my package came in the next day, and they signed me up. To give you a sense of how little money there is involved in this sort of thing, in 1991 I worked with a company that syndicated my cartoons in twelve newspapers. The smallest was the *Philadelphia Daily News*, while the largest was the *Los Angeles Times*. I was doing three cartoons a week for them. And I don't think I broke two hundred dollars a month for three years. These are well-known newspapers, so you can imagine how much less it is when you're dealing with alternative papers. My favorite is the *Washington Post Weekly Edition*, which is a tabloid version of the *Washington Post*. It pays ten dollars a cartoon. You split that with your syndicate, so they get five bucks. That leaves you five—Uncle Sam takes two, so that leaves three. Oh, and they subtract the cost of mailing it to them. So it's a buyer's market when it comes to political cartooning. And it doesn't help that most of our peers in mainstream political cartooning are doing such a shitty job that nobody respects the profession anymore.

I kind of live in both the mainstream and alternative worlds, not by choice. I do what I have to do. I don't target it to any particular audience, and people like it or they don't, and so I have a very eclectic range of outlets. I don't know why the New York Times runs me—they just do. In terms of the compromises you have to make, generally I don't make any compromises to be in newspapers, they just don't run my stuff if they don't like it. In terms of magazines, that's a whole different animal. Magazines are very edit-intensive. Not just for political reasons, but also for reasons like Peter said. You just end up with the strangest reasons to get censored. I did a really stupid cartoon when they renamed National Airport after Ronald Reagan, depicting all the air traffic controllers asleep, and the planes crashing and burning. And I got a call on Saturday night from the magazine editor of Time, and he's like, "We're killing your cartoon." It turns out it's because he's friends with Reagan. I'm like, "Reagan can't tell. He doesn't read anymore." [laughter] That's the kind of thing you have to deal with.

Like most of us here, I can't really complain about the finances now—I cobble together a living. And the advantage of it is that I do a lot of different things. I do freelance illustration, I write a column, and so on. Only in the world of cartooning would freelance writing be considered a cash cow! I used to have a radio show, and I'm about to start a new one, and so I do a lot of different things and put together a living. And the advantage is that you only get fired by twenty percent of your paycheck at any given time, so it does give you a certain degree of independence. The disadvantage, of course, is that you're not a name anywhere. You know, you're not Herblock of the Washington Post, you're not whomever of the Los Angeles Times, you're just this guy who sends out stuff, but that doesn't really matter. I'm just lucky to have gotten what I think is a voice of anger and progressive politics into mainstream venues.

For two years I ran in Fortune magazine and they never edited a word. I did a cartoon specifically making fun of Steve Case, the CEO of America Online, and published his personal email address in the cartoon. And Fortune never censored me. I get more censored working for so-called progressive publications than I do for rightwing ones. The rightwing outlets, maybe they view a lefty as like a token, and so they don't get in the way. But we're meanest to our own, and I'll leave it at that.

Tom Tomorrow: Well, Fortune asked me to contribute, looked at my stuff, and said, "No fucking way!" So I don't know if I buy into that. I do a strip called This Modern World, which mostly runs in the alternative press. I don't go through a syndicate, which means you don't have these mafia people taking half your income in order to lick the envelopes. But it also means I mostly don't get into daily papers. Fortunately, the alternative weeklies sprang up with a culture that they would actually buy cartoons without going through the syndicates. None of them pays much, of course. I was very poor for a long time, and then I started to make a living, and now I'm OK. Yeah, so I do this cartoon each week, and there's not that much to complain about . . . it's a great way to make a living. There's very little distinction between my life and my work—whatever I'm talking about and whatever I'm thinking about, that's what get channeled in to my work, and that's just the routine of my week, and I guess I'm about as happy as a congenitally pissed off, bitter person can be.

Matt Wuerker: I just came up on the train from Washington, DC this morning, where the Republicans are busy renaming everything after Ronald Reagan. It's not just the airport—they want to name bridges and schools and drinking fountains after Reagan. Which make it really easy to get lost in DC now! But in answer to the question—is this a good time for political cartoonists—what's bad for the country is often really good for the political cartoonist, so things are great now that we have a Bush back in the White House. My interest in cartooning is also graphic, in that I really like drawing. I'm a bit archaic in that I do carefully rendered, crosshatched drawings like something from the nineteenth century, which is really out of fashion. But my other main interest in cartooning is humor. I really believe that as an activist, as an artist, that humor helps us get places with our politics. Being strident doesn't allow us to get anywhere.

There was a great Monty Python movie, *And Now For Something Completely Different*, which featured a skit, set in World War I, in which British intelligence has figured out the funniest joke in the world. If you hear this joke you will literally die laughing. They realize what they've got and they carefully have it translated into German, each piece broken down, and then they set up all these big speakers across the Western Front, and they read the joke in German. And all these Germans start laughing in the trenches, and they fall out and die, and the war's over. And everybody lives happily ever after. This is a nice metaphor for the power of editorial cartoons. It's dropped leaflets behind enemy lines, and opening peoples' minds, and lightening things up. There's a new facet that has opened up with the world of the Internet that sort of makes that power exponential. Some people call it viral marketing. You know, the email joke that gets spread around the world because everybody forwards it to their friends. Cartoons will spread around once everyone learns how to do attachments with their emails. You don't need to get into a newspaper, you don't need to get your work into the *New York Times*, for everybody to see it. Which is a really interesting phenomenon.

KW: I have a few more questions, but I think I'll turn things over to the audience. I'm hoping that at least a few audience members will have questions for our panelists, and I'll try to make sure that everyone on the panel gets a chance to respond.

First Audience Member: As a cartoonist you have to be an artist as well as somebody who is able to discern the irony and humor in everyday situations. It seems to me that both tasks are difficult. The first question I have is, do you think you have to be a great artist if you're funny and clever? And the second part of the question . . .

TT: There are several great artists up here, but they don't include the two of us [he points to Ted Rall].

First Audience Member: And the second part of the question is, keeping in mind how difficult it may be to find funny and clever things to say, do you have mixed feelings about George Bush's election?

KW: Why don't we take one or two more questions.

Second Audience Member: I know that Tom Tomorrow worked on the Ralph Nader campaign, and did some interesting work that was shown at some of the rallies. I wondered if he might like to talk about what that experience was like, and if anybody else has done something similar for a political campaign.

KW: Another question?

Third Audience Member: I'm a member of the older generation. What part does computers and computerized art play in your work?

KW: Good question.

Fourth Audience Member: I wanted to ask Ted to say a little more about the problems with mainstream editorial cartooning.

KW: Okay, we have enough questions. Mac, do you want to start things off?

MM: I don't use computers with my work. I mean, I try to avoid it. My lettering is not the best in the world, so I typeset a lot of stories I work on with the computer. I may make my homegrown posters and stuff with my little outdated Macintosh, but I try to stay with pen and ink. I guess I'm avoiding reality for as long as I can.

ST: With regard to the relationship between artwork and humor, I'll have to admit I'm not a real funny guy. However, with regard to the relationship between drawing and writing, that is a really demanding aspect of comics. The fact that you're working from a text that you write, or trying to tell a story, as opposed to just coming up with a nice design, or an attractive single image, is technically pretty demanding. When you say, OK, I want to draw a picture of such-and-such happening and then next thing that happens is X, and the next thing after that is Y, then you have to be able to create whatever X and Y are. So I think that in technical terms drawing and writing comics is pretty demanding. With the best comic book artists, their work may not look terribly sophisticated, but they actually draw really well. It's perhaps more demanding to be a good comic book artist than to be a good illustrator, although there are people with very simply technique who nonetheless can convey a lot with it. And good can come in many forms. I mean, take Peter Bagge, who does a comic book called *Hate*. I don't think he ever developed a realistic drawing style, but he had a certain stylized approach, and as his work developed it became incredibly expressive, and he can do all kinds of things with it. It's a really demanding field.

As far as computers are concerned, just about everything I did in my last book I had to put into digital format in order to get the book into print. That's been difficult for me, because it has made the printing process more complex in certain ways. Particularly if your artwork was originally designed to be shot without computers. Now I'm starting to learn the positive aspects of working with computers. In the future a lot of people are going to do their drawing with the aid of their computer because you're going to have to put it in the computer to print it out.

With regard to George W. Bush, I have a story about that. I did an introduction for the next edition of the book *Fortunate Son*, which is a biography of Bush that was first published by St. Martins Press, which then decided to burn all of their copies. Soft Skull Press then published it, and then they were sued for some of the material that appeared in the introduction. They hired me to do a cartoon introduction to the book. And, at about this the time that this happened, I got a visit from the Secret Service, which had intercepted a letter sent to the *Daily News*. The letter was written on the back of a flyer with my artwork on it, typed, and the letter writer was threatening to kill Bush. The letter said, "If that murderous bastard George W. Bush comes to New York City I'll kill him, if I have to get a bomb and blow up two blocks of New York City to do it I will, I swear to God I will." That's how you know I didn't write it, it said, "I swear to God I will."

And then it said, "I'm not afraid to tell you who I am," and it had my name and address. And it was not signed; it was typed. So, you know, we had to go to the Secret Service office in the World Trade Center. We had to go the WTC, and ask them if we could clarify this. That was with my lawyer, Stanley Cohen, the world's premiere criminal defense attorney, and they wouldn't let us in. They said, "You don't have the security clearance," and I said, "Look, I don't want to be here. You're looking for me." So they finally let us in, and then the guy said, "What was it that we wanted to see this guy about? Oh yeah." They brought out one of the millions of files on people they're bothering, and they found the flyer with the typewritten letter on it, and on the back of it was my artwork, and the guy says, "You know, we saw this drawing painted on your floor." I said, "Yeah, you did. It's by me. But I have a plane ticket that says that I wasn't in New York when the letter was sent." And they said, "Well, Mr. Tobocman, do you have any enemies?" [laughter] And I said, "Well, maybe anyone who thinks that [political prisoner] Mumia Abu Jamal is guilty," and my lawyer is, like, "Seth, shut the fuck up." So we left, and that was the end of that. I don't know if it had anything to do with the fact that I was working on *Fortunate Son*, but I do know that the publisher is getting quite paranoid. He's making certain that he pays his taxes, and stuff like that, because he thinks he'll get hassled. And I have no idea who would have produced the letter, whether it was someone connected to Bush, or someone who just doesn't like me, or whether it was written by a misguided lunatic who likes to do things in my name. I do know that it made me feel very nervous about going to the inauguration and being anywhere near Bush. So I think that political cartooning can be a very interesting profession to be in. That's my answer.

Fly: As for Bush, I don't really have mixed feelings. I think that he shouldn't be in office. But I think that the system of government needs to be restructured anyway, so that's a whole other story. As for using computers, I've been using them for about fifteen years now, and originally did graphic design, and I think they're great, personally. I do a lot of the actual drawing with a brush and ink,

An example of Kuper's *Eye of the Beholder* comic strip, which began its run in the *New York Times*

and then scan it into Photoshop, and it's great because I can change things around, and tweak it, and maybe create some animation, or put grey tones on, or color it. Instead of having to send something FedEx, or Priority Mail, I can send it through the Internet to various publications. A lot of printing presses are becoming digital now—as Seth was saying, he had to put his whole book in digital format. I like the fact that I can have everything on a disk, and I can manipulate it very easily. And compared with having to repaint something, or, you know, create a sequential piece by repainting over and over again. So I really enjoy the whole computer thing. I know it has its problems and its glitches but I, for one, like it.

PK: As far as Bush goes, as a cartoonist it was fine with me that he became president. But when all this medical stuff came up with Cheney I realized all of a sudden that he's just a heartbeat away from the presidency.

One of the problems of being a political cartoonist is being forced to keep up with the news. Once in a while I would just like not to hear about any of this shit, and just look out the window and enjoy the view. But it necessitates you having to keep up with all the idiotic, dangerous, horrifying things that are taking place on a daily basis, and then turning around and trying to say something interesting, or pithy, or whatever. I'm with Matt on the question of humor. Humor is a fantastic weapon, one that the right doesn't seem to have much of, so that's one area where we do have a stronghold. But I've also been influenced by a wide cross-section of things, including German Expressionism, and I like doing an image that's just a straight up slap in the face.

On the computer side of things, I've found that I was very much a neo-luddite and resisted it for as long as possible. I still resist the idea of doing artwork on the computer. I have never, ever hit a button and lost a drawing. They're all on paper, and they've never gone *puff* on me.

TT: What would that button be again?

PK: I think it's delete.

TT: Oh, I'm going to push delete! Stop me!

PK: I told you I was a neo-luddite. Have you never lost a drawing on the computer?

TT: I've never lost a drawing.

PK: You're the only one! But I also just like plain old original art. I like to be able to hold something in my hand. As a delivery system computers have transformed things. Every week, instead of having to take my comic to the *Daily News*, I can just email it. And I email virtually everything. There is the other end of it, which is that there was a time, doing work for the *New York Times*, when they used to have a set of drawing tables in their office, and it was nice to go and actually communicate with other artists, when we were normally living a fairly solo lifestyle. With the advent of computers they removed all the drawing tables, and that whole aspect when into the dustbin. I'm glad to have had the experience, but I'm not sorry about not having to deal with that now.

TR: In terms of George Bush, I'm not in any way, shape or form ambivalent about it, because I would have had a great time with Al Gore too. And I do consider him the president-in-exile. I also think that it's really important for people to not even refer to Bush as president, because he's not. I just want to put that out there.

As far as computers are concerned, like Peter I resisted it, and I like to have original art. But original art can get stolen or misplaced. I used to send the originals to my syndicate, and, strangely, every now and then I'd do a really good one, and they would contact me and say, "Sorry, Ted, we just don't know what happened to that one." And a lot of those pieces have turned up on eBay over the past couple of years. And they've gotten pathetically low bids, which pisses me off! So, the computer thing is actually overall a net plus. The only thing I would say that is problematic is that you have to have a pretty juiced-up computer to run Photoshop, and if I was a struggling young cartoonist, and I was really dirt poor making seven or eight thousand dollars a year, like when I was starting out, I couldn't have afforded a good enough computer. So I don't know if there's an economic issue here, but hey, it doesn't affect me, it affects other people.

The ability to draw things, as Tom has already pointed out, obviously does not affect political cartooning. I'm a terrible artist. Writing comes naturally to me, and I work really hard at the drawing. I've developed a style that works for me, but it's something that I'm never truly happy about. But, if you think about it, there are lots of really great illustrators and artists who are shitty political cartoonists. An idea can make a cartoon. I can think of lots of brilliant cartoonists who couldn't draw for shit—people like James Thurber, and Gary Larson, and Matt Groening. The art itself doesn't do it, as proven by *Prince Valiant*. It's beautiful, but why would you read it? Most of us here on this panel are a reaction to what's going on in mainstream political cartooning. If you look at the cartoons that are in the Weekly Roundup section of *Newsweek*, which presents itself as a showcase of the best political cartooning, or the Week in Review section of the *Sunday New York Times* they really suck. They all have a lot of things in common. First of all, they all look the same. They're drawn in a style reminiscent of either Pat Oliphant or Jeff McNally, who died recently. McNally was a brilliant political cartoonist, but everybody decided that they had to do the same crosshatching things. I mean, the world really doesn't need any more donkey and elephant cartoons. Ever. Labels are so embarrassing.

Nina Paley, who used to do a great comic strip called *Nina's Adventures*, recently showed me this brilliant cartoon. It was a parody of modern political cartooning, and there's a ship of state, labeled "ship of state." And then the waters are swirling around it, and they're labeled "deficit," and on top there's a boat floating that says, "United Nations." And there's all this random shit going on, and you're like, how could you use this to communicate with people who were born after, say, Robert Taft? It's not so much that these people are untalented; it's just that they're coasting on a style that was dead long before their parents or their grandparents died. It's just ridiculous. So, it's like my best friend likes to tell me, "Ted, it's not that you're any good, it's just that everyone else sucks so bad."

TT: I have an old reproduction of a cartoon by Rube Goldberg, who is best known for the wacky inventions that he would draw. I have a cartoon by him that is essentially the same cartoon that Ted just described, satirizing the labels in cartooning. So that was tedious fifty years ago.

There was a question about computers. I use them. I waited a long time, but my work always included a lot of photocopying and a lot of different things, so I was not resistant to the technology *per se*. I just didn't want to deal with the learning curve. It did in fact take me about a year to get up to speed before I really knew what I was doing. But you can do so much with it. I do a regular cartoon for a magazine called *The American Prospect*, and you should check out the next issue, because I just went Photoshop crazy, and had a great time with it. I've got a partner who oversees the animation side of things, and I also have a biweekly cartoon on the web, a three or four minute thing. The address is thismodernworld.com. And, again, this is something that is only made possible through computers. You can have a biweekly animated cartoon without having a TV deal. That's an amazing and wonderful thing. We have a lot of fun with it.

This segues into the Ralph Nader question. We created a Kung Fu-style piece of animation where Ralph Nader fights his way into the debates, along with my character Sparky the penguin. Nader did his own voice for that. But part of the Green platform is completely opposed to violence, so they weren't too sure about the cartoon. So we sent them the script, and everything was approved. Then we travelled down to DC, and got five minutes with Ralph Nader. Nader looks up and says, "Well, they told you we can't have the violence, right?" And my animation partner and I just looked at each other and froze. And my partner said, "Well, OK, it's all good. We'll just record the lines as they are, and then we'll take out the violence, and we'll have you outwitting them with your brains, and it'll be OK." But we wanted to keep the part where Ralph Nader and Sparky the Penguin were still throwing knives, or whatever. And there was still a question as to whether this thing was too violent. But the campaign finally decided that they wanted to show it at the super-rallies, so we ended up screening it at the massive Madison Square Garden super-rally, although, again, up until maybe five minutes before it happened we weren't really sure it was going to happen because the cartoon was too violent. But it's a cartoon penguin! There are worse things in the world to worry about than the violence of a cartoon penguin. People, are you with me on this? But anyway, yeah, so I supported Ralph. I am still proud to have supported Ralph. And I ended up speaking at a few of the rallies, which was a tremendous experience. There was a lot of optimism and energy there, until it all just sort of got crushed by the boot heel of history. But it was a remarkable moment.

As far as Bush goes, let's not fall into the trap of kidding yourself that things would have been so much better under Gore. One of my pet peeves right now is this bit about arsenic in the drinking water. It's almost as if George Bush is going down to the reservoir at night and dumping arsenic in the water supply. Let's remember what happened here, OK? In 1999 a study came out suggesting that the current allowable levels are too high and should be reduced. The Clinton administration was so concerned about this that they signed an order lowering those levels on January 17, 2001. In other words, three days before he left office, which meant that it was easily overturned by the Bush administration. Now, you can say, "Oh, the Republicans are so evil, and if only Al Gore had been . . ." But it's bullshit. If Al Gore had been elected I doubt if he would have signed the thing. The thing was only signed as sacrificial propaganda, knowing the Republicans would overturn it. So now every time Maureen Dowd writes a column about the Republicans wanting you to drink arsenic and die, if the Democrats were so concerned they should have done something about the problem before January 17, 2001.

In a lot of ways I prefer Democrats because it makes people think a little bit more when you're trying to go beyond the acceptable boundaries. I mean, most of the cartoonists Ted is complaining about are Democrats, and they don't like the Republicans. There's this two-party mentality that just keeps people from looking at what's really going on. In a way it's more fun when Democrats are in office, because you have to work a little harder to get people to think a little harder.

MW: I think Tom deserves a round of applause for taking a stand in support of Ralph Nader, which wasn't always the most popular thing. [applause]

TT: Thanks.

MW: I'll just touch on the question of whether or not it's better to have a new Bush in the White House. Tom's right, you have to make people think more when you're criticizing a Democratic administration, but as a cartoonist it gets more complicated. My experience during the Clinton years was this strange thing where as someone who was criticizing Clinton from the left all the time, you find yourself in the situation where your cartoons were then picked up by the right because they were interested in beating up on Clinton. It was a very strange feeling. The worst experience I had was early on. In about 1993 I did a cartoon with Clinton as Pinocchio with a big nose, when he was first breaking his campaign promises on Haiti, and gays in the military, and some other stuff. And it got picked up by a lot of rightwing magazines. I got a call from a guy who really liked the cartoon and has started making real marionettes based on my cartoon. A marionette of Clinocchio, with the big phallic nose. They were a big hit in flea markets all up and down the West Coast.

KW: Did you get one?

MW: No, I never got one. If anyone has one of these, or sees one on eBay, I want one! But this guy made several hundred and was selling them up and down the coast, and someone sent one to the Rush Limbaugh TV show. And Rush loved it too, and they wanted to take it on the air, and at that point the guy figured maybe I should ask the cartoonist's permission, so he calls me up. And I told him my legion of lawyers would descend on him like locusts. And he didn't take it on the TV show, thank God. But it does get complicated when you're picking on the Democrats because a lot of the time you're handing ammunition and fodder to the rightwing. And sometimes it blows back in your face.

KW: We can take one or two more questions.

Fifth Audience Member: There seem to be two main avenues in political cartooning, and I'll use examples from people who aren't here, so as not to promote jealousy across the panel. There's a documentary style, like Joe Sacco's *War Junkie*, and there's also a fictional narrative style, like Jason Lutes's *Berlin*. One is more documentary in nature, the other based more on imagination. My question is whether this is a personal or political decision—to be more documentarian or to be more insightful, but inventive?

KW: There was another question from the front row.

Sixth Audience Member: As you know, in recent years the circulation of *Mad* magazine has fallen dramatically, and there has been a lot of talk that satire is going mainstream, and is not really a viable tool for criticizing society anymore. Do you think that's true, and what might the decline of *Mad* mean for humor in cartooning?

KW: Great question.

MW: I feel bad about the decline of *Mad*. I don't think satire is dead, I think it's just diluted. There are so many outlets. When I was a kid there weren't many outlets. There wasn't cable television, there weren't so many alternative publications, and so *Mad* was it. I think satire is thriving. I think it's just like everything else, diffused. And in some ways it's stronger. It's easier to get in print because there are so many different publications and outlets with really different flavors.

TT: *Mad* was hugely influential on me as a kid. It was a wonderful, subversive thing. There's a lot of satire right now, but most of it sucks. *That's My Bush*, I will say it proudly and loud, is one of the worst things I've ever seen on television. And while I am in my rapidly declining years, it's as I've been pointing out to my wife, I would have thought that thing sucked when I was 22. I would have thought that my contemporaries were morons for enjoying it. It's just terrible and un-insightful, like most of what's on *Saturday Night Live*. So I don't actually think that satire is in any danger, because most of it is so bad that if you're still trying to do something thoughtful then you're in a really small niche, and I think you're OK. Now, what was the other question?

Fifth Audience Member: What is important to you—inventiveness or documentary realism?

TT: I wake up each morning and I say, "I will be inventive and insightful today." No, it chooses you, you don't choose it. It's no choice at all. Your art chooses you. You're just the vessel.

TR: Tom's right. I can't believe I agree with you on this stuff. But yeah, your method of experience is completely based on how the ideas come. I've done comic books, I do weekly editorial cartoons, and some things just lend themselves to a different format. I did one book that was about a three-year problem I had with a bully in junior high. That's not the kind of thing that fits into a single panel. So it deserved a graphic novel. I'm editing a book that's coming out next spring that contains the work of over twenty alternative political cartoonists, including four of the people on this panel. And there's a lot of good satire going on politically in this country. Most of it, I'd say, is appearing in the alternative weekly press, with some exceptions. Very little on television, certainly. As for the demise of *Mad*, I think, like most of us, I loved it when I was a kid. It's grand failure was the failure that a lot of political comedy suffers from, especially on television, which is that it didn't keep up with the times. You know, the times became angrier, and smarter, and more bitter. And *Mad* coasted.

TT: *MAD* still uses words like "nutty."

TR: Right. Exactly. Instead of "fuck" and "shit" and "piss." I got the word "pussy" published in the *New York Times*. Times have changed.

TT: And there's a breakthrough. We should all applaud. Talk about the revolution.

TR: And one more thing I wanted to go back to—the question about shitty cartoons—because this is something I like to preach when I get a bunch of people in a room who are too embarrassed to walk out and leave early. I would ask that when you leave here today, the next time you look at a political cartoon, and you try to decide whether it's any good, don't worry about whether or not it's funny. Judge it by whether you can tell if the person who drew it is a Democrat, an independent, a Green, or a Republican. Can you tell what their political ideology might be? Do you have any idea if you haven't seen their work before? The odds are, you probably can't. If you look at the cartoons that are in *Newsweek* there is no fucking way to tell whether they were drawn by Democrats or Republicans. They're jokes about the news. They're just gags. They're like something out of the *New Yorker*. They don't make any political point whatever. Forget about whether they make the point effectively or intelligently or humorously. They don't have any point, so they're not really political cartoons.

PK: I'm with Tom in that the art chooses you. It all depends on the topic, and whatever it is that I'm working on, and what frame of mind I'm in at a given point of time, because there are stories I want to tell that have to be done in a much more personal way, while there are other stories that I have to talk about in a more journalistic way. My favorite stuff tends to fall in-between the two camps. I recently served as an expert witness on an obscenity trial, and I did a comic strip about it. And so I could have me in the strip, talking in a semi-humorous way, but I was also dealing with the trial itself.

As far as *Mad* goes, I work for them every month. For the past five years I've been doing *Spy vs. Spy*. And I'm actually happy to reach that fresh, ten-year-old mind. *Mad* still has 475,000 readers, or whatever, which is not terrible.

KW: That's a much bigger circulation than any of the political opinion magazines have achieved.

PK: You get this really wonderful, pimply, teen audience that I wouldn't have reached otherwise, and periodically they do something that I think is really cool. I'd say that most of us have been hugely influenced by *Mad*, and I feel in a lot of ways that *Mad* is why I do what I do, which is to try and find that in-between space between humor and politics, that says something really dopey, and while you're laughing you go, "Wait a minute, what's he talking about? It's something important." And they seem to do that. My hat is just eternally off to them, and I don't mind making a living off of *Spy vs. Spy* while I'm at it to.

Fly: Well, I used to love *Mad* when I was a kid. It definitely influenced the direction of my life. But I haven't read it for quite a few years, so I can't really comment on its demise. I didn't even know that it was demising.

KW: It's contracting, not demising. It's that their circulation has fallen dramatically in recent years.

TT: They started taking ads. That was the big oomph in the stomach that said they're on their way down.

Fly: Well, the universe is falling in on itself, or something. Anyway, the question about satire, I think that sincere and true satire is always going to be an effective means of political criticism. I think that there's a lot of pseudo-satire, or wannabe satire, going on in the mainstream media. This is partly to do with the fact that they want images or idea that appear to be risky or edgy, but they don't really want the risk or the edge, so there's a lot of this pseudo-edgy stuff around. As for using documentary styles or not, my comics are more in the documentary style because I'm documenting stories that have happened—my lifestyle, my experiences, living in squats, living on the streets, whatever. Some of the comics that I do are more based on reality than others. I do a couple of different strips, and some of them are very much based on reality, and others are kind of pseudo-documentaries. They're based on an imaginary reality, which is actually much more satirical than reality itself.

ST: I find myself agreeing with Mr. Rall. So this is the second time people on this panel have agreed on something. I find, working for major publishers, that they want political cartoons to express virtually no opinion. They want them to be as inoffensive as possible, and as muted as possible. I find this both with when I've done illustration for big papers and also when I've tried to write for the large comic book companies. They become very nervous about material that takes a clear stand and that provides real information. And I think that has to do with what people in this room are very aware of. It's the corporate ownership of all of these media outlets. During the Gulf War, for example, the only place I was able to put out really good information was in a small local paper. Why? Because they didn't take advertising from big corporations. On the other hand, when I brought the same paper material about an issue involving models and professors here at Cooper Union, they were terrified because, of course, this paper is local, so that Cooper Union could sue them or withdraw advertising. So they never published the material.

You have to deal with the people you're working for, and what their interests are. There are very few disinterested parties who will take anything just based on merit. That's why we have independent publications like *World War 3*, and small press publishes like Autonomedia and Soft Skull Press. On the aesthetic issue that you brought up, about documentary comics versus imaginative comics, for the first ten years that I was putting out comic books, I always tried to use a broad, general metaphor universal human being. Often

I'd use stick figures. I thought of this as a universal person. I later looked at it and said, "You know, it really kind of looks like a white guy." But I thought of it as a universal figure, and I did this because I didn't feel that I had any specific experience that was that much deeper or more interesting than that of other people. And so it was better for me to speak in metaphors than for me to start saying, well, this is what happened last week. I certainly had experiences that filled me with emotion, but I didn't feel they were particularly of interest any more than anyone else's, so I stuck to a kind of metaphorical art, which other people have been able to fit into their lives, and that work was reasonably popular and could be applied to a lot of situations.

At the end of the 1980s I was involved in the squatter movement here on the Lower East Side, and I had a lot of specific experiences where I suddenly one day looked at my life and said, "You know, this is actually a story." In fact, other people were writing about the movement. Stan Mack, for example, was coming around writing about our struggle. Other people thought that this was interesting and they were writing about it from the outside, not knowing a lot about it. So I decided to do *War in the Neighborhood* [2000], which was a docu-comic, although I don't know if I like the term "documentary." It sort of implies somebody, like a reporter, coming in from the outside and feigning objectivity as they phone back and forth to their editors and try to make sure their editor pays them for the work they've done. I've always been very clear about my subjectivity, and the fact that I'm an artist and not any type of journalist or scientist who's bound to an oath of objectivity. On the other hand, I did try to get the details right, and to convey the complexity of a specific situation. So in an odd sense I probably went in the opposite direction of a lot of other artists. I started out with symbolism and abstraction and surrealism, and moved into realism.

Quite a few comic book artists in recent years have experimented with realism, in fact. Some of it I like, some of it I don't. Harvey Pekar really developed that field, through his comic book series *American Splendor*. He does comics about real life, and in particular about working class life in Cleveland, Ohio. And some artists who've done that have done very good work. It really depends on whether you have a story that's unique and interesting and would matter to someone. I would still hold myself to that standard. I wouldn't do a real life story unless I had a real life story that was worth someone's time.

MM: I find doing documentary-type stories really interesting. I love Joe Sacco, and other people like that. When I first started out I wanted to draw superheroes. I was a kid. I thought I was going to work for Marvel or DC. When I got older, I got discouraged with the whole superhero thing. The political things around me mattered much more. The guy down the block, my neighbors, and my world. These were the things I wanted to draw about. I found it a lot more interesting. And when I find people who draw, who do stories about real people, it makes me excited. I have learned a lot from their work, and I find it very exciting to delve into the world, into realism.

KW: I want to thank all of the panelists for a great presentation. [applause]

The *World War 3 Illustrated* Roundtable

KENT WORCESTER / 2006

From *The Comics Journal* #276. Reprinted by permission.

Kent Worcester: Is it unfair to describe *World War 3* as the most militant publication possible?

Kevin Pyle: I don't think that *WW3* is consciously the most militant magazine out there, but we are willing to give a voice to people who have that attitude, whereas a lot of media outlets aren't, because they feel they have to be objective to a certain degree and we are not really about objectivity, we're about a certain viewpoint. There is some political art out there that doesn't really want to tell you what it thinks. We're not attracted to that. I don't think we would turn down a strip because it was too militant.

Seth Tobocman: *World War Three Illustrated* is obviously on the left. But within that leftism we try to be pluralistic. There are many different points of view expressed in this magazine. There are liberals, libertarians, anarchists, feminists, squatters, renters and a lot of people who don't fit under any category. We've featured a range of material and that includes some people who are very anti-state and very direct action oriented and some people who might not be. Of course we don't print work by homophobes, racists, and Nazis. But as an editor, I may choose to print something I disagree with if I think it has integrity. For example, I just got back from New Orleans. I found a lot of people there believe that the government dynamited the levees, intentionally flooding the 9th ward. Personally, I don't agree with this theory. But if there is an artist who can put forth this position convincingly and with passion, I will be open to his work. In the current issue there are two pieces on the Israel/Palestine conflict, one by Eric Drooker and one by Sabrina Jones. I think you will see that their viewpoints differ a great deal. There is no "party line" at *World War*

Three. No matter how "radical" a party line might be, the overall effect of having a "party line" is to inhibit creativity and thus make people more conservative. Artists work best when they are free to express what they feel.

But I do want to add that *World War Three* is not all that extreme. We just *look* extreme compared to the American media. People are used to a really dumbed-down standard of what an opinion piece is. The range of opinion that is expressed in the American media is hardly a range of opinion. People are used to hearing two guys debate who are basically saying the same thing, with slightly different intonations. We allow more to be said than the larger media usually does and I'm quite happy with it.

Peter Kuper: There are times, such as with the current issue, when somebody approached us with a piece that they couldn't find anyone else to publish it. In this case it was a fumetti, a photo-comic, by Penny Allen. A U.S. soldier based in Iraq had given her a bunch of material and there was no other publisher who would touch it. Even when we are not aggressively looking for these kinds of pieces sometimes they find us. For that matter, there are times as editors we can't find anywhere else to publish some of our own work because of the content. I've made strips that I've hoped to publish elsewhere and quickly learned that the only place that will publish it uncensored would be *WW3*. The only alternative might be to self-publish. As far as an "institution," *WW3* is one of the places that allows you to do that.

KP: The 9/11 issue was a case that is obvious to me. Art Spiegelman had something that he couldn't publish anywhere else. He had a viewpoint that now, four years later, would not seem so radical but at the time people weren't willing to go there. There were a lot of artists who contributed to that issue who have said, "9/11 has me thinking about these issues but I don't have anywhere to put this stuff, because everyone is holding back."

PK: Including some of the more radical-ish or left-leaning publications. There was definitely a chill in the air. One of my first coherent thoughts after 9/11 was, "Hmm, this would be a good time to be working on an issue of *WW3*." Having the magazine there to put my thoughts down in was one of the things that helped me recover from the horror of that event.

Sabrina Jones: For me, just talking about how radical we are or aren't is like a cold shower to creativity. It's just anti-erotic. We should focus on specific issues, such as the Middle East. We've always emphasized the importance of first-person narrative. I'd like to see a strip about the bicycle protests, the crackdown on the Critical Mass rides.

If anything, we have been identified with street politics on the Lower East Side. Not exclusively, because don't all live on the Lower East Side, and we're not always activists all the time. It's nice that we have that image as the wild Lower East Side squatters, but most of us rent and more and more of us own our homes now. [laughs] The thing that makes it exciting for me is the fact that we give people the opportunity to tell real stories.

Nicole Schulman: It's interesting. A lot of what is often called "radical politics" is often just logic. The war in Iraq is ridiculous and stupid. This isn't a radical idea, but it has been consigned to the radical left.

PK: Did you say that oil is bad? There would be no heat! [laughs]

NS: I'm the young one here. My introduction to radical politics for the most part was through hanging out with the folks on *World War 3* and hanging out on the Lower East Side when I was a kid and attending squat benefits and picking up whatever zines were around, and *WW3* was one of them. It warped my little mind.

PK: I'm confused. So you weren't converted before you started reading *WW3*? We weren't preaching to the converted?

NS: I wasn't converted or unconverted. I was just a fuzzy little green-haired kid. That was the extent of it.

KW: There have been two terms you've used to describe the magazine. One is as a "zine," and the other as an "institution." Is WW3 a zine that is also an institution? An institutional zine? Are you trying to preserve this sense of spontaneity and eroticism in something that is now actually an institution, at the same time that you are working toward the fiftieth anniversary?

KP: I don't think we were aware of the twenty-fifth anniversary until it was more or less upon us. [laughs] I think we are much closer to a zine than an institution.

PK: I used the term "institution" extremely loosely . . . though perhaps some of us should be *committed* to an institution. Over the years, enough people have grown up reading it—I occasionally hear people say, "Oh yeah, my mother turned me onto it"—and I sense *WW3* being perceived as more than just a magazine. We don't really think about building a house style or a single point of view, but we are all drawn toward similar areas in art and ideas. Every time we come together to put out an issue we are re-forming, as if it's the first issue.

KW: With slightly different people each issue? How does that work?

ST: The continuity of the publication has to do with a couple of things. I've been involved over the years with a lot of different groups and projects and squats and affinity groups and this and that. And this is the one that seems to stay together, as opposed to existing for a couple of years. Part of the reason is that we at a very early point we established a kind of sweat-equity model of editorship. Basically, decisions about the magazine were made by the editors who worked on the issue. Editorial decisions were made collectively by people worked not just on the artwork, but all the stuff that was involved in getting it published. And it's a very stable model. It means that who ever is making the decision has a real stake in it.

The magazine has also continued to publish because there is a need for a comic book that challenges the conservative bent of the society we are living in, which really hasn't changed in any good way in the last twenty-five years. There continues to be a need for a voice like this, and there are always new people who say, "wow, there's something I want to say that nobody wants me to say," we've become a place for that. That's why it continues. Because there is a need for it, and because compared to a lot of things it's been well run.

KW: Does it feel like it is still happening or does it feel like the framework is pretty much set?

NS: There are a core a people, who are sitting here, and core artists, like Fly, Mac McGill, Ryan Inzana, and Christopher Cardinale, but there are also folks who come and go. I remember the first meeting I went to, in the NoRio zine library [a long-running squat and art center on the Lower East Side]. It was so crowded. There was no place to sit. I was on my knees by the door. Seth was in the corner, talking, and everyone was introducing themselves to each other. That was my introduction. That was for the Land and Liberty issue, six or seven years ago. A lot of times I felt like I was riding on people's coattails. It felt like there was this established model. At the same time, the magazine has changed. Folks thirties and younger are getting involved and eventually might take it over.

PK: After they kill us. [laughter]

SJ: I came in somewhere in-between the "founders" and the second genera-tion. What am I, a younger sister or something? For me, there was a golden age for *WW3*. It was the late eighties and early nineties. Personally, it was when I turning into a full-time cartoonist rather than a painter who dabbled in cartoons on the side. Comics was becoming my dominant form of expres-sion. I was learning how to become an editor, and getting a lot of support from these guys in taking on that role. We had a group of about four of us every issue. We were trying to come out more often. It was very intense. It had a rock band feeling, where we were spending a lot of time together. [laughs] I felt so privileged to hang out with you guys, Seth and Peter, along with Scott Cunningham, and everybody else.

PK: Eric Drooker was also in there.

SJ: And I thought I was hanging out with the smartest and hippest people in town. This is so cool. [laughs] "I don't need to go to grad school, I don't need to visit a gallery, I need to be, at this meeting, seeing each others' sketches. We wanted to come out quarterly. That was unrealistic, as it turned out. There wasn't the money for us to quit our day jobs. We wound up having to turn it into something more flexible, and open up our little clique, as it kinda became, to other contributors. We finally realized we had to start rotating in and out other editors and break up that little foursome.

KP: That's actually when I started editing, in 1993 or thereabouts.

KW: Did you feel you were entering something that had just passed its golden age?

KP: I started doing strips for the magazine in 1991. It didn't feel like an in-stitution. I was surprised how approachable it was. I was friends with Scott Cunningham, and I was running a gallery in Brooklyn called Minor Injury in 1990–1991, which had a political bent. We had a small press convention two years in a row, and I met a lot of people through that, including *WW3* folks. I guess at that time, I felt I needed to educate myself about the Lower East

Side, because the magazine did seem closely tied to the history of the area. Just by chance, I'd been at the Tompkins Square riot, only because I happened to be out, drinking with a friend. He got beaten by the police that night, had his ankle broken and his elbow chipped. He was visiting me from Israel. I was like, "Oh well!"

KW: "I guess this *is* my neighborhood." [laughter]

KP: This is the world I live in, now. One of the first issues I was in was the first Gulf War issue, and it seemed like there was plenty to talk about.

KW: Do you like what Sabrina referred to, the magazine's tendency to focus on daily life, on personal stories? Do you see that as part of the formula?

KP: I see it as the tradition at *World War 3*. It's not the kind of comics I chose to do, but that has to do more with my particular aesthetic. But I'm still attracted to that legacy of *World War 3*.

My biggest contribution as an editor was when I edited a prison issue with Scott Cunningham. We got prisoners to write letters, stories, and poems, and then we handed them out to different *World War 3* contributors to draw them. It was a tightly thematic issue. And I think we've become tighter and tighter with each issue. If you want to look at the comic as an activist's tool I think that's important. Being a sweat-equity organization, there is a lot of leeway for each editor to accomplish what they would like to accomplish with a particular issue.

ST: There are a couple of reasons for turnover. In the case of some contributors, *WW3* was the first place they could get their work out. At some point they acquired a certain level of recognition and could publish elsewhere and they moved on. We have a long list of people who published in *WW3* that would surprise people. I doubt that anyone knows that Peter Bagge published in the first issue.

KW: An anti-Reagan strip.

ST: A really good one, too.

KP: The first issue I looked at it had Steve Brodner in it, and he's in the most recent issue (#36).

A sampling of three decades of covers from *World War 3 Illustrated*

PK: There's actually a lot of that, where people circle back. They'll wander out into the more mainstream world of magazines or the art world and they'll keep returning to *WW3*. James Romberger, who did 7 *Miles a Second* with David Wojnarowicz for Vertigo and has work in the Metropolitan Museum of Art, Eric Drooker who has covers regularly on the *New Yorker* and some incredible graphic novels with big publishers, both of them had some of there first published work in *WW3* and keep returning through the years. For that matter Sue Coe, probably the greatest living political artist . . . Sue Coe did the cover for issue #10, and she just did the latest cover for #36. If you also look at some of the people who have passed through, such as Peter Bagge, or Ben Katchor who was our first typesetter and hooked us up with the paper supplier on our first issue. He had done a bunch of comics on the side but I don't believe he had even self-published them yet. If you make a list of who intersected with the magazine over the years it would be a very interesting list.

I used to have the feeling that I had just missed all the art movements. The Beat generation, or the underground comics that collapsed just when Seth and I were about to get into them. Same thing happened when I traveled around the world. I'd always arrive somewhere, and somebody would say, "You should have seen this place ten years ago." Looking back, *World War 3* has been that missing thing for me, even if it has been in a small way. It's been place where there has been this interaction between artists. As an artist you are very often working by yourself, in solitary confinement and to have this interaction is hugely important. We're all schooling each other in that respect. There's a lot of give and take that you normally don't get in your career. And to be so closely involved in the actual production of the work is a useful experience.

KW: Let's focus on the issue of the Lower East Side. There have been lots of cultural magazines on the left, and alternative magazines, many of which go out of business after their first few issues. Has *WW3* survived because it is part of a specific neighborhood with a specific history? How has the magazine developed as that neighborhood has changed, and become less a center of radical politics?

ST: It was important for us, and it was important for me, and I think for some other people, to be able to put ideas into practice, to not just turn out ideas and commentary, but actually get out in the cold air and deal with the issues. For another generation of people that might have been the Students for a Democratic Society, or the civil rights movement, or the movement against the Vietnam war. For us, we were living on the Lower East Side at a time of enormous transition, from the burnout of the neighborhood in the 1970s to the influx of new money in the 1980s. For us that offered both a challenge and an opportunity to see how our ideas worked out in real life. I learned a lot from that.

I went into *World War 3* as a liberal, and eventually I came out an anarchist. I became an anarchist not because of reading something but because the anarchists around me were actually doing something. The anarchists were taking over buildings, and providing housing to homeless people. They were protesting police brutality in Tompkins Park, you know? I can't remember any other publications, apart from *WW3*, and anarchist magazines, that covered the squatters' movement in the early and mid-1980s. That was very important in a certain period.

KW: Let me press Seth before I turn to other people. In her introduction to the Fantagraphics collection of *WW3* material, published in 1989, Lucy Lippard says the Lower East Side was "the microcosm, reflecting locally the global struggles in Central America, in South Africa, in the Middle East, and in your brain." Is the Lower East Side still a "microcosm of global struggles?"

ST: Nicole would probably agree with me when I say that the Lower East Side does not exist anymore, not as we knew it. The Lower East Side is part of New York, and New York is part of America, and America's increasingly globalized. Besides, if you look at the map you'll see that the district boundaries have been redrawn, and the district doesn't officially exist anymore. In a certain way, the notion we had at that moment, which was almost a kind of nationalism of the Lower East Side—that's not possible anymore. That was wiped out. We have to work with what's here; another type of society, another type of situation, and just like we didn't sit there in 1987, and talk about recreating the sixties, I'm not here trying to recreate the late 1980s. What we learned from that was the connection between the individual and the collective. Something that is happening in your life *is political*; something you see in front of you *is political*. I think we applied that very well in the 9/11 issue.

Just the fact that you had to say that the Lower East Side is a microcosm of global struggles implies that there were people walking around thinking that their life has nothing to do with politics. Somehow, your relationship with people in your community is not as political as the war in Iraq. And that's an alienated point of view. We were successful in creating affordable housing for about 500 people through the squatters movement. Some of the squats on the Lower East Side were eventually legalized and became people's houses. We were not successful in stopping the gentrification of Manhattan [laughter], and we were not successful in solving the homeless problem. Nicole might have something she'd like to say about the politics of the neighborhood.

KW: Did you grow up on the Lower East Side?

NS: I grew up on East 23 Street. I'm a third generation New Yorker. I'm thirty years old, and I was five when the magazine first came out. It's . . . interesting. When I started hanging out downtown in the little nascent punk scene, I'd come home because of my curfew, and I'd turn on the TV, and see pictures of the riots at Tompkins Square and say, "damn, I missed it." [laughs] It all seemed so cool and romantic. But at the same time, a close friend of mine grew up in a squat. It wasn't like an anarchist squat, it was an insane Jewish version of the Michigan militia. Her father is a good friend of Bernard Goetz. I was the only person who wanted to hang out at her place, ever. I remember when we were kids, going to a show at NoRio, and some of her friends were giving her shit because she wasn't up in the appropriate punk uniform. Even though she was actually a squatter, going to a squatter benefit. It was a very bizarre thing. My very first piece for *WW3*, "You Can't Go Home, Again," tells that story.

ST: That kind of thing used to happen a lot. Sometimes I would meet punk rockers who were actually wearing patches with my artwork on it, and they would see that I wasn't dressed like a punk and be rude to me, not knowing I was the guy who designed their patch. It was a minor annoyance.

NS: It's a long story about the fashion of anarchism versus actual anarchism. Growing up in New York, it's like your hometown, but you have no connection to anything. My grandmother was born in Brooklyn, while my mother was born in the Bronx. Both my parents were; now they live in Manhattan. I can't afford to live in the neighborhood I grew up in. My parents couldn't afford to live there if they were not living in a rent-stabilized apartment and they were over sixty. If you do away with those laws, my parents are out in the cold. By the time I was of age to have my own place, you ended up getting pushed further and further from the city's center. First we were on Fifth Avenue in Park Slope, which was still kind of a working class, Latino neighborhood, it's all trendy bars now. Now we live out in Kensington where the Hasids are, you know? Vox Pop is out there, which is a nice thing. But it's very frustrating, because I feel like the city I grew up in doesn't exist anymore. It's unrecognizable.

KP: Your question, though, is whether *WW3* survived so well because it was tied to the Lower East Side. But I think it survived because of the commitment of Seth and Peter, which was kinda superhuman at times, to be honest . . .

KW: They're gods! [laughter]

KP: Well, they're not gods but it's a lot of hard work at times. Whenever it needs something, one of them is there to make it happen. You can't over-estimate the amount of work they've put into the magazine over the past twenty-five years.

PK: I don't think you should underestimate how much work you guys have put into it.

SJ: Seth and Peter also know how to delegate.

PK: The thing about the magazine is that it is not about making a fast buck and getting out.

KW: It's not a cash cow.

PK: It's not a cash cow.

SJ: Also, it doesn't need real estate. It doesn't have an office. You can't lose your space because you can't pay the rent. With an art gallery, if they raise the rent you are out of business.

PK: Precisely. It floats. None of us have said, "We want to turn this into a business." I know I don't want to sit behind a desk signing checks! Essentially, we keep plowing whatever money comes in back into the magazine, and we keep plowing our own money into the magazine, to keep it going. It's an unintentional punk aesthetic, sort of anti-success, which is probably why we're still around. We want to do the magazine. We don't need to take it to some other level. On the other hand, for a lot of people working on the magazine helped lead to other things. Sabrina, for example, was producing *Girl Talk* for a while. Because of her editorship at *World War 3*, Nicole was asked to be an editor of the Wobblies book, which has done quite well.

KW: Smash hit.

PK: Seth was developing his graphic novel, *War in the Neighborhood*, and Kevin was developing his graphic novel *Lab U.S.A.* in *World War 3*. It has provided a lot of nourishment for people to continue their work, but not in a direct, here's-your-check kind of way. It's only been out-of-pocket—no payday. Nobody can say that Peter and Seth made a ton of money on it.

ST: Someone can say it, but it ain't true.

PK: Of course you want anything to be successful enough, but what keeps it alive is not necessarily that.

KW: Let's talk about distribution.

SJ: Another cold shower. [laughter]

KW: Presumably, part of the hidden story of *World War 3* is the story of its distribution. Any magazine faces an uphill struggle. Have you guys depended on alternative bookstores?

KP: Every major city has an anarchist or non-consensual culture bookstore. Baltimore, Philadelphia, Madison, Chicago . . .

PK: One of people involved is Susan Willmarth, who has also edited the magazine, and she works at St. Marks Bookshop. She's very aware of how distribution channels work, and she's been able to make sure we're in touch with the right distributors. For the last few years we've been listed in the Diamond catalog, and we are currently distributed by Top Shelf, which is another aspect of getting out there. But distribution is our biggest stumbling block. It's always causing us heartache.

SJ: We're not quite a periodical, but we're not quite a book either. We're something in-between. We only come out once or twice a year.

PK: We've got it nailed down to once a year.

SJ: We're an annual magazine.

ST: There are two forms of distribution. Actual distribution in terms of sale, and then pass-along. In terms of physical sales, for a long time we were distributed by Mordam Records, which put us in a lot of small punk shops that primarily sold independent music. We also got into Tower Records, where we still sell copies. That got us out to a completely different people than might go into a comic book shop, or even Barnes and Noble. The other thing is that the people who picked up the book very often passed it along to other people. And some of the images that appeared in the book later showed up on t-shirts, flyers, posters, and so on.

PK: In Italy I saw a gigantic mural that was based on one of Seth's pieces, and in Mexico I saw a flyer that had lifted a Seth graphic. As Matt Groening pointed out, copyright infringement is the highest form of flattery.

ST: It became like a media campaign. I don't think we have any gauge on how many people have read an issue of *World War 3*. We know how many copies we print, and how many are sold, but we don't really know how many readers we have.

KW: Does anyone else want to weigh in about distribution?

SJ: Somebody has to take a few copies to Printed Matter. [laughter]

PK: There you go. The distribution headache never ends. Seth and I started out by selling copies off a table at Pratt Institute, where we went to school, and walking copies around to bookstores and comic shops. We're still doing that.

KW: Has there ever been anyone on the editorial board who wasn't an artist?

SJ: Never.

KW: There's something specific about an artists' collective. Do you work together as artists independent of the magazine? Has it changed the art that you make?

NS: I've developed a lot because of everybody here. I started off doing regular black scratchboard when I graduated from college. And then I started doing printmaking. I was never into mainstream comics. I never read comics as a kid, except for a few issues of *Tankgirl*. None of the big names mean anything to me.

KW: Kirby. Ditko. Toth.

SJ: Who?

NS: I started off doing underground comics, and developed technique-wise and subject matter-wise partly as a result of everyone who is here. Also, just learning how things reproduce in a magazine that is printed by a company that mostly specializes in foreign language newspapers printed on cheap paper. [laughs] You have to take extra care with the images, and so you learn to do reproducible art.

KP: My role in the last few years has been a lot of the production stuff. We were probably the last comic magazine that was still pasting up mechanicals and shooting stats, and things like that. In terms of the impact of working together in a collective . . . I don't think I would have produced the book I did, *Lab U.S.A.*, if it were not for this magazine. Working under steady deadlines really helped, and the style I used in that book was closely connected to things I'd done for *WW3*.

KW: Do you feel a positive competitive pressure? Do you think to yourself, "boy, Sabrina is working on a prison comic, I should be doing something? Maybe I should be working harder . . ."

SJ: Peter has an army of clones.

KP: Knowing that something is going to appear in print makes a big difference. In some ways, however, my comics have been defined in opposition to things I've seen in *World War 3*. That I had a different way of thinking about the underlying reasons behind certain government policies. A lot of my comics are about institutional brutality, and that's a lot of the way I think about politics. I see a lot of things in *World War 3* that I understand, but that doesn't look at the same things I like to look at. The great thing about a collective is that everyone is working from different angles to produce something that will hopefully offer a unified voice, ultimately.

SJ: The collective does keep you going. It definitely helps fight off the feeling of alienation. But for me the exciting thing is the comics medium. The medium was a revelation for me. The narrative sequence. I had done activist art and had collaborated with others but I still considered myself as a painter. In the gallery world there is this nebulous thing called "the body of work," where you do one painting and then you have to do a bunch of others that are sort of like it, but different, so that the galleries can sell more paintings. You shouldn't show galleries your work until you have some things that kinda go together. I kept stumbling against this formula. I would do an image for a reason, and then it was difficult for me to keep riffing on it, until I had another reason to do a different image. Whereas in comics, you do a series of images, and they're all different, but they all fit together for a reason. Suddenly my brain clicked into gear. I need the picture that gets me from here to there. With comics I was able to work in a way that was much more vital, engaging, and challenging than the start-stop pattern of the elusive body of work in painting.

ST: Putting out the magazine in the early 1980s was kinda like putting up this flag, and seeing who noticed it. All sorts of people started to show up. Some people needed an anti-Reagan comic book. It wasn't that we had done the best one—there wasn't one, and we did one, and people wanted to be part of it. Eric Drooker affected me a great deal. He affected my political thinking. Josh Whalen affected my thinking about alternative communities. Sabrina's affected my thinking. Kevin's affected my thinking. Eric Drooker introduced me to the cartoons of Naji al-Ali, the first Palestinian cartoonist I had ever come across. People brought stuff to us, and educated us, about different parts of the world.

PK: Seth and I go way back, because we grew up together. We did a zine when we were eleven, which helped make the idea of doing a magazine not so remote to us. When we started *WW3* we knew it wasn't going to be super-heroes, and yet somehow would be toggled to comics as a medium. I always felt that the comics I produced for *WW3* had to have a clear idea about what they were saying. That was a voice that was coming from both inside and out. It made me feel that I wanted to be clear about the point of view of the piece. Is there a reason for this piece, or am I doing one more fantasy piece? That has been a real driving force. At the same time, I've relaxed into a more humorous approach over the years. "Gee, it's a really heavy topic, but it can be addressed with humor?"

The magazine is all about communication, and reaching out on different levels. Different people on the magazine can make different approaches work very well. One person who approaches things with their fist in the air can work like dynamite, whereas when somebody else tries to do that it comes out contrived. Each of us must find our own footing. As Kevin was saying, he sometimes functions in opposition to what's appeared in the magazine.

KW: "I want to see more footnotes in this thing!" [laughter] "I want to prove what I'm saying."

KP: When I first got involved with *WW3* I tried to do an actual *World War 3* comic. I did that for three issues, but gave it up. I was doing a character called the Odious Omnivore, who just ate and shit on everything. He was the ultimate symbol of capitalism. Actually, it was a lot of fun, but I realized I was compartmentalizing myself as an artist. I had to ask myself whether that was what I thought I was supposed to be doing rather than what I wanted or needed to do.

KW: Any other comments on humor and its role in the magazine? Let me put it this way. There are a lot of great cartoonists who have contributed to *WW3*. Take one example: Ruben Bolling is not on that list.

PK: We asked him to contribute to the last issue.

KW: Fair enough. To me, he's one of the funniest political cartoonists around. His work might start with a superhero parody, but he'll turn it political. Should the magazine embrace that kind of cartoonist?

PK: If you look at our recent issues we've had Spiegelman's stuff, Tom Tomorrow, Ward Sutton's funny, Steve Brodner's hysterical.

KW: But none of them are as goofy as Bolling.

KP: It's hard to be goofy with the title *World War 3*. [laughter] In some ways we really do want to be sincere. What sets *WW3* apart from a lot of comics is that we are not really ironic. We're not hiding what we are thinking. It's not really about "entertainment." Obviously when you are working on a strip you want it to be seductive, and for people to read it all the way to the end. But you don't want to take short cuts just for the entertainment value.

NS: Satire is used in political commentary to sneak it by the censors.

KW: You guys have no censors so you don't need to dress it up in funny clothes.

NS: And we are all too neurotic to do real humor.

KP: The people who are doing those kinds of strips don't think of bringing them to us. It's not that we wouldn't print it, it's just that they don't think to themselves, "Oh, I did this really goofy strip; I'm going to bring it to *World War 3*."

ST: You can list a lot of things we don't have in *WW3*; we don't have a whole lot of gags, or superheroes, or a whole lot of zombies. Occasionally, a couple of zombies. [laughter]

KW: Zombies are good.

ST: You can identify a lot of things that you would expect in a comic book that aren't in *World War 3*. And that's good, because most of the time when people are doing, say, a humorous piece it's for a humor magazine, or they're doing a superhero piece for a superhero company, or they're doing goth things because goth is fashionable. We produce the magazine so that we can say what we want to say. I don't think we should be required to say, "Oh, why aren't we doing what someone else is doing?" Well, we're doing it. We offer a comic book that has a kind of social commentary that is straight up. I'm not embarrassed about making a political statement. I don't think I have to soft pedal my message because I'm not embarrassed about what I have to say. You can agree with it or disagree with it, but that's what I'm doing. I don't feel inclined to have to explain why there are not capes and tights, or big noses, or anything else.

KP: I thought mine were horror comics. [laughter]

PK: The whole thing in a way is a horror comic.

KP: I think it is.

PK: But I'm really interested in humor, and how to mix humor and politics. *Mad* magazine had a big effect on me and helped "convert me" quote-unquote. It would occasionally punch you in the face with something that was not funny in the slightest. "When Johnny Comes Marching Home," and it's a soldier with a giant syringe coming back from Vietnam addicted to heroin, and there's nothing funny about it whatsoever. As a reader I'm thinking to myself, "OK, I'm looking under the rock for the humor, it's not here, but it's in a humor magazine . . ." I enjoy being able to explore political subject matter from a lot of different angles. I also enjoy reading a good piece that is fact-based, journalistic, or what have you. We're all looking at the work, and there are so many ways to address these issues. Right after 9/11, we were a little paralyzed, and there was work coming in that represented that frame of mind. The second Gulf War has elicited some powerful pieces. The ground is always shifting. There are life and death matters, and things that affect each of us on a daily basis, and I can't think of anything more exciting, interesting, and important to deal with as an artist.

ST: Does anyone know any good September 11 jokes?

PK: I've heard a few horrible ones.

SJ: There's the one about the guy who calls his wife . . .

KW: Do you want to comment on humor, or should I keep going?

SJ: I think it's a gift. We can't just decide to be funny. Some people like Peter are funnier than others. I can be funny on occasion but it's not a driving force of my strips. [looks at Seth] He's not very funny. [laughter]

KW: Wouldn't you say that *World War 3* is more in the tradition of early *Mad* magazine than, say, Jack Kirby?

ST: Actually, we did show Jack the first issue of *World War 3* at a comics convention and he loved it. He liked the title and the cover. He liked the energy and directness of some of the art. But he particularly liked a piece that James Romberger was working on at the time, called "Jesus in Hell" (it later appeared in issue #5). He said to Romberger "You're the best! This is a great work of art! But don't take this to the comic book companies. They won't understand it. This should be in a museum." And James did take Jack's advice and go the fine arts route for a couple of years. And he does have some work in the Metropolitan. Although James has also done some work for Vertigo, most notably the graphic novel, *7 Miles A Second*. Me, Peter, James, Eric, we grew up on comics made for kids. And I think our work grows out of those comics. We've just tried to take it to another level.

KW: Would you consider doing a humor issue, to shake up readers' expectations?

ST: If that's what the moment called for.

SJ: It sounds like what you'd like to read. A funny *WW3*.

KP: In the context of a particular issue, you definitely think about the emotional tenor of each strip. If you have a couple of hard-hitting strips in a row, you will definitely want to put in a more humorous piece.

KW: Does that work formally? If you have a couple of stories with small panels would you break out with something with, say, full-page panels?

KP: Definitely. We put a lot of thinking into the best way of organizing each issue.

KW: Let's talk about putting together an issue. Take us from the first idea to the completed product.

ST: We've done it different ways, but a standard thing is for a couple of the editors to say, "Right now, it really feels like we need an issue on such-and-such." The editors will then get together, and after that contact the much larger group of artists and writers and potential contributors, which can be as many as 50 people. In some cases we've organized meetings and tried to get as many people in the room as possible, and in other cases we might decide to deal with everyone on the phone. Depends on the issue. One way or the other, the call goes from the editorial board to our artists. "What are your thoughts about September 11th? What kind of piece would you like to do?"

PK: There's also the possibility of seeing something on the street somewhere. Scott Cunningham, who became an editor, became involved after Seth saw his work on a lamppost. Sometimes people forward us work that they think we might be interested in. In the earlier days we used to have these enormous meetings, sometimes without any unifying theme. The most potent meetings were right after the Tompkins Riots. One thing that was always fascinating was that the person who spent the most time talking invariably never came through with a piece. This is why these meetings started to seem less and less interesting.

KW: Let's say you've picked a topic and solicited contributions. What if you get 1/3 more material than you need? Do you print extra pages? Do you have a standard rejection letter that you send out?

SJ: No form letter for rejections!

ST: This is a problem for us, because we have limited resources and there is a lot of good material out there. There's a bottleneck. We can only print what we can print.

SJ: Sometimes, if we get twice as much material as we can use we'll split it in half and print two issues. Half of those artists think they're getting blown off slowly, but their stuff will show up in the second issue.

ST: Like the issue we did on genocide in Yugoslavia. We started receiving work that did not really fit in with what was being published elsewhere. So we said, "OK, there's a bunch of stuff about Yugoslavia, so we will have to make the next issue about Yugoslavia. That built up into a whole thing.

KW: So contributors must be patient. But you must sometimes reject material.

Interior art for Kuper's *Sticks and Stones*

KP: We try to do it at the sketch phase.

KW: As early as possible.

ST: The key thing is to review the concept as early as possible and reject it. That is what ought to happen, and sometimes hopefully does, but unfortunately it doesn't always work out that way. Some people don't like to communicate about their work—they like to hand you a finished product—and sometimes because you expect a piece to come out better than it does.

PK: There's also the process of working with somebody and having them work on it, and you are hoping they are pulling it along. As an editor there can be a lot of working it out with the artist. The back and forth can happen all sorts of levels. I worked with Ryan Inzana co-editing the latest issue, and he was working on a piece, and I made some suggestions, and Seth did too, and he did some rewriting. It wasn't like it wasn't going to run—it was a good piece anyway. One of the useful things about having thematic issues is that we can turn down something on the basis that it's off topic.

KW: "We regret to inform you . . ."

SJ: It is really the dirty work of editing. It is a job that we dread. We'll sit around and say, "OK, who's going to tell Joe we're not going to use his piece?" Usually it's the person who's worked with him the most.

KW: Do you guys hold votes? Do you go by rule of the majority?

SJ: We're not that formal.

PK: Ideally you have three editors. That can help us avoid the loggerhead where two editors don't see eye-to-eye. But editing is always difficult. As an editor you are often working closely with an artist and you might be too close to the piece yourself, while another editor might come in, and say, "But it doesn't do anything for me." And you're like, "But, um, er . . ."

ST: On the other hand, there is something to be said for publishing something that is a little awkward, especially by someone who is starting out who definitely has a certain passion or feeling that they want to express. They may come back at some point with something great. There are a number of artists whose work developed in the context of *WW3*.

KW: And the assumption is that there are some things you can only learn by seeing the work in print.

PK: And also the sheer encouragement of it.

ST: I'm saying more than that. I'm saying there are a lot of people who need a context in which they can develop. There's not a lot of encouragement out there for this type of work. By having the experience of being in print, a dialogue develops. We try to give people a chance, based as much on what we knew about them as the work in front of us. Sometimes the gamble doesn't pay off.

"Sorry guys, I should never have brought that guy in here." But sometimes the guy is great.

PK: It's virtually a lifeline that we are throwing out. There was a time when writers and artists were more nurtured than they are now. Publishing used to be much more forgiving and nurturing of novelists, for example. Now there is such an emphasis on creating hits, and if your first novel isn't a hit they drop you.

SJ: We can afford to publish a certain percentage of work that is not 100%. That's part of our folksy charm. We tend to give people that kind of chance with a shorter piece.

KW: That's actually useful. Somebody might read this interview, and decide to not send you their fifty-page nonfiction comic.

ST: Yes.

KW: Don't send it to *World War 3*. But let me ask you, if we have one page left when you are putting together an issue of the magazine, do you go to a famous cartoonist who will get back to you right away, or do you take a chance on a complete unknown?

KP: You have to look at the issue as a whole. The interesting thing that happens in *WW3* is that sometimes we'll print a piece that is by no means up the professional standards of the pieces around it, but what it is saying is much more on target. Sometimes you'll get a piece that's really well done, but it doesn't really say anything. There are probably some potential contributors who say, "Look, they rejected my piece, but what about this thing that looks like it was drawn with crayons!" Yeah, but read the piece. We certainly make editorial decisions where what the piece is saying is definitely more important than the quality of the line-work.

PK: Take Peter Bagge's piece in the first issue. Seth had to show it to me a couple of times. I looked at the artwork. It was his early attempt at being a cartoonist.

KW: His line is loose.

PK: Yeah, but it wasn't loose, it was looser than loose. [laughter] I was hung up on the drawing, but that was as much my own fussiness as anything. But when I read the piece some bell went off, and it ended up being one of my favorite things, because he managed to address this heavy topic in a funny way. There is so much material out that is extremely glossy, but at the same time vacuous. There are so few things that have something real to say.

ST: Part of the fun of being an early Talking Heads fan was seeing them learn to play their instruments in front of the audience. They started out as people who should not have been in a band, and yet ten years later they were *the* band.

Another aspect of this is that we started *WW3* at a time when no one knew what an adult comic was. Spiegelman had just come out with *Raw*, Ben Katchor had the first copy of *Picture Story*, and Harvey Pekar was putting out *American Splendor*. But there was no real definition of what a comic book would be if it was not the stereotypical comic book. So you had people show up who would say, "I'm a competent comic book artist," and we'd say, "Yes, you are competent at doing what everyone has been doing for the past several decades, and we're trying to break out of that tradition." It was really important for us to draw on other, non-comic book influences, such as painting, music, and so on.

Now you have people who have a notion of what a comic for adults might look like. There are courses at colleges and universities on the graphic novel. People know what it is. That limits the possibilities, in a way, because it's just got to look like Chris Ware, or Joe Sacco, you know?

SJ: But those are already two very different approaches you can point to now that didn't exist then. When the magazine started there was either the mainstream, or the undergrounds. There weren't that many options.

PK: There was *Heavy Metal* floating in this nebulous region between the mainstream and the underground. It was slicker than what we were into.

KW: Both Spiegelman and *Heavy Metal* were looking to Europe for inspiration, whereas that wasn't what you guys were into.

ST: We couldn't afford the airline tickets.

PK: Even without visiting, though, German expressionism was part of our mix.

SJ: Another influence was the work being done by political artists with stencils and graffiti. A lot of that work was showing up on the Lower East Side. That's something that both Peter and Seth picked up on.

NS: In terms of activist art, an important influence was old Russian propaganda posters. The key thing is the need to reproduce your art as easily and quickly as possible, making it accessible to people who need it. We all got into comics because they are easy to reproduce and cheap.

KP: From me the aesthetic is a straight line from punk rock graphics to political comics. I grew up in the mid west, and my parents were not the type of people who took their kids to galleries or art museums. For me, the local record store was the art gallery. I was redrawing Iron Maiden covers in eighth grade and bought my first Dead Kennedys album for the artwork. Man, when I saw *World War 3* it was a punk rock music magazine without any music. And for me, that is a uniquely American aesthetic. It didn't come from Europe. It came from rock and roll.

KW: [turning to Peter and Seth] When you guys founded *World War 3*, did you think of it as a continuation of the underground comics tradition, or as a break from that tradition? And were you conscious of the sexism of the undergrounds?

ST: I don't think we thought that through at all. Peter and I were both frustrated with *Heavy Metal*, because they wanted soft-core porn from their American artists. We had some questions about that. We grew up in the seventies in a period when the counterculture had already collapsed. The Vietnam War is something I saw on television as a kid. Commercialized hippie stuff was all over the place, but it was really quite empty. There were very few outlets for talking about what was really going on. Even a decade later, with the first Gulf War, there were very few magazines that were willing to dig below the surface. What the Web did was to make it possible to find any point of view that's out there. I can go online and find out about all kinds of outrageous stuff that's going on the Middle East that the administration and the media would not want me to see. I can always find things that are completely fabricated, and things that are from a completely reactionary point of view.

KW: Whatever you say about the Internet, it's not just another mainstream media.

Even post-apocalypse, alternate side parking will remain in effect

ST: Right. So that changes our role. We can no longer say to our readers, "You will never find out this information if we don't print it." It's more a question of developing our point of view.

PK: And also doing it in comics. Using comics as a political medium. After 9/11 there were all these comic books that came out that addressed the issue. But that was the area we were swimming in for twenty years, so our magazine already had contributions lined up who knew how to combine comics and political ideas. For some people that is an uncomfortable fit.

KW: Spider-Man in the rubble of the Twin Towers.

PK: Or Superman with a flag, saying, "We're going to come and get you, Osama." Being able to merge information and personal commentary in the comics form is *World War 3*'s métier. Jesus, I can't believe I used the word "métier." I apologize.

My point is, that following 9/11 it was hugely important to have an outlet to express what we were going through and how our government and society was reacting. By self-publishing we were able to have a book out within a few months that examined many of these aspects in an uncensored way.

In a lot of ways all our years of experience came to bear at that juncture in time and as we discovered from sales and an incredible turn out at our release event, people were desperate for that kind of information presented in that form.

KW: That's a good defense of both comics and *World War 3*. Would anyone else like to say anything before we wrap things up?

SJ: I want to know who's editing the next issue. [laughter]

Diario de Peter Kuper

CHRISTOPHER IRVING / 2009

Previously unpublished. Printed by permission.

Christopher Irving: What would you consider yourself: An editorial cartoonist, a cartoonist, a cartoonist with editorial leanings . . .

Peter Kuper: I just say plain ol' cartoonist. It's a real conversation starter—"You're a what? A *cartoonist*? Cool, that must be fun!" At least, that is truer these days. Before, people would assume I did Superman or Garfield, and then move quickly away. Now they at least pause before asking if I do Superman or Garfield and moving quickly away.

CI: Your new book, *Diario de Oaxaca*: what can you tell me about it?

PK: It covers the two years we spent in Oaxaca, Mexico, a small town way in the south of Mexico. We went there originally and primarily to expose our daughter to a second language, and to get away from everything after our 2004 "elections," such as they were. I was ready for a little time out. Also, when I was ten, my father had a sabbatical and we moved to Israel for a year. It was part of my sense of an important learning curve for a kid. My wife and I were talking about it for years, and that we'd do it before our daughter was eleven, because it's so much easier to learn another language before that age.

CI: Why have her learn another language?

PK: It's brilliant to know another language. It opens a door on a secret world of communication. I'm only sorry that I don't know more languages myself.

CI: How many do you know?

PK: Mostly, one—I'm still working on my English! Spanish I'm passable, I know some Hebrew. I went back to Israel a few times over the years and what I learned when I was a kid came back to me. When I saw the animated film

Waltz with Bashir, which is in Hebrew, I found that listening to it and reading subtitles my forgotten Hebrew was coming back to me.

Back to Oaxaca, we moved down there for what we thought would be a break, and it turned out that the town was in the middle of a political explosion. There was a teacher's strike that expanded into an international incident when an American journalist was killed a few months after we arrived. There were 4,500 federal troops flown in to quell the strike and the whole city was under siege. That defined the first six months that we were there—so much for escape! Though we had another year and a half in Mexico, and the rest of the time wasn't as fraught.

That time period was an incredible opportunity for me to draw everything, and got back in touch with drawing in my sketchbook as I had on previous jaunts around the world before our daughter was born.

CI: It sounds like you'd been planning this with your wife for a while, and then the Bush "reelection" pushed you over?

PK: That helped. The timing was, in fact, great since the events of the strike allowed me to apply my art in a way I've always wanted and our time in Mexico was before the world economic crash. Even given the turmoil, we were in our little pre-crash bubble down there and able to worked full-time and send our work back to the U.S. by email.

CI: Were you working on *Spy vs. Spy*?

PK: That was my guaranteed monthly gig, along with some other illustration work I got. I had a couple of books come out when I was down there; I finished up *Stop Forgetting to Remember* in our first months in Oaxaca which came out in 2007. Before we left I'd finished a children's book (*Theo and the Blue Note*), which came out in the fall of 2006.

I was also called to do more talks than ever before while I was down in Mexico, so I found myself flying back and forth to the United States and Europe. I was invited to Belgium with Scott McCloud and Kevin Huizenga, Angoulême in France and came to NYC to promote my books a few times. I also had a brief residency at the University of North Dakota during a writer's conference, which included being on panels with Salman Rushdie and Junot Díaz, which was a thrilling experience.

CI: What was your feeling every time you came back to America?

PK: Sometimes it was happy to get a shot of New York City and the American scene, but there were other times when I came back and felt like the twenty-first century was racing forward, and I wanted to move slower. It was the feeling that everyone has a cell phone, and that everyone has an iPod and society is going to hell in a hand basket. In Oaxaca the pace was just slower, though it wasn't devoid of modernity. It's a pretty cosmopolitan town for being from the sixteenth century. On several of my visits home I felt like things were really escalating towards the crash. Apparently I wasn't mistaken about that vibe. It was the height of the economic boom and having been away I could especially feel the electricity of people in a money frenzy. As a temporary outsider, I was probably seeing more than if I was right in the middle of it.

When we finally returned to NYC from Mexico, the transition was very difficult. On the plus side were the elections and the end of the Bush administration, but that was hand in hand with the mess they left and the financial crash. On top of this, both my parents died which had my head spinning. I also went through some artistic shifts from the Mexican experience that I am still sorting through as I try to explore new directions with my work in this difficult economy. Bottom line, transitions are a bitch!

CI: Your stencil style: How do you go about doing that?
PK: Speaking of transitions! I photocopy my pencil drawings, and then cut a stencil out of the photocopy paper. I spray them with enamel spray paint, not an airbrush, so I can pick up one can, put it down, and then spray another fast.

CI: How did you first arrive at using stencils for comic book art?
PK: It was a leap from doing them as illustrations. My lifelong pal, Seth Tobocman turned me on them. I was looking at an illustration he did this way and it rang my bell. It was apparently a very loud bell, because that was in 1988 and here, to this day, I'm still doing stencils. At this point, I feel like I want to move away from spray paint because of its toxic nature. The irony of doing pieces on our degraded environment using aerosol sprays is too much.

CI: *Spy vs. Spy* is done in stencils, right?
PK: I did it in stencils when they asked me to try out for the job figuring they wouldn't go for it. I didn't want to try to mimic the style of [Antonio] Prohias', I thought that "If I'm going to do this, I'll do something that's different. I thought they'd thank me for my kooky approach, bid me adieu and I'd go on my merry way." When they said, "You got the job," I thought I'd probably just do it for a year. I'm in my thirteenth year of *Spy vs. Spy*.

CI: Do you do these stenciled comics a panel at a time, or a whole page?

PK: I do it a page at a time. I usually spray a base in red and black. I spray the red paint first and then spray the black on top of it, which gives a glow of the red under the black. Occasionally I do more than one stencil per piece, but not that often. I'm experimenting now with rolling or brushing on acrylic paint with a stencil. I want to move toward painting a little more, and bring new things into my work.

Part of the digesting from Mexico is having spent all this time drawing in my sketchbook, I want to transfer some of what I've been doing there into my work. I think the next comic I do will be pen and ink with watercolor, which is something more akin to my sketchbooks. As far as illustrations go, I haven't really looked for illustration work since I've gotten back. I was propelled by what was going on in the Bush administration to draw about the subject matter, but now there are fewer outlets for political art. And, I'm just a little bit burnt out on the subject matter. I have drawers filled with stencil art on that history, and I'm now interested in what other kind of work I can do, not devoid of politics, but something I might want to have on my wall. Just staring at the problems and horrors of the world can get pretty depressing to look at!

CI: Editorial art isn't typically something you want as a reminder everyday on your wall.

PK: I'm pretty lucky because a lot of the illustration jobs I did were really close to my heart, as far as the subject matter goes. I directed my work that way and I got known for doing that kind of political subject matter, and those were the calls I'd get. It was fantastic—doing work on topics I could sink my teeth into.

I removed the part where I compartmentalized my art. Before I would work in the magazine I co-founded, *World War 3 Illustrated*, doing political comics was separate from my illustration work. After some years I managed to push those worlds together, both stylistically with stencil comics and content wise with by only taking jobs that were on political subjects. The illustrations I did in magazines and newspapers like the *New York Times* were dealing with political topics that could comfortably fit in *World War 3*.

CI: I doubt you ever thought *World War 3* would last this long.

PK: Next year is our thirtieth anniversary. It's a mini-miracle—our secret may be the punk aesthetic of anti-success. Not that that was a goal! But we were always interested in keeping it going more than worrying about it becoming a huge money making enterprise. It turns out that if you do too well with a cooperative, there are issues of money and who's doing better than whom. Since no one is getting paid, and it all comes out of pocket, being editor just means you do extra heavy lifting and more bottle washing, and that has kept us all on a pretty even keel. If you can get something out of it, it is the magazine itself, and being involved with it is a great association. I'm really proud to have the long-term connection to something like that that people have come to know around the world.

CI: How has it evolved since your conception of it twenty-nine years ago?

PK: The magazine has gotten some color, and the paper quality has gone up a bit, and there has been some design tweaking. When we've made more money, we've always put it straight into having a better production. From the editing stand point, these days I can send out a call to people from a complete range to students to as big as you can get in illustration and comics, and get them to contribute. That's really nice and an opportunity to publish artists whose work I love.

There's a lot about the process that remains the same, and we haven't altered the process dramatically over the years. Maybe the biggest thing is that we don't have huge meetings for each issue, as we once did. We work via the Internet, emailing ideas back and forth, which makes it slot into my life between other things more easily. We figured out how to break down the responsibilities and share them so we don't get burnt out. If too much work falls on too few people it is easy to burn out on a long-term project like this.

CI: It seems a new group would also bring in new influences and new voices that can play the devil's advocate.

PK: That definitely happens, among us, too, where there are differences and points of view. It's really interesting because there are people who grew up reading it. The last issue was coedited by Kevin Pyle, who is a fantastic cartoonist. He grew up in Kansas and came across a copy there. He said it was like a call from New York, and a lifeline and was one of the reasons he moved to the city.

It's part of what we're trying to do, we're trying to send out this message in a bottle that connects people and gives them a sense that there is a vast group of people who share these sentiments of concern about what is going on in the world. For many of the people involved in this magazine, *World War 3* was their first opportunity to get published and start in the field, and get some feedback from other artists. *World War 3* helped launch many of our careers.

When I started in comics I thought what a rip-off it was that there was the Beat Generation, the hippie movement with the underground comix scene, but they were gone by the time my generation showed up. I'm finding in retrospect that what we've done with *World War 3* was to create a group like that of our own. As an artist, you're mostly isolated and *World War 3* was a way of breaking through some of that isolation, so that even before the piece went to print, you had other artists giving feedback on your work.

CI: You had that feedback?

PK: Yeah, and as an editor I do that with the contributors I work with. There is always a good amount of back and forth in the process. The last issue was wordless, so I was actually drawing my editorial comments to explain the changes I thought the work needed. Kevin Pyle and I co-edited that issue and we spent seven months putting it together. Since it isn't paid work naturally we have to slot it between other jobs.

CI: Going back a bit, you were an assistant to Howard Chaykin?

PK: That's way back. Even further back, I was inking Harvey comics' *Richie Rich*.

CI: How long were you working for Howard? I think you were 21 at the time?

PK: I was about 20 when I started working for him at Upstarts Studio and continued for two and a half years. I was in art school at the same time, so I'd go to art school during the day, then run over to the studio, and work evenings and on the weekends. In that studio were also Walter Simonson, Jim Starlin was there, Val Mayerik, James Sherman and Frank Miller came in when he was starting on *Daredevil*—I got to see working artists, and Howard was a super workaholic, so I learned that when I got out of school, it wasn't like, "Now I can relax." I discovered that working for myself meant working at a higher velocity than school. That was really great, because there were no surprises in terms of what being a working cartoonist was about. It was an important learning experience.

I came to New York with very little technical ability. I barely drew, but I was really interested in comics and had been a real big fan of the medium. I met Howard when I was twelve, at a comic convention, and he was a nineteen year-old fan artist. He got into the field, and every year I'd cross paths with him at the New York comic convention.

When I moved to New York and bumped into him again, he happened to need an assistant and gave me a shot. I needed to get my technical chops together and working for Chaykin at Upstarts Studio was a pressure-cooker chance to do that.

CI: I know Howard had evolved and reinvented himself. How did you see him evolve, personally, over all of those years?

PK: He was always doing something in the mainstream that was, relatively speaking, alternative-minded. He was one of the early graphic novel guys, working on *The Stars, My Destination*, by Alfred Bester. He jumped around with different things, but evolutionarily, it's hard for me to say. He started *American Flagg* at the tail end of my being there.

CI: How did your own viewpoints towards comics develop after leaving Upstart Studios?

PK: My interests were shifting around the middle of my being there. I had been into superheroes in my teens, but had grown tired of them. I was nonetheless reading all the comics everyone in the studio was doing, and that was having some impact. Towards the end of art school though, I discovered a whole new set of artists that interested me, particularly Saul Steinberg, German Expressionism, Ralph Steadman—and rejected most of the styles I had grown up reading in mainstream comics. Already for a long time the underground comics, especially Crumb, had been what appealed to me anyway, both stylistically and in their subject matter.

Though working at Upstarts I was immersed in the mainstream field, I was moving away from those kinds of comics. I was starting to get illustration work even when I was in art school. Fortunately at the end of school I started working for the *New York Times*, and that was not the type of work anybody in the Upstart studio was doing. I started doing linoleum prints and collage, working in forms that weren't anything like mainstream comics. Even as I rejected superheroes as something I might want to draw I still enjoyed many aspects of what Chaykin, Simonson, and Frank Miller were doing with the form.

But the muscle bound superhero style I moved away from completely and nothing I aspired to do. It was clear to me that I wouldn't be doing anything new by regurgitating my superhero sources. Even though Jack Kirby is still an influence on my work, and I still get charged up looking at his work, I don't want to do those kinds of comics.

There are so many other comics that I do return to. I'm continuously rediscovering how much I love early turn-of-the-century strips, like Winsor McCay's work, and Lyonel Feininger. There's so much information in their work I want that influence to wash over me as often as possible.

Thanks to my time in Mexico I've gotten a new infusion of artistic influences, from looking at Diego Rivera, and other muralists. Though I wasn't intending to copy them stylistically my sketchbook pages became more and more like murals with a cross section of different images built up to form a single spread. I think that is very much a result of the environment. The simultaneity you find there of past and present history.

CI: It's almost as if these different experimental processes were really pointing you towards the non-superhero direction, as well as the content, early on.
PK: I grew up reading thousands of superhero comics and I was looking for the next step, and underground comics were that, and then I wanted influences outside of comics. I'm still exploring, if for no other reason than out of boredom. The water's rising; I want to jump to the next higher rock. If I stand in one place too long I get bored and need something new to refresh me.

Going to Mexico was certainly a refresher, but its influence is still gestating. With my career, I went from doing line drawings to lino prints to scratchboard to using the stencil approach, and back to pen and ink. I was doing collage in my sketchbook while traveling around on my other trips in Africa and Southeast Asia, like gluing down maps and that got integrated into my illustration work.

I wasn't trying to create a style; it was an organic process. The beauty of working in a sketchbook is never thinking about style. If it comes out being a style where people then say, "I recognize your work." That, to me, is fine, but it has to be organic. That I can work in any medium, but because of my sensibilities, it's going to come out looking like something I did is nice. If I'm painting, stenciling, or carving wood, I hope all has the feel of being part of a whole.

CI: Why did you decide to use a pseudonym in *Stop Forgetting to Remember*?
PK: I thought that was the honest approach. What I'd done was move the pieces of my life around a bit, and not worry about sticking with a straight-up story. It was interesting to me as a story. My experiences in many ways are universal experiences, so it wasn't as important that it was "my story."

However, having said that, much to my surprise, I got a lot of people saying, "Is it really you?" I thought I was being obvious it was. There's a French edition coming out now, and I made myself "Peter Kuper" again through the whole book dropping the pseudonym. Perhaps it was an error on my part, in the assumption that it would be so obvious that this was my autobiography. Apparently people prefer to be lied to. I should have learned that from the George W. Bush years! Making myself a character freed me up to do other things, like have the whole book be about my character trying to finish this one graphic novel. In truth I did ten books in that same time period, but I thought reducing it to the one, made for a better story. That's the last time I'll be honest!

CI: It seems you experimented with many different approaches in your work.
PK: Throughout my career I've tried to defy what people—especially non-comic readers—have assumed about the form. By removing things like word balloons and panel borders, or doing comics in stencils, I hoped that people would discover that their presumptions were wrong. This seemed to work especially with wordless comics like *The System* and *Eye of the Beholder*—which was the first regular strip to appear in the *New York Times* and which then ran in alternative papers for ten years—and also happily landed me the *Spy vs. Spy* gig.

I'm also interested in exploring comics as a language. I like the idea that I can go to other countries, hand someone a wordless book and say, "There you go, my Russian friend, enjoy!" In general, there are so many aspects to comics that I'm interested in exploring. From journalistic comics, to autobiographical, political, humorous . . . you name it. Then there are adaptations, like the ones I did of *The Metamorphosis* and *The Jungle*; I just keep on finding new areas and going, "That'd be cool; I want to try that." As a medium, it's so wide open that there'll never be enough time for me to explore all the things that are possible, but I'll die trying!

Drawn to an International Comic Art Career

MICHAEL DOOLEY / 2013

From printmag.com. Originally posted June 3, 2013. Reprinted by permission.

Peter Kuper's seen it all. And he wants us to see it, too. So he draws it for us. His visits to Latin America, the Middle East, and beyond have been providing him with perspective and inspiration for *World War 3 Illustrated*—America's longest-running radical comic book anthology, since 1980. His various comics autobiographies include *ComicsTrips: A Journal of Travels through Africa and Southeast Asia*. And his graphic novel adaptions of classic literature by authors such as Franz Kafka and Upton Sinclair have been translated into French, German, Swedish, Portuguese, Greek, and several other languages.

Peter's accomplishments include creating the *New York Times*'s first regular comic strip feature. With his mastery of multiple art media and a flair for rendering powerful, riveting images, he's produced award-winning covers for *Time*, *Newsweek*, and numerous other publications. And he's most known to the public for *Spy vs. Spy*, which he's been drawing for *Mad* magazine since 1997.

This summer, you can find Peter at his regular spot in San Diego Comic-Con's Artists' Alley, selling his original *Spy* artwork and rare collector's items. He'll also be promoting *Drawn to New York: An Illustrated Chronicle of Three Decades in New York City*, which just released this week.

Our conversation begins with his views of Manhattan and Mexico and covers a lot of ground, including his comics class at Harvard, his success at gaining a broad readership and reaching foreign markets, and his thoughts about print vs. digital media.

Michael Dooley: How would you describe *Drawn to New York* and *Diario de Oaxaca*?

Peter Kuper: Both books are odd birds, falling between categories. They're more like visual diaries of time periods in my life, reflecting the influences of specific locations.

MD: And how are they different from each other?

PK: New York, relatively speaking, seems to be in black and white, with its towering modern steel and glass structures in stark contrast to the humans who inhabit the city. Compared to most other places in the world—especially the laid-back nature of Mexico—the pace in Manhattan is intense—which I love—so the books reflect those vast differences.

Drawn to New York illustrates 30 years, including an era when the city was much more dangerous, down and dirty, then later, as it was gentrified for better and worse, through 9/11 and other stormy experiences—*literally* with Hurricane Sandy.

Diario de Oaxaca is a sketchbook journal primarily about a town in Mexico where I lived from 2006 to 2008. Oaxaca is an incredibly colorful place, sunny and warm 90% of the time, with sixteenth century architecture and nearby ruins of ancient civilizations. There *was* a huge teachers' strike, people killed and a military presence during the first six months of my stay, which added a dark dimension, but that left the remaining year and a half to draw the glorious details of life in Mexico.

MD: The pages of both these books appear quite vivid and luminous on electronic devices; do you see this as an advantage?

PK: For the limited way I've used eBooks, this is the main benefit. It is really striking to see the pages illuminated this way, but not worth the loss of the tactile experience of a print book. I haven't taken advantage of all the things that can be done within the form of eBooks, like open sources, linking to videos, or adding animation.

MD: So, print's your personal preference?

PK: I'm really a print person, and need the feel of a book in my hands. I feel obliged to explore the options of digital since it's clear that this is a direction books are headed. And of course, there are, and will be, many exciting things to be done in that medium, too. Like many people, I have a real love/hate relationship with computers and everything that they've changed.

MD: What've been your most successful works in foreign markets?

PK: My adaptation of *The Metamorphosis*, thanks to the popularity of Kafka, has been translated in ten countries—including Israel, Turkey, Brazil, and the

Cover art for Kuper's graphic adaptation of *The Metamorphosis*

Czech Republic—so that's the winner. But since I lived in Mexico I've done five books with my Mexican publisher, Sexto Piso, and that's opened the door to a much wider relationship with Latin America, which is another kind of success. It's also translated into many invites to book festivals throughout South America.

MD: And what've been your experiences with overseas printing and publishing?
PK: At this point most of my books are printed in Asia, and working directly with those printers and seeing what's possible has given me many ideas for more elaborate printing: debossing, tipped-in plates, paper-wraps, etc.

As far as working with foreign publishers, it's been generally fantastic, but the pay is much smaller than the bigger U.S. publishers. Still, I'm thrilled to have the opportunity to reach new audiences with my work. And my relationships open other doors as well, with illustration work. I've been art directing and illustrating a weekly political piece for the French paper *Libération*, which came through one of my publishers there.

MD: What did you learn from the reception that *Stop Forgetting to Remember: The Autobiography of Walter Kurtz* received?
PK: Avoid faux autobiographies! I had the "clever" idea of making it the autobiography of a fictitious cartoonist. This seemed reasonable, since I wanted to make adjustments to my story without cheating the truth. It seemed that the play was the thing and it was less important that it was *my* story. But some people were flummoxed by this.

It was later published in Spanish and French and I decided to drop the doppelgänger in those editions.

MD: How will your approach to *Ruins* be different?
PK: *Ruins* is a very different book for me. It will be my longest graphic novel, at about 300 full color pages. And it is a work of fiction, though I'm applying my experiences in Mexico and my interest in entomology. Nobody will mistake it for autobiography.

MD: What first motivated you to express your political beliefs through visual commentary?
PK: Fear was a big motivator. Ronald Reagan was about to become president when I was in art school, with a hostage crisis in Iran and his itchy trigger-finger ready to launch the bomb. I was desperate to have some kind of response, which was a big reason my friend Seth Tobocman and I started publishing *World War 3 Illustrated*. That title choice says it all!

MD: How has *WW3 Illustrated* evolved over its 34 years?

PK: One of the ways our magazine has expanded has been through bringing in younger people, including some of the students Seth and I have had at the School of Visual Arts. They bring a whole new set of ideas and connections. As a result we've ended up with more contributions from abroad, like cartoonists from Egypt. Many of these artists have never been seen in the US and they're bringing stories based on first-hand experience, which is an area of journalism ideally suited to comics.

I'm currently editing a new issue, with dozens of contributors and a rotating group of editors.

MD: What topics will it tackle?

PK: This issue has an unusually light, upbeat subject: death. We have stories ranging from the history of hell to a personal account of life on Death Row. There are comics about losing family members, and a look at how other cultures view death, like Mexico's Day of the Dead. And there will be a series of photos of murals in Egypt commemorating people who died during the Arab spring.

Mortality is something we all face and comics are a great medium to express all the angles.

MD: What makes a successful political cartoon?

PK: One that stops you in your tracks, enlightens, and makes you consider a perspective you hadn't previously entertained—maybe even to the point of taking some positive action steps. If it can also have humor, it's win-win.

MD: How did you come to teach at Harvard?

PK: There were enough students interested in comics that Harvard was pushed to include a course. How my name got thrown in the hat is still a mystery to me. Once I was asked—even though it's a daunting commute from New York City to Boston and back every week—I couldn't say no.

MD: What was the nature of your class?

PK: It's really the same class I teach at SVA. It gives students all the building blocks necessary to create a solid comic page, from the most basic aspects of page design and lettering to the elements of a solid visual narrative.

All the assignments are strictly in black and white and complete beginning-middle-end in one page. I help them find stories worth telling based on personal experiences, dreams, adaptations, and journalistic approaches. I include a lot of comic art history through presentations and get them to each give a talk on an artist of their choosing. I also bring in guest lecturers; Steve Brodner and Ben Katchor visited Harvard last semester. And at SVA over the years Peter de Sève, Gabrielle Bell, Seymour Chwast, and Matt Mahurin, among others, have given presentations to my students.

MD: How did your Harvard students differ from your SVA students?
PK: Generally the SVA students are all cartoon or illustration majors. On rare occasion they're in film, but all related in one form another to art.

Of my Harvard students—twenty-three applied and I had to select twelve, the maximum per class—only half were coming from an arts background. I had an economics student and an English literature major and one who was doing medieval studies. They brought some interesting ideas to the table even though they were sometimes artistically starting from scratch.

Students like Jonathan Finn-Gamiño and Kayla Escobedo were in Harvard's art program, so they were already producing developed work. For the ones that were first-timers I help them hone their skills through inspiring assignments and Gulag-esque critiques. They were all pretty responsive to this approach, though several said it was the most demanding class they took at Harvard!

MD: How would you evaluate your course's success?
PK: Some of my students formed a comics club and began publishing a magazine when class ended, so my enthusiasm for the form must have rubbed off!

MD: Which art media do you feel most comfortable with?
PK: I like media that allows me direct contact with materials and that has an unpredictable outcome. Stencil and spray paint has that in spades, so I spent several decades working in that approach. Until I lifted the stencil, I wouldn't know exactly what the result would be. Unfortunately, I do have a pretty good idea about the long-term effects of working with toxic materials, so I stopped using spray paint.

I also love scratchboard since it, too, has surprising results, like a fluid form of woodcut. Quality scratchboard, however, has been difficult to find, so I'm finding myself forced to dig up new mediums that will bring that element of mystery.

One of my recent favorites is a multicolored pencil with seven different colors in the tip; always an unexpected color with each scrawl.

MD: How do you feel about the "cartoonist" and "graphic novelist" labels?

PK: It used to be I'd rarely mention I was a cartoonist since it brought calls to reproduce some kind of "Superman" style. That used to be the main way people viewed comics. These days I'm able to refer to myself as a cartoonist without people presuming superheroes. And it's a great conversation-starter at parties!

We still haven't really found the right title to describe what we do. "Graphic novelist" is just the one we currently agree on. In the future it may be another moniker like "People of cartoonal" or "Comic-con Americans." I don't care, as long as I get to ply my trade.

MD: What's your advice to cartoonists who want to reach a broader readership beyond the usual fan base?

PK: First advice is: learn about the history of the form. There are so many old masters to be discovered that serve as inspiration beyond the flavor of the moment: Winsor McCay, George Herriman, Lyonel Feininger, Harvey Kurtzman, etc. I've found, consistently, all successful cartoonists know their history.

Next—as much as I hate aspects of computers—the Internet provides many opportunities to reach a wider audience. Or so I've heard.

Third, it's unavoidable—unless you win the art lottery—to end up doing a lot of free work. This is hard to face, but to create work that demonstrates your abilities often requires producing without remuneration. Most of my early comics—and plenty of recent ones—were done without pay, at least initially. *WW3 Illustrated* has never paid anyone, which may be the secret to our success!

I'm not glorifying poverty: it's just important to not give up if the money isn't there. If you do work from the heart that you really enjoy, fandom—and hopefully, filthy lucre—will follow.

MD: Speaking of fans, do you have anything to say to yours?

PK: I was as surprised as anyone to be chosen *People* magazine's "Sexiest Cartoonist/Illustrator Man of the Year," so thanks for all your votes.

MD: And finally, what will you be debuting at San Diego's Comic-Con in July?

PK: *Drawn To New York* will be the big new thing, but as always I'll have new *Spy vs. Spy* original art and a number hard to find collectors' items encased in unbreakable plastic.

Kuper & Tobocman Celebrate *WW3 Illustrated*

ALEX DUEBEN/2014

From comicbookresources.com. Originally posted 12/15/14. Reprinted by permission.

Alex Dueben: Peter, Seth—it's been thirty-five years since the debut of *World War 3 Illustrated*. Looking back to the series' beginnings, where did the concept of the book come from? What was the impetus in creating the anthology?

Peter Kuper: Seth and I grew up together in Cleveland, Ohio—we met in first grade and lived a street apart until the end of high school. We discovered comics around the age of seven and when we were eleven did our first zine with several to follow through our teens. We attended many comic conventions in New York each summer and got to interview everyone from Jack Kirby to William Gaines. Inspired by these trips, we separately made our way to New York City in the late 1970s. Seth had gone there to be a filmmaker studying at NYU and I came a year later based on an animation job offer. Neither ever materialized and we both found ourselves at Pratt Institute in the late 1970s. We were still fans of comics and had become serious about creating them, but there were few venues to get our work published. The undergrounds were mostly gone and the alternative movement didn't exist yet. Since we'd done zines, the idea of self-publishing wasn't remote. Beyond publishing our own work we also wanted to print work that moved us—much of it was on the street posted on walls and lampposts. It was work that was talking about our reality in 1979 with a hostage crisis in Iran, the Cold War in full swing and a B-actor about to have his itchy trigger-finger on the nuclear launch button.

Seth Tobocman: There was no place for an intelligent comic book artist to get published back in 1979. So it was inevitable that we self-publish.

I think what spurred me to make a political comic book was the Iran Hostage crisis. I knew a lot of Iranian students who were at school with me. So I knew about how the Shah of Iran was put in by the US and how my Iranian friends were afraid of the Savak, the Iranian secret police, even while walking

Peter Kuper (front row) and Seth Tobocman (back row) in their first grade class photo, from 1965

around NYC. So when the Shah fell and Iranians took over the US embassy, I understood why they did that. But for many Americans this was an outrage, like 9/11, and there was this wave of patriotic hysteria. So I felt, if all these ignorant people can express themselves, so could I. I decided to throw my hat in the ring.

AD: Publishing a single issue is an accomplishment in and of itself, but what pushed you to turn it into a series? How did it become an ongoing anthology?
ST: Growing up in the 1970s it seemed like any time you found something cool, you immediately discovered that it was over. It was very disheartening. So I didn't want to add to that big pile of negativity by making yet another thing that blew over. What has also made it continue is that wave after wave of younger artists has come to the book. Today there are people working on it who were born the year we started.
PK: We were presented with [the subject matter] every day. We felt desperate to communicate the things we were seeing in the world around us and the things we were experiencing directly and we were not alone. Issue after issue more people joined the magazine. Every time I thought I could find other venues that served a similar purpose I discovered catches. Either they wanted to censor the ideas, or simply couldn't devote the space for a full-length piece.

Really for the first decade or so that we were publishing *WW3*, interest in com-ics— especially with political subject matter—was near zero.

AD: You're both busy people doing a diverse amount of work, but you both continue to contribute to and edit issues of the anthology. Why?
ST: There is no place where I am so free to express myself. I just did a pretty honest piece describing my mother's death, with all the ugliness of a hospital room included, for the latest issue of *WW3*. I don't have anyone telling me I can't do that here. Yes, I could find a publisher for that at some point, but that takes a lot of negotiation, and meanwhile the idea is getting old in my head.
PK: *WW3* remains one of the very few venues that provides complete freedom of expression. At critical points like after 9/11 no other publication was willing to touch the subjects we wanted to discuss— like the stupidity of our rush to war in Iraq. When I lived in Oaxaca, Mexico during a teachers' strike, there was no other publication willing to give me the space to tell the full story. This is true for many of the contributors including artists from places like Egypt. I also feel like we are still relatively unknown and doing this new anthology was a way of codifying *WW3*'s history and the history we've spent the last thirty-five years writing and drawing about.

AD: At what point—assuming there was one—did you begin to see *WW3* as something bigger than the two of you?
PK: When we heard from people around the world who had somehow found copies, when people joined the magazine who had seen it in a record store in another state and were inspired to move to New York and do comics, and when a teenager came up and said "I grew up reading *WW3*—my *mom* showed it to me!"
ST: I always wanted it to be bigger than me. I wanted it to be a collective, and part of a wider movement that encompassed both art and politics. But in the 1980s that often felt like wishful thinking. To me, the moment when my hopes began to be realized was the 1988 Tompkins Square riot and the wave of protest that grew out of it, because that was the first movement in which my generation of activists, and artists was in the lead.
    In 1988 the city tried to impose a midnight curfew on Tompkins Park in New York's Lower East Side. Such a curfew targeted several groups of people. Young people who liked to hang out late, long time area residents who sort of viewed the park as their back yard, and homeless people who slept in the park. Resistance to this curfew resulted in several nights of rioting. Large numbers of police came into the neighborhood to try to enforce the curfew. The cops

wound up attacking everyone who was on the street. But after several rough nights, the bad publicity from video of cops attacking bystanders embarrassed the city into lifting the curfew. A movement of locally based radicals was born out of these riots. This movement fought the city over issues of housing, homelessness, and police brutality. There was a very deep connection between *World War 3 Illustrated* and this scene.

AD: Which comics are you most proud of being involved with during your tenure with *WW3*? You can choose whatever criteria you want, but what are a few stories that stand out?

ST: I'm very proud that so many of the early graphics by *World War 3* artists got picked up by political movements to be used on flyers and posters. With regard to my own work, that would be the "Why are Apartments Expensive?" series that describes the causes of gentrification. There were a couple of years when I saw that reprinted everywhere. More recently, a young cartoonist named Ethan Heitner put us in touch with comic book artists in Egypt and Lebanon who now have work in the magazine. We are one of the few English-language magazines carrying these guys.

PK: In the new anthology we published a color piece by James Romberger called "Jesus in Hell." He brought that to us in about 1984 and we ran it in black and white—which was all we could afford. We've always wanted to see it in full color and it finally happened after thirty-five years! Artists like Mac McGill whose amazing work may have never seen the light of day but for *WW3* and Sabrina Jones who has gone on to have a full-blown career as a graphic novelist, thanks in part to the opportunities the magazine provided for her growth. Really, for all of us, *WW3* has been a place to experiment and interact with other artists, which has made everyone's work that much better.

AD: Talk a little about this anniversary collection. What did you want to do and how did you end up at PM Press?

PK: We wanted to put together a collection that showed off great examples of what we've been doing over the years—work that demonstrated the possibilities of comics as a medium for political and personal expression. Hopefully we've created a book that winds up in schools and libraries so we reach a whole new audience into the future. We first assembled the book back in 2008—Abrams had expressed ongoing interest and we hoped to have it out to coincide with a thirtieth anniversary retrospective that we mounted at a gallery in New York called Exit Art. With the crash the publishing industry was in a shambles and the idea of a 320-page full-color book of political comics

Stencil art from the pages of *The System*

was next to impossible. (Actually a French publisher stepped up with interest and will do it next year.) I had begun working with PM in 2009 and they not only said they wanted to do the book, but that it could be hardcover. When they saw the bill for the collection though, they realize it was over their heads, so we agreed to do a Kickstarter campaign to help them with the costs, which happily exceeded expectations.

ST: I'm glad that there is an anniversary anthology, but I'm even gladder that there is an anniversary. For me, the magazine is what matters. I am glad it's still coming out.

An answer to a question you really didn't ask, "What matters to me about this?"—it isn't the anthology or even the magazine or any of my own art-work. What matters is that I see a lot of young cartoonists now using comics in a way that was very rare thirty years ago. To talk about social change in a very practical and direct way. So this is a new language, now spoken by many people but once spoken only by a few. So I think this magazine has been part of bringing that language into existence. I think we did that. I hope it has a positive effect.

AD: Peter, you have another book coming out from PM Press at the same time. People might remember *The System*, which came out from Vertigo in the nineties as part of their short-lived Vertigo Verite sub-imprint.

PK: *The System* was a remarkable fluke. Vertigo hired an editor named Lou Stathis and encouraged him to bring in new and different projects. I had worked with him for years at every other magazine he'd been with and he asked if I had any ideas. *The System* had been percolating for about eight years and it flew. I was really trying to push the boundaries of the form, so I did the whole book in stencils and spray paint (a medium that Seth first introduced me to), chose real-world themes and made it wordless. I wanted people who assumed comics—especially coming from a mainstream publisher—had to have word balloons and be in a certain style, would be forced to reconsider their assumptions. Right after it was published, sad to say, Lou died and the door on Vertigo slammed shut again. This is among my favorite projects and I was distressed that it had been out of print for fifteen years so many people had never seen it. PM was up for not only getting it back in print, but also doing it as a larger hardcover that I redesigned. By the way, *The System* was the work that *Mad* magazine saw that led them to ask me to try out for *Spy vs. Spy*, which I've now done for seventeen years.

World War 3 Has Raged for 35 Years

STEVEN HELLER / 2014

Previously unpublished. Printed by permission.

Steve Heller: Tell me how *WW3* got started, and why?

Peter Kuper: Seth and I grew up together in Cleveland, Ohio—we met in first grade and lived a street apart until the end of high school. We discovered comics around the age of seven and when we were eleven did our first zine with several to follow through our teens. We attended many comic conventions in New York each summer and got to interview everyone from Jack Kirby (co-creator of Captain America, X-Men, etc.) to William Gaines (publisher of *Mad*). Inspired by these trips, we separately made our way to New York City in the late 1970s. Seth had gone to New York to be a filmmaker studying at NYU, and I came a year later based on an animation job offer. Neither ever materialized and we both found ourselves at Pratt Institute in the late 1970s. We were still fans of comics and had become serious about creating them, but there were few venues to get our work published. The undergrounds were mostly gone and the alternative movement didn't exist yet. Since we'd done zines, the idea of self-publishing wasn't remote. Beyond publishing our own work we also wanted to print work that moved us—much of it was on the street posted on walls and lampposts. It was work that was talking about our reality in 1979 with a hostage crisis in Iran, the Cold War in full swing and a B-actor about to have his itchy trigger-finger on the nuclear launch button.

SH: How have you managed to keep the energy going all these years?

PK: We've been compelled by the history that's unfolding around us. New wars, new administrations making the same old bad choices, a desire to capture our personal histories as we age through these experiences and a deep, deep love of comics as an art form that can tackle all of the above. We also have been joined by a great number of like-minded artists and writers in editing and producing each issue, without whom we would have run out of steam a long time ago.

SH: During the course of your tenure, how has your attitudes changed both in terms of content and art?

PK: Personally, I'm always exploring new ways of communicating about what's happening in the world. Sometimes using humor, sometimes journalism, sometimes in your face screaming graphics. Looking at early issues, which date back to 1979, there was a high degree of anxiety as we wrote and drew about Ronald Reagan, the possibility of nuclear war, environmental destruction, the housing crisis, homelessness and so on. These days we write about those same things with a high degree of anxiety, only Ronald Reagan's name doesn't come up as often.

SH: Has the motivation changed? Are you still "alternative"?

PK: Our original intent was to document our history, one that often wasn't covered in the mainstream. That hasn't changed one bit, though aspects of what we do have been embraced by the mainstream. In the 1980s very few people gave comics a second glance as an art form. Now comics and graphic novels are all the rage. Yet, talking about social and political subjects in comics remains quite alternative and there still are very few venues for political art. With the disappearance of comic shops and independent bookstores, distribution has only gotten harder. So, like it or not we remain into the alternative world.

SH: How many issues have you done?

PK: Forty-five in thirty-five years and this is our third anthology collection. We have also had several retrospective shows in galleries and museums and provided graphics for political actions from the anti-nuke movement of the early 1980s to Occupy and a couple of other things last week.

SH: What have been the three most important, influential, and radical issues?

PK: Hard to boil thirty-five years down, but here are some of my picks:

Importance: In issue #3 we started talking about the events right outside our door rather than world issues we read about in the paper. It was the beginning of a more journalistic, autobiographic type of work. #14 as Seth mentioned, #32 was our 9/11 issue that was the best example of what started with issue #3.

Influence: The 9/11 issue since it was a rare creature in the aftermath of that tragedy, given there was a virtual shutdown in any commentary that didn't go along with a war fever. Suddenly our release parties had hundreds of people attending, desperate for alternative perspectives. Artists like Art Spiegelman also started contributing since they couldn't get their ideas published in other mainstream venues.

Radical: Issue #10 was the "Fascism" issue from 1987 that covered a range of actions from Germany to Reagan to Israel's dealings with the Palestinians. The 9/11 issue would also be on that list as well as issue #34 that opposed the War in Iraq before it began and included a parody I did on George Bush as Richie Rich. That story was later reprinted and US customs seized it as piracy. The Comic Book Legal Defense Fund then came to the rescue, with a bank of lawyers proving it qualified as parody and customs relented.

SH: Has *WW3* always been on the left or have you allowed for other polarities?
PK: We certainly don't all agree on the subjects we tackle or how we tackle them, but consistently it's from a left-leaning perspective. The right has no shortage of mouthpieces right up to the *New York Times*.

SH: With this thirty-five year volume, have you decided to call it a day? What could come next?
PK: Thankfully, since all the problems we have been addressing since 1979 have been solved through the power of comics, we've decided to kick back, relax and enjoy the fruits of our labors. Unfortunately the fruit turned out to be genetically modified by Monsanto, we got evicted from our hammocks and retirement isn't until sixty-five—2065 that is.

What could come next is everybody's guess and we all need to be guessing hard and taking action based on those very educated guesses. Though the revolution may not be televised, it *will* be illustrated.

SH: How has the publication been received?
PK: You must have missed the 5th Avenue *WW3* parade—very exciting with all that ticker tape, until we realized the ticker tape was our shredded economy being thrown out a window. *En serio*, our reception has been a slow build, but an enterprise like this never knows its impact. We find we have readers all over the world and that some of them have been rescued by its content. Which is to say that they saw in the pages of *WW3* that other people shared their concerns that gave them hope and in some cases encouraged them to create, take action

and join us on the magazine. As individual artists we can really only count on an audience of one and hope our work travels far beyond that.

SH: How do you think it fits into the comics renaissance that started thirty years ago?

PK: Actually, I think we fit more into the renaissance from one hundred years ago with publications like *The Masses* and *Simplicissimus* and the exploration of cartoonists like Lyonel Feininger, Windsor McCay and woodcut picture story novels by artists like Frans Masereel and Lynd Ward. I'd also like to wishfully think we're part of the political cartooning tradition of Thomas Nast and his "damn pictures," Art Young and back to Daumier and Goya.

SH: Seth, could you talk about how *WW3* got started and why?

Seth Tobocman: As Peter says, we read and drew superhero comics as kids. As an adult I still wanted to draw comics, but I wanted a different type of subject material. This made self-publication inevitable.

We started *World War 3 Illustrated* because in 1979 there was simply no place to publish comics that explored serious political issues. It was an unheard of thing. Mainstream comics publishers of course wanted capes and tights. But the remaining underground comics publishers also had a formula to sell their books that was pretty narrow. Book publishers had not yet learned the phrase "graphic novel." There were a few interesting publications coming out of the punk scene. We either had to publish ourselves or give up on our ideas.

We also started the magazine because we disagreed with the direction the country was headed, with the rise of Reagan, the "Moral Majority," and their domestic and foreign policy. We felt like we were watching the whole society rush like lemmings off a cliff. What was most disturbing was that a whole lot of people who knew better were going along with it. We didn't want to go along, we wanted to say "No." The magazine gave us a place to say that.

SH: How have you managed to keep the energy going all these years?

ST: The magazine sort of generates its own energy in that there is a constant stream of new artists joining the group. People need this forum. You have to understand that *WW3* isn't just Seth and Peter. There is a whole editorial collective that divides the work and discusses the decisions. And this is an intergenerational group. There are today people working on the magazine who are younger than the magazine itself.

SH: During the course of your tenure, how has your attitudes changed both in terms of content and art?

ST: When I started out my ideas about art were very much influenced by the kind of comics I read growing up. My ideas about politics were sort of vague and liberal. I was horrified by nuclear war and concerned about the environment. But I had no idea what should be done about such things.

But the simple decision of a small group of young cartoonists to come out against the rightwing in 1979–80 was a very dramatic thing. It was like we had raised a banner and all kinds of people rallied to that banner. Not just comic artists but writers, painters, graffiti artists, socialists, anarchists, squatters. And these people educated us. I learned about stencils and street art from Anton Van Dalen and Michael Roman, about civil disobedience and moral commitment from Tom Keough, about community organizing from Eric Drooker and Paula Hewitt. Josh Whalen introduced me to the squatters' movement and the business side of the Punk scene. Charles Frederick taught me how to run a meeting. And I can continue down that list all the way up to the present where younger members are teaching me about social media and the Egyptian Revolution. The magazine is my school, constantly teaching me something new.

So I became a more experimental comic book artist and a much more radical activist from this process. No regrets.

SH: Has the motivation changed? Are you still "alternative"?

ST: It's not so much us who have changed but our environment. Today there are a lot more places where you can publish adult comics or political comics and a lot more acceptance of this kind of work. Also, the left in the 1980s was so damn small. Starting around 1995 a whole new generation of people got involved and there were huge actions like the protest against the World Trade Organization in Seattle and Occupy Wall Street. So maybe what we are doing is no longer so rare. But I think it is still important to have a place where a cartoonist can bring a really radical piece of work and no one looks at you funny. This year I did a piece about my mother's death. It was pretty brutal and realistic. I suppose I could get that published somewhere else, but it would involve a big negotiation. What I can show and what I can't. It's great having a place like *WW3* where it's just, "Cool, go ahead and express yourself."

SH: What have been the three most important, influential, and radical issues?

ST: In my opinion:

Issue #6 is where we really developed our position on homelessness and squatting. I think both the artwork and writing in that issue helped jumpstart the squatters' movement here in New York. I think many of the organizers would agree.

Then there is issue #14 which came out right after the first Gulf War and which collected a lot of graphics used in the anti-war movement. In those pre-internet days it was possible for the mass media to hide the casualties of the war and hide the protest movement, which was substantial and energetic. So *WW3* was there to disprove the war hype. In that issue Eqbal Ahmad predicted that an American victory would lead to "Many Vietnams in the Middle East." Prophetic, I think.

More recently issue #42 featured the work of a new generation of comic book artists in Egypt, Lebanon, Jordan, who have emerged out of the Arab Spring. These guys are amazing and I hope to be working with them for many years to come.

And then there is the most recent issue that Peter Kuper and Scott Cunningham produced on the theme of Death. Not Goth-fantasy death, but death as people really experience it. This is a brave issue and opens up a new area of exploration for comic artists.

SH: Has *WW3* always been left or have you allowed for other polarities?
ST: There has never been an official ideology of *WW3*. There is a diversity of opinion among contributors. We treat each artist as an individual. But most of the work is somewhere to the left of the Republicans. We have had a few right wing contributors, like Peter Bagge who is a libertarian. I'm not afraid of a difference of opinion and I'd love to publish something by Steve Ditko.

SH: With this thirty-five-year anthology volume, have you decided to call it a day? What could come next?
ST: There is an ugly cliché about people being radical for a few years while they are young then throwing in the towel. That isn't us. We are in this for the long haul, because society really needs to change and art is part of that. And if Peter and I get tired there are lots of young artists at *WW3* ready to take it to the next level. Our next issue, edited by Paula Hewitt Amram, Sandy Jimenez, and Hilary Allison focuses on youth activism.

That said, there is a big problem that everyone in publishing is facing with a change in the way magazines are bought and sold. The record stores and bookstores that carried our magazine are vanishing. So we are working on

This is not a comic

ways of making it easier to buy the magazine directly from us either over the Internet or at events. It's a struggle, but it always has been.

I sometimes think that the title *World War 3 Illustrated* kind of dates us, but that dating is also a mark of integrity, it shows we been at this for a while. We're the OGs. Anyway, the Russians are in Crimea, the Americans are back in Iraq. The title is unfortunately still relevant.

SH: How has the publication been received?
ST: You know, I got over worrying about that years ago. There are always going to be those condescending reviewers who think that anything political can't really be art. But there are also those people whose lives are changed by this magazine. Who have art by *WW3* contributors taped to their wall or tattooed on their skin. We are taking strong clear positions. You do that, and someone won't like you. We are here to communicate, not to be universally accepted.

SH: How do you think it fits into the comics renaissance that started thirty years ago?
ST: Back in 1980, there were, in my opinion, only four American comic books that were aimed at an adult audience. Ben Katchor's *Picture Story Magazine*, Harvey Pekar's *American Splendor*, Art Speigelman's *Raw*, and *World War 3 Illustrated*. Of those four, we were the only one with expressly political intentions. Today there are hundreds of such publications. We pioneered the idea of a comic strip that deeply investigates a social or political issue. Today they are calling that graphic journalism. For example, in 1988 we published an interview with slain Palestinian cartoonist Naji Al-Ali, then Tom Keogh went to Palestine and did a piece called "The Gaza Strip" for the very next issue. A few years later Joe Sacco went to Palestine and did comics about that situation too, and what he's done with that is truly great. Sacco nailed it. But big things start small. And a lot of big things started small at this magazine. I am constantly meeting cartoonists, and other artists, who tell me that picking up *WW3* when they were young had a big influence on their work. So I think we are participating in a process of evolution. Maybe we are making a big contribution, or maybe a small contribution. But we are part of it. Comics have changed, and the world is going to change. And I am optimistic about those changes. It gets better from here.

Thirty-Five Years of *WW3*

NICOLE MARIE BURTON / 2014

From adastracomix.com. Originally posted on February 2, 2014. Reprinted by permission.

Seth Tobocman: In 1979, I started the magazine with the help of Peter Kuper, Christof Kohlhofer, and Ben Katchor. I've been constantly involved as editor and publisher since then, as well as contributing a lot of my own artwork and comics.

Scott Cunningham: I started submitting comics to *World War 3* after the Tompkins Square Police Riot of 1988. This was a pretty famous event— at least around the Lower East Side where I was living at the time. I did a series of street posters protesting the police's violent behavior, and Seth saw the images and was trying to track me down to contribute to the magazine. Which wasn't easy, since I didn't sign the posters—postering being illegal and all. But I went to a fundraiser for the magazine around that time and met Seth—and the rest is history. At least, *my* history. After contributing comics for a couple of years, I stepped into a co-editor role.

Kevin Pyle: I co-edited quite few issues starting in the early nineties, through 2010. For a chunk of that time I was the primary production person who brought *WW3*—at least the actual hard copy—into the digital era. Thankfully, that role is now shared by many people who have the expertise to expand our online presence.

Nicole Marie Burton: How did you find yourself using art to carry a political message?

ST: Politics is a natural part of how I look at the world, so it has to show up in my art. The world around me gives me constant inspiration for new work. For sure, there were events that made a big impression and effected the direction of my art—the invasion of Grenada in 1983 led me to do my first stencil graffiti, in that such an illegal act required an equally illegal response. The housing movement in my neighborhood offered me a vast area of subject material to explore. More recently, the Occupy movement showed up to confirm that we had been on the right track all along.

SC: My background was in fine art painting. That had become less satisfying to me in my late twenties. Essentially, to become successful in art, you need to sell your work to rich people. I worked at a gallery for a couple of years and developed a distaste for rich people who collected art. So, I sort of was trying to figure out what to do next. Then the riot around protesters supporting the homeless living in Tompkins Square Park happened. I knew people who were beaten by police during that time. The Lower East Side came to look like a war zone and suddenly you see these cops everywhere . . . and they didn't look like the regular beat cops. They looked like soldiers. Very militaristic. I guess you could say the event politicized me. Looking for an outlet for my rage, I started postering on the street. Then I discovered *WW3* on a magazine rack and thought I could do work for them, if I could figure out how to do comics. Luckily, the editors were willing to help me with the process, translating my posters into something that could work as a narrative. The first piece I did for them wasn't all comic-like—more like a series of posters. But I learned how to do regular comics over time.

KP: I did a few posters for political groups in college, but it was really seeing the work of Sue Coe and issues of *WW3* that got me moving in that direction. I was a big fan of German Expressionism and I think when I saw contemporary work that shared that aesthetic, I started looking deeper at the reality it was portraying. I also think doing op-ed illustrations for newspapers got me interested in writing about the things I was illustrating. My first book, *Lab USA*, was kind of what I thought should be the newspaper.

NMB: What are some of the ways that *World War 3* has gained an audience over the years? What was your strategy?

ST: For the first few issues, it was pretty difficult. But then we were picked up by an indie record distributor, Mordam Records, who were very much involved with whatever Left existed in the American punk scene. So we were carried in all these little music shops and venues in the 1980s. That sustained us all the way up to about 2002, when the music industry collapsed. Since then, we have been innovating and finding new ways to reach the public. Our work with PM Press is part of that innovation process.

NMB: Can you tell me any particular anecdotes about the challenges of starting and maintaining the world's longest-running radical comic anthology?

ST: The first two issues were put together in a really weird way to save money. It involved printing the guts in one place, the cover at another, getting the paper at a short end paper supplier. Then stapling it and trimming it by hand . . . At one point I cut my finger trimming a copy and had to go to the hospital.

KP: I wasn't there at the beginning, but in the early days before everything was digital, we would have to go look at the negatives at the printer out in Queens. Because of where it was located, the easiest way to get to it would be to go down to the end of a train platform, cross the tracks and a rubble and trash-strewn vacant lot. It had the feel of some covert act.

SC: Peter Kuper always says that the only reason we've survived this long is that no one gets paid! Not that we don't fight over ideas, or the quality of the art that goes into the magazine, or the balance of perspectives that the magazine embraces . . . But what we don't fight over is how much you got paid. And those [seem like] the kinds of fights that can really make your blood boil. Money . . . the root of evil, right?

We've got this Kickstarter campaign going right now to raise cash for the anthology, and it makes me a little nervous . . . because if we reach our goal, the magazine will actually have some bucks to work with for the first time, rather than struggling to make enough from sales and ads to crank out the next one. I guess that gives you some idea about where we're coming from. *I'm worried we might have too much money.* But I shouldn't worry too much. I'm sure we'll still never get paid!

NMB: What kinds of political discussions do contributing artists have through *WW3*? Can you give an example of a controversial issue that has led to debates between artists, or a comic being refused for political reasons?

ST: We have always had a number of different points of view, from liberals to anarchists to people who don't want any label. It's important to make it possible for all of these people to have a voice.

We had big arguments about feminism back in the day because the comics scene was so overwhelmingly male back then. It was hard to get women comic artists—many of whom were trying something new that they had never imagined doing before—to feel welcome.

SC: I don't know of any comic refused because of the political ideas in it. I mean, we don't have neo-Nazis submitting work, which helps to cut down on the amount of stuff we would reject. In some ways, the debates that stick in my mind over the years, had to do with "quality." Someone has a good idea, or interesting perspective, or personal story that seems worth telling, but they don't have the chops to turn those ideas into a good comic. Editors will often work with those potential contributors to try to make the story better, or pair them with an artist who *can* make it better. But different editors have different ideas about what's good, bad, and acceptable, and that's the zone where the debates can get the most heated. I have a feeling that other *WW3*ers answering this question might think differently about it . . . That's why it's good that we have a broad range of people who edit the magazine.

ST: [I also remember] discussion of aesthetics. Eric Drooker, Paula Hewitt, Peter Kuper, and I were all looking at woodcut artists of the 1930s—Lynd Ward and Frans Masereel. At one point I said to Eric, "Hey, it's cool to be influenced by this, but our stuff shouldn't look *exactly* like theirs. Because times have changed." and Eric replied, "But that's the whole point! Look around you! Times haven't really changed!"

NMB: In the Kickstarter video, September 11 is specifically mentioned as a time when American artists experienced a lot of doors closing to free expression. As a New York-based magazine, what was the response like to those first issues that came out in response to 9/11 and the subsequent setbacks?

KP: I remember it being really positive. The release party for that first issue after 9/11 was absolutely packed with all sorts of folks I hadn't seen at other events. I think people were hungry for a different perspective and they knew we would have one.

NMB: I really want to point out the quality of the narratives in *WW3*— I picked up my first copy at an indie record store in Illinois when I was about thirteen or fourteen, and loved it. I picked it up again, for the first time in fifteen years, in 2013, and the content was just as good as I remember. I'm wondering if you've had any favorite stories over the years?

KP: One of the earliest issues I edited was mostly made up of *Shit House Poet* stories by Sandy Jimenez. Given that, as editor, I spent a lot of time with stories, Sandy's gifts as a writer, [plus] the fact that it was so personal, I was deeply affected by that work. It may have even inspired me to explore the material that became *Blindspot*. I think Seth's work that was part of *War in the Neighborhood* fits your description in that the politics of it are intertwined with the complexities of human relations.

ST: I feel like Sandy Jimenez is one of the best writers in comics. I think his story "Skips" which is in the anthology is a good example. He shows us how people are affected by social conditions, but never loses sight of the individual. He is able to show human beings with all their failures and still maintain some compassion for them.

I like Fly's piece on her first sexual experience, "K-9s First Time." It gave me a new way of looking at sexuality, from a point of view I had never understood before reading it.

I also liked Peter Kuper's "Promised Land," Eric Drooker's "Throwing Stones," and Tom Keough's "The Gaza Strip." These were some of the first American comics to take on the Israel/Palestine conflict. That was brave work.

I like the work of Hayley Gold in the new issue. It's a very personal comic dealing with anorexia. Hayley is one of the new generation of cartoonists who are not burdened by the idea that comics have to be kids' stuff. Here she is, a college junior, doing very sophisticated material.

SC: I don't want to play favorites here. But I'll single out James Romberger's comic on the life of artist David Wojnarowicz as one that really stood out to me, about how Wojnarowicz worked as a male hooker when he was just a kid. That ran years ago, and was an excerpt from a longer story that was eventually published as 7 *Miles a Second*. It was recently republished by Fantagraphics. We also published a story by the controversial artist Mike Diana called "Grasshopper Boy," which I thought was one of his best.

NMB: *WW3* prides itself on showcasing new and emerging artists. Can you give us any examples of first impressions about folks who have gone on in the art/comics world?

KP: I can't think of any first impressions but I always love to see *WW3* contributors out there with their own books. Part of me always wonders, with a new contributor, if we'll see a lot from them or just a little. I know, for myself, *WW3* was very important for the simple fact that you had a deadline, a place you knew something would be printed, and a group of people you respected who would read it.

ST: When I met Eric Drooker and Paula Hewitt, they were handing out free copies of their own "little red book," a 4¼" x 5½" comic book called *The USA at War at Home and Abroad*. The drawing style was crude and people today would not recognize it as the work of the same artists. But the message was right on the mark. In fact, the analysis in that pamphlet would affect my work for many years to come.

I met James Romberger in 1981 at a comic convention. He was showing this amazing pastel comic strip called "Jesus in Hell" to none other than Jack Kirby. Kirby said, "You're the best, kid! But don't take this to those guys at Marvel and DC. They won't understand it! Take this to a museum!"

More recently, I was handed a leaflet at a demo with an interesting comic strip on it. I asked who was the author and was introduced to Ethan Heitner, who now works on *WW3*.

Back in 1983 no one knew who Eric Drooker, James Romberger, Peter Kuper, Seth Tobocman, or Sabrina Jones were. And today, how many people know about Ethan Heitner or Hayley Gold? But *WW3* gives people a place to start where their integrity isn't compromised by someone's bottom line.

SC: Absolutely *everyone* on that list above would qualify. *WW3* has been a great launch pad for a number of important artists over the years.

NMB: Can you say how many subscribers you've had or issues you've printed and sold since 1979? What can you tell me about the breadth and reach of *WW3*, today and over the years?

ST: Our print run ranges from a low of 2000 to a high of 6000 depending on the issue, but I think our influence has been greater than those numbers would indicate. Copies of the magazine are shared between many people—and then the artwork is shared again, as it is copied into flyers and posters, made into murals and tattoos. When I meet readers of the magazine I find they are some of the smartest, most creative, most socially active people in the world. Many are artists themselves, or work in community organizations. So we have had a big effect on many different social movements, from the Squatters in the 1980s, to the people who rebuilt houses after Hurricanes Katrina and Sandy. I am very grateful that these people have made my work a part of their life and activism.

KP: All told, it's been 45 issues and two—soon to be three—anthologies. I know I've shown *WW3* in a few classes I've taught about activist art, and sent plenty of issues abroad. I was at a language school in Guatemala that had some comics in their library, and I could tell from the selection and conversations that they were lefties, so I sent them off a big old box of magazines when I got back home. I sent a lot of the prison issue (issue #24) into prisons. But the best was when I used to read letters sent to the P.O. Box (back before the internet) from small towns in the Midwest saying things like, "I love your magazine! I never knew there was anyone who thought like me!" It reminds me of Peter Kuper's response to the accusation that we're preaching to the converted—the converted need comics too!

NMB: Being a young punk kid growing up in the Midwest, one of those letters was probably from me! What else do you do as artists, activists, and educators?

KP: I've been jumping back and forth between pamphlet-sized activist comics, like *Prison Town* and *Wage Theft*, that are designed as outreach tools to specific groups in need of social justice, and graphic novels aimed at kids 12 and up. My graphic novels, like *Blindspot* and *Take What You Can Carry*, aren't overtly political but somehow end having those themes run through them anyway. I also do a lot of short comics workshops in public schools.

SC: My new book with Kevin Pyle is what we call *WW3* for kids. *Bad For You* is pretty political and meant as a way to educate kids about a lot of issues that affect them. It's an attempt to instill critical thinking at an early age, to make kids question various forms of authority that are telling them what is bad for them. I don't think I would have done a book like *Bad For You* without my experience working on *WW3*, and editing issues of the magazine with Kevin helped us in the collaborative process on the book.

ST: I have been drawing my own comics since I was a kid and have a number of my own books out. I have also done illustrations for books and magazines and posters for radical organizations.

"Thirty-five years of *World War 3*" seems to be a loaded statement. Literal meaning aside, what does that mean to you? Are social justice activists and artists still engaged in the same "war" as three and a half decades ago?

SC: For me, since the day I was born (and years before it), America has been on the lookout for the next war, the next enemy, the next reason to feed the gaping mouth of the military industrial complex, instead of using its *huge* resources to feed its people instead. We should be helping to educate kids instead of pouring money into weapons designed to destroy them. What a fucking waste. But that's the 1984-ish, perpetual war that America has decided to wage since the 1950s.

That's *WW3*.

KP: I think it speaks to the necessity of having something like *WW3* in existence. The fact that it is constantly rejuvenated with new energy and talent who jump on board with nothing more than a promise of hard work and a vehicle to express their anger, concern and humanity, tells me that it survives because it is tied to something deeper than your average comics anthology.

Younger editors like Ethan Heitner and Hilary Allison help carry the torch from the wave of energy people like Rebecca Migdal, Sandy Jimenez bring (alongside others, too numerous to mention). At the center of it is Seth and Peter, who have always been there as constants to keep the magazine going. But the ultimate constant is the need for a place for the artists who have something uncomfortable or challenging to say about the world we live in.

ST: When I was a teenager, I kept running into cool things that were already over. Someone had done something really interesting, and then abandoned it before it amounted to anything. It was very disheartening. So I didn't want to add to that great pile of disillusion. That's why it was important to set this magazine up in such a way that it would keep coming out.

There is an ugly cliché that radical politics is something you only do when you are young. While I have made plenty of mistakes and I hope my understanding of people has deepened, I do believe that, in a broad sense, the positions we took thirty years ago were right. We said that comics could be a serious art form. We said that deregulating the economy would lead to another depression. We said pollution would lead to global warming. And the list goes on. So what part of this am I supposed to take back? There is no reason to stop publishing this magazine.

The Long Haul

KENT WORCESTER / 2015

Previously unpublished. Printed by permission.

RUINS

Kent Worcester: Let's start with *Ruins*. A lot of your work is short-form—illustrations, comic strips, one-page stories, and the like. *Ruins* is 328 pages. Was this something you'd been thinking about for a long time?

Peter Kuper: The first ideas that I had for the book came in 2007, when I was still living in Oaxaca, Mexico. I lived in Oaxaca with my wife and daughter from 2006 to 2008. I had a general idea for a book that was going to be auto-biographical, but as time went by it became clear that the story wanted to be bigger than that and needed to step outside my direct experience. I was looking at my contract recently and it said that I was expected to deliver 224 pages. I turned in something that was over a hundred pages longer than that. The ultimate shape of the book depended on what the material was saying, and it kept expanding. It's definitely the most ambitious work I've ever done, by at least one hundred pages. And it explores areas that I've avoided until now, for the most part. I've tended to avoid fiction, in favor of autobiography. Of course, it draws on things I've seen and done, and people I've met, especially in Oaxaca.

KW: Do you feel as if you hit a wall with short form cartooning? Are there things you haven't been able to say via short form cartooning? And isn't it the case that the longer format automatically pulls you away from a strictly political approach?

PK: I never thought about it that way. It gives you more room to stretch so that the story can wander in lots of different directions. It doesn't have to make a single point, in other words. *Ruins* is actually two or three books—there's the flight of the monarch butterfly, and that's done wordlessly, and then there's the lead story about the two characters who move to Mexico, and then there's a story within the story, about one of the character's books. Then there are stories about secondary characters who turn out to be pretty interesting in their own right. I'm fitfully trying to explore comics as a form, and I'm interested in all of the different avenues I can go down. I'm still excited by the possibility of comics—adaptation, nonfiction, fiction, political, humorous . . . with *Ruins* I can incorporate lots of different approaches. I'm throwing the kitchen sink into it, as it were, and thereby demonstrating to myself as much as anyone what you can do with the form. I've been playing with word balloons and panel shapes, as well as the way that color can inform character, place, and time frames. Stylistically I've made use of all of the images I recorded in my sketchbooks when we lived in Oaxaca, drawing from life and capturing details. I really wanted to have that in *Ruins* so that it conveys the flavor of life in that part of Mexico. At the same time, I wanted to make certain that I had a solid and clear story to tell.

KW: A lot of your early work is in black-and-white. It's not clear from, say, the pages of *Bleeding Heart*, that color was central to your thinking. Was there a moment when you suddenly thought, "I should be doing more with color"? Was it mostly driven by financial considerations?

PK: Financial concerns are part of it. For a long time most of the opportunities I had were for smaller publications such as *World War 3 Illustrated* that had to be in black-and-white. And for a long time the idea of using color was pretty daunting. Simply creating longer comics was a big step by itself, and the idea of doing something that was as long as *Ruins* and in color was something that I hadn't even considered. For the most part I focused on developing my chops within the short comic format and in black-and-white. Color adds a whole other dimension.

When I teach I only allow students to use black-and-white. I don't want them to become overwhelmed by the choices that color engenders. It's nice to have the relative simplicity of black-and-white to work with. It's like with film—something was lost when film went to color, because of the subtle approaches that people had developed for bringing the most out of black-and-white. Sometimes it serves the work if the imagery is in black-and-white. But color is increasingly affordable, and in my case sketchbooking had a big impact on the way I think about color. I was travelling in Africa and Southeast Asia for eight months and I played around with watercolors in my sketchbooks. When

I returned to the U.S., one of the first projects that I worked on was an adaptation of Upton Sinclair's *The Jungle*, and the coloring that I had developed in my sketchbooks was in there. In *The Jungle* I also made use of the stencil-based technique that I was beginning to develop. I showed the editor at First/Classics Illustrated an example of my stencil art, and we decided to use that approach for the entire book, even though I had never done anything with stencils on that sort of scale before. It was a leap of faith, as it were. The book ended up combining this stencil-based technique along with a color palette that I had developed through sketchbooking, although my use of color was bolder in the book than in the sketchbooks. For *Ruins* I used pen-and-ink and watercolors, rather than stencils, but the book's color palette itself is ultimately based on things I learned as a sketchbook artist.

KW: It sometimes seems as if you are almost two artists. When you're working in black-and-white your view of the world seems more pessimistic [laughs], whereas when you use color you're often invoking natural landscapes. If I see a work of yours that is in black-and-white I can almost assume it's going to be about politics. There's a grim side to your black-and-white comics, and an exuberant quality to your colors. Adding color has seemed less like an extension of what you've been doing and more like a departure.

PK: That's an interesting observation, because when I got back from Mexico I went through a period of thinking hard about what kind of work I wanted to produce next. I had spent a couple of decades mostly doing very politically minded illustrations and short nonfiction—much of it intended to be as eye-catching as possible, so that if you saw it from across a room you'd immediately realize what you were looking at. A lot of my work was iconic, poster-ish—a fast read in a lot of ways. When I was in Mexico there was so much subtlety in the color and the imagery of everyday life, as well as in the Mexican artwork that I saw in galleries and museums and in people's homes. I knew I couldn't honor Mexico in *Ruins* without having a subtle color palette. Also, I was beginning to get bored with the type of work I was doing, and a little burned-out. The timing of it was interesting as well. Bush was leaving office, and Obama was just starting his presidency. Obama's been a mushy president and it's been a pretty mushy period, politically speaking. It's not as if everything has been fixed but some of the urgency of the Bush/Cheney years dissipated. I experienced some of the same thing when Clinton became president. This is not to say that either Clinton or Obama have been great presidents, and that everything is fine when a Democrat is in the White House. But sometimes the attack is so much clearer when you have more obvious villains in power.

Cover artwork for Kuper's graphic novel *Ruins*

KW: Obviously we'll return to these political issues but let's talk about color for another minute. When I think about some of your generational counter-parts—the Hernandez brothers, Dan Clowes, Peter Bagge—they also moved from mainly working in black-and-white to doing more things in color as the technology became more affordable and as they started to work with bigger publishers. But for the most part these folks have tended to use color very differently than you have—flat colors, and limited palettes, whereas you use a very distinctive palette that is extremely subtle in its effects. Was there a period of time in which you were thinking about color as color or has it always been connected to storytelling?

PK: Drawing from life is almost inevitably going to require bringing in these other palettes. There are subtle patterns and colors in the real world that you don't find if you're sitting in front of a computer. My experiences in Mexico, and traveling in Africa and Asia in the late 1980s and 1990s, definitely helped shape my use of color. At the same time, I'm basically schizophrenic—I put on a lot of different clothes. Doing "Spy vs. Spy" is one of my personalities, and it's almost like being an actor. I go through a process where I'm "getting into the role" of drawing, say, "Spy vs. Spy." Sometimes I'm more of a German Expressionist. I like to respond to the material, of course. If it's an adaptation my linework and use of color will reflect what I'm getting out of the writing. Obviously I have a voice of my own but I'm also trying to be true to the mate-rial. It's important to leave that door open. I'm always trying to leave enough room so that my approach can shift depending on what's happening in the story. That doesn't mean that my work has to change stylistically from panel to panel, although Dan Clowes does that in *Wilson* and *Ice Haven* to some extent, and in a way that definitely works in the context of the story. I like to keep those parameters pretty wide so that I can move into different areas and explore stylistic variety but in a way that doesn't make it difficult for the reader to follow.

KW: If we look at your early work, it's pretty easy to identify some of the art-ists who influenced your work—the artists who contributed to the *Masses*, for example, Lynd Ward, Frans Masereel, political art from the sixties and seven-ties, and so on—but it's not as easy for me to identify the artistic inspirations behind your more recent work, such as *Ruins*.

PK: I didn't look at other artists for the color palette that I've developed in recent years. That came from travelling and using sketchbooks. But I will say that I've learned a lot from looking at David Mazzucchelli's *Asterios Polyp*, es-pecially in terms of reminding me about what not to put in backgrounds and so on. I've also learned a lot from teaching comics—I always tell students to "make their own adventure" and not to use the same panel designs, fonts, and so on, over and over again. It's such a long catalogue of things to think about. It's definitely been the case that I've looked at someone else's work and gone, "Oh right!" and was reminded about something that I thought I already knew. But at this point it's unlikely that I'm going to be knocked off my game by looking at someone else's work. My work isn't suddenly going to look like someone else's. But it's important to look at a variety of work, and sometimes it's useful to take a break from looking at other people's work, and comics in general.

KW: Having completed *Ruins*, are you planning to do more of this sort of novelistic work, or are you itching to get back to autobiography?
PK: As usual, when I finish a project I want to move onto something very different. A wordless short story would make sense about now. There was a lot of autobiography in *Ruins*, of course.

KW: Now that I've had a chance to read it, I would say that George is a very different person from you. He's less you than I thought was going to be the case. For one thing, he's much more neurotic.
PK: I fall somewhere between George and Samantha. I related to both of them. That's ideally what happens when you're working on a story. More than with any other project I identified with several different characters at the same time. I was putting on these different clothes, and stepping into these different personalities. That's one of the many things that was great about working on *Ruins*.

EARLY DAYS

KW: Did *Heavy Metal* help subsidize your career when you were starting out?
PK: Definitely. It was one of the few places that would consistently publish my work, and that would allow me to create all sorts of oddball pieces. And they were paying commercial rates. You couldn't live on what they paid for very long, but it was way better than what I was making from alternative publishers.

KW: Were you ever tempted to do work for places like *Screw* and other kinds of porn outlets?
PK: Actually, I think I did do some illustrations for *Screw*. I never had a problem with them; they were a nice outlet for many cartoonists. I did some political

illustrations for another men's magazine called *Swank*. I also did a lot of work for *Twilight Zone* magazine. My confounding schizophrenia . . . I started out doing a lot of art with linoleum, and I started to get work on that basis, and then I got tired of linoleum and wanted to do something else. Saul Steinberg became a huge influence on my work toward the end of my art school studies, and his influence was particularly important in terms of my sketchbooks. His impact threw everything up in the air and he helped me rethink the whole approach of what I wanted to do. Just at the time when I was heading out into the illustration world my work was pointing in several different directions. I was doing drawings on rocks and airsickness bags, and wanted to do a crazy patchwork of things, and that made it hard for art directors to get a handle on my work. For a long time I would do work for almost any political magazine I could dig up, and I even approached political organizations that would let me do my thing.

KW: Should we assume that, along with Hitchcock and Chaplin, that Harvey Kurtzman had a big impact on your work?

PK: Yes. Absolutely. And Winsor McCay, Ralph Steadman, Saul Steinberg, Tex Avery, and of course R. Crumb, to name just a few. I had a big cross-section of influences. At one point I was an inker on *Richie Rich* comics, and that became an influence on my work. One thing I can say for *Richie Rich* is that the storytelling is very clear. And that helped inform my storytelling. Kurtzman's war comics—*Two-Fisted Tales*, and *Frontline Combat*—also left a big mark on my work. When I was starting out I read the big black-and-white reprint books of his war comics; I wasn't looking at the original color comics. But I also grew up reading superhero comics, and while I was inking *Richie Rich* during art school I was working at a studio called Upstarts for Howard Chaykin. Walt Simonson also worked there, and he helped me a lot with my work. One of the things he was working on at that point was an adaptation of the *Alien* movie with Archie Goodwin, and Chaykin was working on *The Stars My Destination*, and *Swords of Heaven, Flowers of Hell*, and a number of advertising jobs. Later Frank Miller came to the studio too and was working on *Daredevil* and began *Ronin*. All of this left an impression on me. But at the same time I also wanted to break free from the mainstream and more commercial work. Many of the things I created for myself were a counterpoint to the work that I was seeing. Being in that environment helped me figure out what I didn't want to do as much as what I did. I felt like I had to move away from the comics I grew up reading if I was going to bring anything new to the form. Around this time I began working with linocuts and scratchboard and eventually stencils and spray paint, I had spent so many years of looking at mainstream comics I needed to have a complete break from that stylistic influence.

As I said, whatever you see and do when you're at a formative point in your career will leave a mark. I often ask my students to make copies of work they like or are interested in exploring. Doing that ensures that it'll get into their fingertips. It's a good exercise for pretty much anybody.

KW: Let's return to this issue of commercially viable work. Contemporaries of yours, such as Dan Clowes and Peter Bagge, still talk about how much they hate superhero comics. Spiegelman too. The question for these folks is whether superhero comics are fascist or neo-fascist. That's the debate. I don't remember your saying definitively that you hate superheroes, but unless I'm mistaken you never tried to get a job at Marvel or DC.

PK: It's not that I hate all superhero comics—Jack Kirby's work makes my blood flow faster, and I'm still blown away by the storytelling qualities and the energy that is in his work. I generally don't read superhero comics, but I don't spend a lot of time thinking about them negatively either. Like any genre how good or bad it is depends on the quality of the writers and artists. There was a time, however, especially when I was starting out, that you had to distance yourself from the superhero world because you were constantly being lumped in with superhero cartoonists as if it was all one form. It was like being put in a room full of musicians where the rock guitarists are completely drowning out the jazz guitarists. Alternative cartoonists were playing jazz. It just doesn't mix. The public perception that this was all one form was a real problem if you were trying to do something other than superhero or adventure stories. That's my issue at least, and it was a real problem for the first few decades of my career. Libraries and bookstores wouldn't carry comics and review publications sneered at the form as an indistinguishable blob. Superhero comics created the stigma that comics were a for-kid's-only medium. For many years I didn't call myself a cartoonist, because in the illustration world that meant a superhero style. Eventually that changed and the hipper art directors were looking for comics that were political, personal and far from mainstream styles.

As it happens, I inked and colored a few pages for Marvel at one point, and I did some work for *Crazy*. Larry Hama called me up to work for *Crazy*—oh God I did such terrible work—so I had some experience with the commercial end of the comics business. It was around this time that someone asked me if I was interested in working as an assistant editor at Marvel. Fortunately it helped me realize what it was that I didn't want to do. But taking on commercial work isn't always the wrong decision. To jump forward a bit, when the editors at *Mad*

From *Spy vs. Spy*. © E.C. Publications Inc.

magazine asked me if I wanted to work on *Spy vs. Spy*, in 1996, I just about said "no" on the spot. I had just finished doing *The System*, and I was feeling my oats, and I thought to myself that I do my own things and my own characters, and that to take over someone else's characters was a step backward. I probably also thought that it was a little juvenile. But the editors urged me to try it out, and I came up with something that I thought they'd be certain to reject. I used stencils and spray paint, because I really didn't care about getting the job at all. I think back on that moment sometimes and I realize that *Spy vs. Spy* has become another hat that I wear, with pointy shoes. [laughter] But it's kind of like revisiting my adolescence to get into the frame of mind to be able to come up with new *Spy vs. Spy* stories. I'm really glad that I didn't decide to say no to

Mad. I feel really fortunate to be able to work on such a well-known feature, and it's been a boon to my career. And there's a lot of room when it comes to making *Spy vs. Spy*. The parameters are incredibly wide. The characters can fit a lot of situations—they can travel through time, they can be cavemen, the stories can be completely absurd, and of course it's a wordless comic.

KW: Aren't there words sometimes in *Spy vs. Spy* stories—in fake advertisements and so on?
PK: Rarely, and mostly in the sound effects. The whole point is that it's a wordless strip. And of course the basic storyline fits nicely with my work—two sides of the same coin battling for domination.

ANIMATION

KW: Let's talk about your experiences with Hollywood. What's the first time you came into contact with the worlds of animation, television, and movies?
PK: Well, I came to New York in order to become an animator. I had great enthusiasm, but minimal skills. I thought that if I could work for an animation house, even if I was just painting blue backgrounds, that I would be around the field and see how it worked.

I started keeping a sketchbook when I was fourteen or fifteen. I came to New York for one of the comics conventions, and my cousin, who was in the music business, was doing music for an animation house. He introduced me to the owner of the animation house, and I showed the guy my sketchbooks. And he said, "Do you want a job?" I was only fifteen! But it really helped spark my interest in becoming a professional artist. At the back of my mind there was this realization that, "oh my God, I was offered a job in art." [laughter] During the spring break during my hellish year at Kent State . . . did I mention that I spent a year at Kent State?

KW: I knew you were at Kent State for a short time but I didn't realize that it was "hellish."
PK: It wasn't a good fit. It was jock world.

KW: Did your parents encourage you to attend Kent State?
PK: Not at all. It was a total fallback. I had picked a couple of other schools that I didn't get into. Because my father was a teacher in Ohio, I could attend Kent State for free, so it was a default school.

KW: And were you living at home when you were at Kent State?

PK: No, I stayed in a dorm. Dorm life was, as I say, jock world. It was where I came to realize that in the event of a war I'm a hostage. This was not my world; it felt like high school gym class. I tried to fit in by painting murals in people's dorm rooms and things like that. They actually had a couple of good art teachers. But it was an extension of high school for a lot of people. They were partying the way that I had already partied in high school.

KW: It's not a very attractive campus.

PK: Not at all. From my window I could see the spot where the 1970 campus shootings that Neil Young wrote about in his song "Ohio" took place. The highlight of that year was May 4, which was the anniversary of the National Guard's attack on the students during a Vietnam protest. Dick Gregory came to school, classes were cancelled, and I went to the talks that were held. And no one went to them. That was the vibe at the school. Dick Gregory was a great speaker, and that was the summer during which the school started to make plans for building a gymnasium on top of the site. They were going to obliterate it. As a result, Ron Kovic, the Vietnam vet turned antiwar protestor, who Oliver Stone made a movie about called *Born on the Fourth of July*, helped organize a "tent city" to stop the gymnasium project. I spent a few nights out there sleeping in tents.

KW: So the year you spent at Kent State wasn't a complete loss.

PK: But my involvement in the protest was part of the separation process. Here I was at a school where no one seemed to share my interests. By spring break I was telling myself that I had to get the hell out of there. I somehow got a ride to New York, and went straight to the animation guy's office—the guy who had offered me a job three years earlier. But the animation business was in a downturn at that point—1977—and he told me that he didn't have any work for me. He was pretty grim about it. But one of his office mates told me that there were other animation studios, most of which were located in the same area, near 46th Street and Madison Avenue. From his office I called another couple of places, and took my sketchbook to a place called Zander Animation. They were in the midst of working on a Raggedy Ann movie, pre-CGI, all hand-done cel painting, and the owner said that he'd be happy to give me a job. I was practically skipping for joy when I returned to Ohio. I went back to Kent State, finished the semester, and then moved to New York. I was totally excited, and I even wrote to the guy to tell him how much I was looking forward to working for his company. When I returned to New York that summer, I immediately phoned him, and tried to set up a meeting. When I eventually got to see him he pretended to not remember who I was, and then said, "Call me in six weeks." We went back and forth like this for six months. Finally, his phone stopped ringing. There's something very informative about getting into a field just as it's crashing. Underground comics were crashing at about the same time, of course, and in 2008–2009 the floor dropped out of illustration.

KW: Kyle Baker talks about what it was like being at Marvel when people were saying that the "last person to leave the industry should remember to turn off the lights." Some of the old-timers thought that the superhero business only had one or two years left to go.

PK: This is something I've been hearing for my entire career—how badly things are going. I often hear it from publishers who want to pay me less. [laughter] It's like a mantra.

That was my introduction to the world of animation. So, fast forward to 1996, and HBO was wandering around San Diego Comic-Con looking for properties. I had just come out with *Stripped*, which was autobiographical.

KW: Was SDCC a small operation in 1996 or was it starting to balloon?

PK: It was ballooning. But it was still small enough that I could go out there and squat a table in the artists' alley and no one would say boo. Sometimes I could get two tables. It was a different world. So, HBO expressed interest in my work, and we stayed in touch. This was around the time that they were producing the *Spawn* cartoons.

KW: Had they already written you a check?

PK: Not at all. All they were saying was, "Let's stay in touch." One of the people at HBO seemed especially interested in my work. I should also say that this was at the point just before my daughter was born, and I really wanted to make this happen. My wife and I had already been planning a trip to California before she got pregnant, and she told me that I should go by myself and meet with the folks at HBO. So I kind of pretended that I was on vacation and asked HBO if I could stop by. While I was out there I connected with Jason Grode, who was an assistant to Matt Groening.

KW: I thought HBO was based in New York.

PK: Their animation offices were in LA, although they did have an office in New York. Jason then introduced me to his mom, Susan Grode, who is a high-powered entertainment lawyer, and she became my lawyer. I got a meeting with HBO, and it went well, and we signed a contract. I got a check. I also met with Twentieth Century Fox, and they were super-enthusiastic.

KW: Were you beginning to think that your daughter would grow up on Park Avenue? [laughter]

PK: I thought that my career would take a shift, yes. I thought that things would get easier. But one thing I did know was that I wasn't going to move to LA. And that was probably to the detriment of this project. I think that if I had gone out there I could have made it happen. The project almost happened. I wrote three or four scripts for it, for example. We developed a bible for the show. All the stylistic issues got resolved. We also agreed on the music for the show. There was a musician who I wanted to work with, a guy named David Yazbek, who was already working with HBO. At the time he was a complete unknown. He later ended up doing working on various Broadway shows, including *The Full Monty*.

KW: Let's back up. At this point you'd been paid but they weren't yet promising that they would air anything.

PK: Right. They had optioned my work.

KW: Did they option your work for five years? Ten years?

PK: It was quicker than that. It was for a year or two.

KW: Were you paid extra for the scripts you wrote, or for character sketches and so on? Or did that one check cover all of the work you were doing for them?

PK: I got paid extra. They paid me option money, and for scripts. The character design "bible" was probably part of the deal. At one point there were a team of people working on this show. They brought in animators, and they created what's called an "animatic," which is a bare-bones version of the real thing. Nowadays you would use Flash Animation software and it would probably be 100 times better.

KW: Has any of this shown up on YouTube?

PK: No.

KW: So the copyright is still held by HBO? Would you get in trouble if you posted, say, the animatic on the web?

PK: At this point they probably wouldn't notice, but it's not something I would want to show. It was still pretty rough.

LA STORIES

KW: I find the business side fascinating. This is an experience that a lot of people never have.

PK: There were interesting questions that had to do with who would own the work and so on. After all, this was all based on my life story. The whole process made me very nervous. I didn't want to be in a situation whereby if I drew an autobiographical comic HBO would automatically own the rights.

KW: Would HBO have published a book as a companion to the animated television series?

PK: They would have done a whole lot of stuff. *Stripped* itself probably would have gone back into print. A lot of things were in the pipeline. This is what made things so hard when the project didn't come together.

But at this point a lot of people were working on this. There were people working on the backgrounds, and we were even starting to make decisions about who would be doing the voices. The main voice actor, who was playing my character, was Wallace Langham, who had played a writer on the *Larry Sanders* show. They also lined up Billy West, who later worked on *Futurama*, Laraine Newman, who of course was an original *Saturday Night Live* cast member, and Pamela Adlon who's been on the Louis C.K. show. The voice director was Jack Fletcher who had worked on Miyazaki's films. It was absolutely amazing to see these people perform my characters.

KW: Was anyone warning you at this point about the pitfalls of working in Hollywood, that projects don't necessarily materialize and so on?

PK: Yes.

KW: Was your head getting bigger?

PK: I felt nervous and excited. And I was asking myself, "What happens if this doesn't fly?" I had just turned forty, I had just had a kid, and it was a very tense period. As it happens, I didn't tell them that I was a new father, because I feared that they would see me as not being available enough. I literally had conference calls with HBO where I would pretend that I wasn't taking care of a newborn. I just kept the bottle in her mouth so they wouldn't hear a baby crying on my end of the phone!

KW: Was part of the pitch was that this was a story about a single guy in New York?

Kuper's studio is nice, but not *this* nice. Concept art for the HBO animated *Stripped*

PK: It started that way. But I then started to frame it in terms of a father-to-be who was looking back on his days as a single person. And so I told them that I had become a father and they were quite happy for me. There was a sort of gulp moment, but they were totally cool with it.

KW: So you're not angry about this experience.
PK: Not at all. I didn't get jerked around. I was in shock at how much creative control I had. They were rolling out the carpet for me. There was a point, late in the game, where it did start to unravel. They had a head of development at HBO who liked the project, and then a new guy came in. That's a terrible thing for someone who was in my position. The new person is always going to sweep the floor of what was there before and put forward their ideas. The new guy's favorite project was *Sex in the City*.

KW: Oh, your show would have been so much better than that crap.
PK: Be that as it may [laughter], that's what I was going up against. But until that point things had been going smoothly. They had approved three scripts with almost no notes. But they also brought in another writer to work on the show because up until then I was the only writer. The key problem was that at some point HBO decided that animation wasn't working for them. And so people started to lose their jobs. It was really heartbreaking. The producer told

me that she still wanted to work with me, and we shopped the project around, and she even got me an agent at Creative Artists Agency (CAA), which at the time was run by Michael Ovitz. It was the total fake Hollywood experience. My producer wanted fifty percent ownership on everything. My response was, "Sure, if it's an animated show, yes. But if I do my own comics then, no way." Her lawyer stood her ground, and we had a falling out. It cost me several thousand dollars to arrive at a point where we couldn't work together. But CAA brought me out to meet with an animation director named Frederik Du Chau. He saw what we had put together and said that he loved it and that he had ideas for how we could make it work. He was interested in using computers in addition to traditional animation. This was in 1997–1998 so the technology was still in its early stages. He created a beautiful piece of animation for the project, with some acting, some animation, and some rotoscoping. Forest Whitaker's production company became involved, and Forest Whitaker thought that his company would be able to copyright this new technology. He was angry at having spent the money and decided to sue Du Chau, to block us from working together elsewhere. So that fell apart too, and I never got paid for any of the work I did with Whitaker's production company. I spent a year and a half working on this project with HBO, and a year working with Du Chau and Forest Whitaker, and both of them fell apart. About six months later a $4,000 check showed up from CAA. They had basically taken the money and not given it to me. They were in the middle of closing the file and had decided that if I found out about the money that I might sue the pants off of them.

KW: That is such an LA story.

PK: It was pretty classic. The super-drag was when I was still collaborating with HBO, they had people meeting with me in New York to talk about building a HBO website around my work. This was at the time when the web was just taking off. They wanted me to create a new *Eye of the Beholder* every week for this website, along with the animated show.

KW: Is *Eye of the Beholder* in the *New York Times* at this point?

PK: It had finished its run in the *Times* and I was self-syndicating it. And they wanted to be able post not only the regular strip but original content. That ended up being my first website. At this point I had way too much work on my plate. Not only was I dealing with Hollywood, and the website, but I was in the process of turning *The System* into a book, and at the same time I was developing a new book for Vertigo, titled *Wild Blue Yonder*, which was about my travels in New Guinea.

At one of these meetings in New York they hadn't yet heard from LA that the entire project was being put on hold, and they were promising all sorts of things—that they were going to promote me to the moon, basically. It was like a drug. All my creative pistons were firing. Your channels can be opened by all of the success. And when it collapsed, it was all gone.

Karen Berger at Vertigo had me announce *Wild Blue Yonder* at San Diego Comic-Con, but Paul Levitz finally decided that DC wasn't going to publish autobiographical comics. My editor at Vertigo, who had worked with me on *The System*, died . . .

KW: . . . Lou Stathis . . .

PK: . . . got brain cancer. He was a hilarious curmudgeon. And he really loved comics. He had a whole list of ideas for projects we were going to work on at DC. He got sick, he died, and when Levitz turned down *Wild Blue Yonder*, Karen Berger told me that this was the first time that he had said no to any of her projects. A few years later they probably would have given it a green light.

The HBO thing and the Vertigo book pretty much collapsed at the same time and I went from having too much work to too little. And I had a newborn.

KW: There's always *World War 3*.
PK: Yes, there's always *World War 3*. [laughter]

KW: That profit center.
PK: We don't know where to store all the money.

Anyway, I was ready to have a nervous breakdown by this point. It was depressing to get so close to the finish line. And I had to start thinking about how I was going to resuscitate my career.

KW: Before it all went south, were you thinking that you would have a dual-track career, part cartoonist and part animator? Or were you still thinking of yourself as a cartoonist first and foremost?
PK: Comics were always at the center. I was thinking of myself as a cartoonist who happened to be working on an animated show. But ultimately what my experience with Hollywood achieved was to send me running back to print.

KW: Print will never break your heart, because the stakes are so small, and it's easier to maintain control.
PK: Right. My graphic novel *Stop Forgetting to Remember*, which came out a full decade later, is based around the material that was going to be in the HBO show. So I got to finally do what I wanted to do.

KW: You often find ways to use and reuse your ideas, in new contexts.
PK: This was especially the case in my parental years, when I found it very difficult to start new projects. I managed to get some new books out, but I also repurposed quite a lot of existing material.

KW: How much of *Wild Blue Yonder* managed to get into print?
PK: Not so much. There's a short story in *Stop Forgetting to Remember* that is drawn from that experience—the story of going to New Guinea.

KW: When I spoke to Peter Bagge about his experiences in Hollywood he told me how struck he was by the fact that there are people in Los Angeles who make a living coming up with ideas that never bear fruition. Their work gets optioned, they drive around in nice cars, and nothing that they do ever sees the light of day.
PK: Yep.

KW: And it sort of reminded him about how much he cared about getting the stuff out there.
PK: I have exactly the same sentiments.

KW: I thought you might.
PK: That was part of why there was no way I was ever going to move out to Los Angeles. The idea of working on various projects simply to get a paycheck was death to me. So when I returned to working on comics on a full-time basis I thought to myself, "I understand this. The print runs might be small but at least some folks were getting a chance to see the work." Like lots of people I have lots of ideas for graphic novels, children's books, and so on, just sitting in a drawer.

KW: I'm struck by how much work you've managed to produce over the years. You've written about times in your life when you've been depressed, or at loose ends, but from the outside it seems like you're always working. Where does your drive come from? Were your parents like that?
PK: For a long time my fear of nuclear war was a driving force in my life. Things were at a heightened level during the Cold War, just as they are now with climate change. I can't say why these things drive me toward action, but they do. What feels worse—twiddling my thumbs, or getting the work out?

At the moment I'm working on an eight-page story for Vertigo. And, after *Ruins*, it was hard for me to remember how to create something on that kind of scale. It was just, like, gone. I was waking up nervous for a couple of weeks before I could come up with a new idea. With *Ruins*, I had a block that lasted for years. It was such a daunting project. There was so much work involved, and anything with that many pages is going to be financially risky. And for a long time I wasn't sure that people would find the idea interesting. With any project there's always the possibility that finding an audience is going to be hard, or going to take a long time. And with this one I had all kinds of concerns. But in a certain sense grappling with these issues and concerns helped make the book more intense.

KW: When you first showed it to me I responded to the art—the colors, the butterflies, the landscapes. When I actually read it there was a point about a quarter of a way in when all I cared about was the *story*. I'd occasionally go, "Wow, like at that nice page," but mostly I was like, "What's going to happen to their marriage? How violent is it going to get?"

PK: That's great. Any graphic novelist hopes that you'll read their work more than once. There's the 45-minute read that is all about the story, and there's another one that's all about the artwork, and another which is all about the construction of the thing.

OPINIONS

KW: Obviously you have harsh things to say about politicians and corporations and so on but you don't seem to have anything nasty to say about anybody in comics.

PK: A lot of that stuff is useless. It isn't productive. The comics scene is a party that people tend to never leave, and I'm going to be crossing paths with people for years and years. So why would I want to alienate them over differences in artistic interests? But it's also a political question—I like to think that I'm a humanist, and I'm interested in communicating with a wide range of people.

My in-laws are an interesting case. They're from the South, and it's a military family. My father-in-law is a West Point graduate who served in Korea and Vietnam. He was shot in Vietnam and is now wheelchair bound.

KW: Wow.

PK: Do I want to go down there and tell them that they're jerks because they don't share any of my politics? [laughter] They watch Fox News, and sports, and I have no relationship to any of that. Can I communicate with somebody like that? That to me is what's important in terms of fixing the world. If our mode is alienation and non-inclusiveness then we're not going to get anything done.

The good news is that most people are not total assholes, even if I don't agree with most or all of their views. I had some experience with this when my George Bush animated parody was circulated on the web—Richie Bush. I started to get all of this threatening hate mail. What was remarkable was that when I wrote back to these people they often retracted their harsh stance, once they realized that there was an actual person at the other end. But it doesn't always work out. We've been invited to leave the dinner table at my in-laws a couple of times, especially during the Bush years. Sometimes their stance blew my mind. How could they support a president who, among many other things, was busy cutting funds for veterans, for example?

There's something to be said for taking a firm stand, of course. I'm a great admirer of people who are willing to stand up for their beliefs even if they are hated for it—I really enjoy artists who take a stand. Somebody like Bill Hicks, or George Carlin. The kinds of people that are taking the chance that somebody will try to shout them down. Given the nature of my work it's inevitable that a large number of Americans are going to hate what I have to say. I don't spend time worrying about it, and I hope that it's the case that I sometimes put forward ideas that will at least make people think about their assumptions.

KW: Is it the case that when you haven't made any political art for a while you start to get an itch? And is the opposite also true, that if you've been focusing on political issues you think about going in a different direction?
PK: There's that schizophrenia in my thinking, but on the other hand I can't help but think that almost everything touches on politics in one way or another. After all, to ignore politics is to take a political stand. A lot of people say that they "aren't political" but that's like saying you're not into fire when there's a fire in your living room. You can say you're not into it, but the fire will influence you, and if you don't take any action it will burn your house down.

KW: Trotsky once said that, "you may not be interested in war, but war is interested in you." [laughter]
PK: We're all on the same planet, and what happens on this earth is all of our concern. You can ignore what's happening around you, and your role in where things are at, but that doesn't mean that it's not all happening and that you aren't participating, even if it's through inaction. I do get tired out if I spend too long working in a single mode of expression, and sometimes I do like to draw . . .

KW: . . . sunsets . . .

PK: . . . right, sunsets. And they are interesting to draw. They can turn up in political cartoons, of course—I once drew a page where George Bush drove off a cliff and there was a nice sunset in the background. [laughter] That kind of naturalistic imagery can turn up in all kinds of contexts. Also, I really like the idea of creating art that you cannot simply dismiss for purely ideological reasons. If nothing else I want to produce things that are visually interesting. I like the idea of drawing something that can grab people's interest, even if they are repelled by the message once they take a closer look. There are a lot of different ways to talk about what's going on.

I have trouble justifying to myself doing work that is completely vacuous. There has to be something in there that's talking about the world around me. I have a deep sense of urgency, especially in terms of the environment. We're on a sinking ship. And we're not bailing.

KW: Obviously you believe in general things like human rights, ecological awareness, and so on, but a lot of people who are politically minded would use a specific label to describe their views, such as anarchist, say, or liberal, or liberal Democrat, or socialist. Do any of these terms strike a chord for you?

PK: It's tied up with my religion. I'm "antagonostic." [laughter] I'm really angry at the God I don't believe in.

KW: Interesting. I wasn't expecting that.

PK: And that's how I feel about most politicians. I'm angry at these so-called leaders. I utterly reject them and yet they keep having an influence on my life.

KW: Do you call yourself an atheist?

PK: I would, if I had to. I would say I'm a Jew-ish atheist. A questioning Jew-ish atheist, which is to say, agnostic. So to clarify: I'm an antagonistic, questioning, Jew-ish atheist with socialist leanings. The point is, labels really have no value. What matters is how you behave in the world, how you move through the world. There are political people who don't tip well, religious, God-loving people who only spread hate.

KW: Are there certain political writers who you rely on, and return to . . . ?

PK: Noam Chomsky would be at the top of my list. And Cornel West conveys the messages I most relate to. He's a super-humanist. Everybody is "brother" or "sister"—he's going to yell at "Brother Obama" or even "Brother Bush." He's always looking for ways to bring people to the side of righteousness. "Brother

It's only blood

Cheney is a confused cat"—that's the way he'd frame it. Somebody like Chomsky is able to talk about what's going on in the world with an incredibly deep sense of history. He's obviously angry at the state of the world, but he always leaves room for some sense of optimism. And that's a struggle. I struggle to fight off a sense of cynicism. I really do feel that we are doomed. As a result of choices that we've made we've decided to create a suicide pact with the dollar bill. I really have trouble breaking free of pessimism. On a day-to-day level I feel optimistic, because there are so many examples of things going right in my own life. I can't ignore that. I'm able to work on books and get them published. I make a living as a cartoonist, and I have a happy marriage, a beautiful daughter, and great friends. So I can't really say, "everything sucks." It just doesn't make sense. At the end of the day, I don't just see a beautiful sunset as light filtered through pollution.

KW: A beautiful pop song is not just a cynical attempt to take money away from teenagers.

PK: But sometimes it is! We have to fight those people who are just about the money. As Bill Hicks would say, "Soul-less, ball-less suckers of Satan's pecker." The insanity of the corporate world, the perpetual profit machine that crushes everything to make another buck. So crazy they would sell you the rope you would hang them with if there was a last dollar to be made. People have been talking about it for a long time; Steinbeck talked about all of this in *The Grapes of Wrath* (1939) with the faceless banking system that evicted people from their homes.

KW: The 1930s often serves as a key historical reference point in your work— do you think that it's fair to say that the popular arts of the Depression era had a greater impact on your thinking and your aesthetics than, say, the popular arts of the 1960s?

PK: The 1930s, sure, but also the period before World War I, with *The Masses* and so on, before Woodrow Wilson cracked down on anti-war dissent. The work that we've published in *WW3* relates to any period in which there was a sense of great urgency, and a push for social change. And what strikes me is that during these periods change did happen, and the arts played a huge role in helping to move things forward. Knowing something about these periods helps to push back against the tide of cynicism and apathy. My guess is that we're about to enter another one of these time periods, which could result in great changes—but I'm afraid it will include a lot of bloodshed.

KW: Do you spend a lot of time thinking about who to vote for and so on? A lot of progressives fret about these issues—"can we support Bernie Sanders, even though he's running as a Democrat?" or "can we imagine voting for Hillary Clinton, even though she supported the Iraq war?" and so on.

PK: I voted for Obama happily in 2008 and I enjoyed a full week before the good feelings began to erode. I voted for Obama in 2012 to oppose Romney. Obama's been good on some issues but as bad as Bush on others. Having Obama as president has put some people to sleep, as it were—some of his supporters talk as if the only thing that matters is keeping the Republicans out of the White House, as if there aren't substantive policy issues at stake. But other progressives talk as if voting doesn't matter. Clearly it does or the GOP wouldn't go to such lengths to prevent people from voting. Public opinion, and voting, can indeed make a difference. Though the choice between the Democrats and the Republicans generally feels a lot like the choice between Coke and Pepsi, and they have a point. But I still vote.

KW: Are there particular magazines, say, or radio stations that you rely on for news and information?

PK: A cross-section of things. I do still read the *New York Times* every day, albeit with a great deal of skepticism. I subscribe to *The Week*, a magazine that does a roundup of various mainstream publications. I watch *The Daily Show* pretty regularly, and I like the writings of Chris Hedges on truthdig.com. And when I was working on *Ruins*, which took over three years, I spent a lot of time listening to the radio, *This American Life*, and to books on tape, but I also watched a ton of documentaries, most of them political. I probably saw three documentaries about the oil spill in New Orleans, for example. At this point I'm a professional documentary-watcher. [laughter] I'm much better now at reading the point of view of the filmmaker, even if it's supposed to be subtle. There are tons of great documentaries out there. I also listened to comedy.

KW: Who are some of your favorite comedians?

PK: George Carlin is at the top of the list. I would have voted for Carlin for president. Bill Hicks, Chris Rock, Doug Stanhope, Louie C.K., Louis Black, Key and Peele, John Oliver, and Stephen Colbert.

They're all politically inclined humanists and unusually good at calling out bullshit. It's all about pulling back the veil and seeing what's going on. Stand-up comedy is an ideal forum for doing that.

KW: Are there are moments when you attend leftwing events, such as the Left Forum, or street protests, and think to yourself, "oh, the left just does not have its act together."

PK: Well, I'm coming out of an art form that spent many decades on the margins, that was commonly regarded as having very little value. This goes back to attending meetings in Cleveland when I was growing up that would only have five people, and of course the topic was comics.

KW: So you've seen small groups of people change the world?

PK: I recognize that you cannot predict what's going to become important, and when there's going to be a shift, when something goes from being almost completely ignored to suddenly taking the center stage. *WW3* had that experience after 9/11. Before 9/11, our release parties would mainly attract contributors, and they were sometimes depressing affairs. After 9/11, 300 people showed up at the release party we held at the Theatre for the New City. We couldn't keep the issue in print. That was a particular moment in time, and some of that energy has inevitably faded.

It can be frustrating, to be sure. Sometimes I think to myself, "man, this long haul thing . . ." You really have to look into the distance. Some people live and die without ever knowing whether their work mattered. There is a sense in which you have absolutely no say in how the work you're doing will influence and change things. And sometimes you assume that your efforts are not connecting with other people and then you find out that something you've done has made a difference. I've certainly done panels at the Left Forum or elsewhere where five people show up and there are six people on the panel. That can be demoralizing. But I'm always hopeful for more. I've also had the experience where we thought no one would show up and lots and lots of people were in fact interested in hearing what we had to say. It's the same thing with teaching. You say these things and hope that it makes an impression on your audience. Sometimes it feels like I'm showing a dog a card trick—I get blank stares and when the class is over I leave feeling disheartened. But then, years, later, I'll hear from someone who was in the class and they'll tell me that the course made a difference in their lives.

TEACHING

KW: Let's talk about teaching for a moment. Was your first teaching experience at the School of Visual Arts (SVA)? Do you remember your first day as a teacher?

PK: Yes, and I was very nervous. And I had those dreams where I was naked in class, and completely unprepared. [laughter] I had that dream every semester or so for about a decade. And then it just stopped. But then the dream returned shortly before I taught at Harvard. Of course, a little bit of fear is a useful thing. Being invited to teach at Harvard gave me the opportunity to rethink my approach to the classroom.

KW: Should I assume that you are one of those teachers who over-prepares for class?

PK: I certainly have had classes where I had more material prepared than I had time to cover. Some of my SVA classes run for three hours, and the Harvard class runs for four hours, and this seems like way too much time. And yet I still find myself scrambling at the end of class to fit everything in. When I first started teaching I didn't have this problem—with my very first class I ran out of things to say after the first half-hour. I spoke very quickly [laughter]. After that I started showing films to fill up the time. Sometimes we'd watch a Hitchcock film, for example, which always gave us a lot to talk about. Some of my classes almost turned into film criticism classes. I had found Hitchcock to be so useful to me as a cartoonist that it seemed like a useful reference point to share with students.

KW: Is that something you've heard from other cartoonists, about Hitchcock? What is it about Hitchcock's work that stands out for you? Is it the camera angles, the way he uses the camera to build suspense . . . ?

PK: Storytelling is a lot of it. For example, *Strangers on a Train* (1951) opens with the feet of two characters walking toward each other, and bumping into each other, and then there's an image of two crisscrossing train tracks. There are many subtleties that I picked up from reading interviews with Hitchcock, especially the interviews that Truffaut published. One of the things I've emphasized with students is how critical their early influences are in terms of their creative development. It's like with chicks that come out of their shell and imprint themselves on the first creature they see. The same thing is true for an artist. Hitchcock died when I was in art school, and there was a retrospective of his films during that semester—two Hitchcock films each week for an entire summer, starting with his silent films. And I went to all of them. The timing was perfect, because I was at just the right age to learn from his work. His imagery made a big impression on me, especially on my black-and-white work. In one of his earliest films he has a shot where a police van is pulling away, and the van has two big circular windows that almost look like eyes. I used the same effect in one of my Kafka stories, and it helped me realize the contribution that what we might call "secondary imagery" can have on the comics page—a car that looks like a face, or a building that resembles a skull. The effect can be quite subtle, and readers won't necessarily be conscious of the resemblance, but it can help shape their experience as readers.

Charlie Chaplin also had a big influence on my work, especially *Modern Times* (1936). I consider that to be the greatest piece of art ever made, in all art forms. It has humor, politics, and great storytelling. It's a beautifully made film and it's got all that history in it. It's also extremely human. I try to combine these kinds of elements in my own work. In creating political comics it's really easy to come across as ham-fisted. It's really easy to be didactic. There are a handful of artists and cartoonists who make effective political art where they are straight up delivering a strong message. And that can work. But for me personally, I'm always looking for a way to create work that will sneak up on the reader and that can use irony and humor and that can make fun of the message it's conveying, so that it doesn't get so self-important that it's deadening.

KW: There are some issues of *World War 3*—not so much recently—where there's grim story after grim story, and then Kuper. [laughter] You're kind of the outlier. Did that ever feel awkward? Were there people around the magazine who thought that there should be more work like that, or less?

PK: I wanted to contribute that aspect to the magazine; as a reader, I find that if the material is too grim it's a turnoff. But it also has to do with my nature. I grew up with *Mad* magazine and I love the way *Mad* combines humor and politics. If there's commentary it's also done with irony. No one around the magazine ever told me that I was treating a topic too lightly. I always felt that the magazine needed to find the right balance, and I was always looking for people who could add humor to the magazine.

KW: It seems to me as if Coe and Tobocman have had a bigger influence on the younger contributors to *WW3* than anyone else.

PK: Perhaps in regard to not using humor. Actually, it is very hard to find humor in many of the dire things we address in *WW3*. For a while I was compartmentalizing. In my illustration work I was creating a lot of serious-minded political graphics, and of course I was thrilled to be getting work in the first place. And then I was making comics on the side, almost as a hobby because there was so little money in it. There weren't that many outlets for alternative comics when I was starting out.

HARVARD

KW: If somebody had said to you, when you were starting out, that at some point in the future you'd be teaching comics at Harvard, what would you have said in response? It would have seemed science fiction-like.
PK: Yeah, only in Pellucidar.

KW: How did that come about?
PK: When I first received the email inquiry I thought it was a joke. [laughter] And I had a somewhat similar response when I was invited to work on *Spy vs. Spy*. They both seemed very unlikely. The good news is that the Harvard invitation came at a point in my life where I could imagine taking a five-hour commute each way. At a different point I would have told them, "I'd love to do this, but I just can't afford the time."

KW: I assume that Harvard pays better than SVA or Parsons.
PK: Not crazily. It's not like there's Harvard and then there's everybody else. One of the reasons that Harvard has such a large endowment is because they don't spend a lot of money on visiting professors! [laughter]

At Harvard I've been teaching a course called "Graphic Novels." I get to interview the students before they take the class, because the course is capped at twelve students.

KW: Nice.
PK: Last time around I interviewed forty people for twelve positions. Half of the students are in the Visual and Environmental Studies program, and they're usually a shoe-in since that's the program that sponsors the class. Only rarely have I turned down a student from that program. The other students are from across Harvard, including several dissertation students in the English department. The overall quality of the students is extremely high. It helps remind me why I love teaching. I've taught at SVA for many years, and at Parsons, and I've even taught at FIT [Fashion Institute of Technology], where I offered a Masters'-level class in illustration. But just when I was getting burned out on

teaching, Harvard fortuitously came along. The person who hired me didn't know my work, but had heard about me from somebody else, someone I had never heard of. Basically there was building pressure from students to offer a graphic novel class, from various disciplines. I ask them to create a new comic every week. Not just sketches—a complete comic. There's very little drawing in class—the emphasis is on the quality of the ideas and the writing. Obviously I will give them suggestions about their artwork, but the emphasis is on the ideas and how they are expressed. The art is secondary. I use the Roz Chast meter—it's like, if I had Roz Chast as a student, would I look at her work and go, "oh, god, what's with the drawing?" [laughter] But her drawings are perfect in the context of her ideas. In fact, I use her as an example in class—it isn't a question of creating dazzling drawings, since that will stumble you up often as not.

KW: There's a reason you don't see people sitting around reading *Prince Valiant*.
PK: Or *Tarzan*.

KW: As marvelous as that work is, it's not what people go back to.
PK: Yeah. That work doesn't move me at all now. I'm much more interested in Winsor McCay and George Herriman.

KW: This makes me think of David Rees—tremendous writing combined with perfunctory visuals.
PK: So perfunctory he doesn't even draw them.

KW: He spends a little time deciding whether the clip art character is going to be facing to the left or to the right. [laughter] That's the aesthetic moment. And yet his was some of the most important work to come out of 9/11.
PK: Indeed. His work is so smart, and it's all about the writing. Another example I use in class is a comic by Jules Feiffer, who did a two-page piece where all of the panels were black. It's a couple that just had sex, and the focus is on their conversation and the pauses in the conversation. It's much more about the writing than anything else.

KW: There's a bit of a tension between your emphasis on good writing and your interest in wordless comics. You seem to enjoy writing, and you emphasize it in your teaching, and yet you've created quite a number of wordless comics.
PK: It's probably related to all of the traveling that I've done, and my desire to communicate with people through the language of art. There have been

times when I've had to use drawings to get things like food. Probably the main reason I'm drawn to this form is because I have an innate desire to communicate with people, to create a dialogue even though I'm not necessarily in the same room. In its purest state it's an art form that doesn't have to confront the problem of language. It all ripples back to cave art and these really fundamental symbols and connections that all humans can make. There was a time when I was collecting little figurines from all kinds of disparate places, from Indonesia to Greece to different countries in South America, and they all shared common characteristics. In some cases these basic symbols *became* language. In Chinese the word "tree" looks like a tree, for example. When I do wordless comics I'm tapping into some very bedrock ways of communicating ideas and experiences.

KW: Sure.

PK: Some visual symbols became clichés almost instantly. The prisoner on a box at Abu Ghraib became a universal symbol of torture in a matter of days. When I was working on *The System*, I was looking for as many visual shortcuts as I could find. At that point a cell phone represented a yuppie-type figure. Nowadays the image of a cell phone doesn't have the same value. Many symbols are culturally bounded, of course. The symbol of three dots as a symbol for waiting as we do with text messages probably doesn't mean much in many parts of the world. But there are symbols that cross all barriers. It's possible to rely too heavily on visual symbols, of course, to use them to the point where they have no punch and become tired clichés. You have to walk a fine line.

One thing that happens very quickly with political art is that it dates itself. The same thing happens with *New Yorker* cartoons. This touches on something that is much bigger. As we age, we confront the question of whether the values we hold will ripple across time, versus ideas and values that are of the moment. I find when I'm teaching that students don't necessarily value the same things that I do. At the same time, there are some fundamental beliefs and concerns that cut across the generational divide. To give an example, I'm still wedded to the idea of putting comics on paper. I'm never going to work in an all-digital framework. And for some students this means that I'm from another era. It strikes them as anachronistic. But there are certain fundamentals that remain unchanged—the basic need to communicate with other people, for example. One of the things that I stress to my students is the importance of finding a passion. In order to become an artist you have to figure out what matters to you. What do you care about? And this isn't something that matters less just because we live in a digital age.

Passport control in Oaxaca, from *Ruins*

KW: Passion as a kind of hidden asset.

PK: Absolutely. But a lot of the time, when I ask students "What's your passion?" I get a blank stare. I'll tell them, "If you're into horses—fine. If you're into sports—fine." It's not my bag, but if they care about sports then they can make comics about sports. And they might be interested in several different things, none of which are particularly interesting on their own but in combination can become interesting and original.

KW: I've been teaching at SVA for the past several years; what I've been struck by is the sheer number of students who are passionate about Japanese cartooning, as well as Japanese animation.

PK: Yes. That's something I definitely have difficulty with, and it's definitely tied to generational differences. For a long time I was able to keep up with pretty much everything that was coming out of the world of alternative comics. I knew who to keep an eye on and so on. Nowadays there is a flood of material that I haven't been able to keep up with. There's not only a ton of manga that I haven't read but also quite a bit of new work that's aimed at the young adult market, much of which doesn't speak to me at all. In some cases I'll see things which I don't relate to but which I'll recommend to my daughter. People like Raina Telgemeier, Hope Larson, Jillian Tamaki . . . their work doesn't necessarily resonate for me story-wise, but I can appreciate its appeal. Manga, overall, doesn't do much for me, and that's a big area of comics that I don't know much about. I enjoy the work of Osamu Tezuka, Keije Nakazawa's *Barefoot Gen*, Masashi Tanaka who did *Gon*, Yoshihiro Tatsumi, and of course Miyazaki's animation, but that's pretty much the extent of it for me. More students than not are coming into the classroom with a manga style, and it starts to become such a cliché. There are so many stylistic tics involved that it's almost like superhero comics in the heyday of Rob Liefeld and people like that. At a bare minimum students should go to the original source material, so in the case of superhero cartooning they should be looking at Kirby. In most cases students need to expand their repertoire.

COMICS OLD AND NEW

KW: If somebody asked us to summarize what's been happening in comics over the past ten or fifteen years, young adult comics are important, manga is important, but I'd also say that we're in a golden age of reprinting old comics.

PK: That's for sure.

KW: Work that twenty years ago would never have been reprinted is now being published in lavish, full-color volumes. I would assume that of these major trends that's the one that is most agreeable from your perspective.

PK: Yes.

KW: So when you actually go into a store and buy a comic you're often buying a reprint volume rather than something that's new.

PK: Not necessarily. One of the joys of teaching at SVA is having access to their wonderful library. My collecting is now down to nearly zero, and I'm a little embarrassed about that because I'm always trying to get people to buy my comics. [laughter] I prefer to trade books rather than buy them. My wife is a little like Gandalf standing at the bridge going, "you shall not pass" when I'm bringing new graphic novels home. Apartment living has space limits, which I passed a long time ago! If I'm going to buy something it's often a reprint of old material, especially early 1900's comic strips like *Little Nemo* and *Dream of the Rarebit Fiend*. That's true. The things I know that I want to keep in my collection are often generations old. There is a lot of great new work coming out, that I want to read, and I always have a stack of new graphic novels that I'm plowing through, but often they're borrowed from the SVA library. It's almost worth teaching at SVA just to have access to their library! I almost always discover something when I go there.

KW: What's impressed you recently?

PK: There are too many interesting things being done in comics to know even where to start!

Many of the artists that knock my socks off are coming out of Europe. Killoffer's work is mind-blowing, as is anything by Lorenzo Mattotti. Brecht Evens is doing unique work in the form. So is David B. and Joann Sfar. The Dutch artist Wasco, whose first collection of strips is published by Scratch Books, is doing some approaches to page design I have never seen before. I also love the work of by Olivier Schrauwen. There's a marvelous turn-of-the-century flavor to his work. It's confounding in wonderful ways, he approaches storytelling in ways I wouldn't think to do.I thought that the storytelling in Jillian and Mariko Tamaki's *This One Summer* was beautifully realized. Though it didn't speak to my experience, it was very engaging. Derf Backderf's *My Friend Dahmer* was a fantastic work of autobiography, *Climate Changed*, by Phillipe Squarzoni, is an important, powerful, work. Though his drawing didn't excite me at many points, it was was worth the price of admission. He's tackling a very difficult and complex subject, that very few people are addressing, and necessitated lots of explanations to develop the topic. That's very hard to pull off. A completely different take on environmental issues in a brilliant way, is Jesse Jacob's *Safari Honeymoon*. It's incredibly inventive end to end and a great way to address our relationship to the environment from a brand new surrealist angle. Naturally, I keep returning to work I've loved for a long time. I re-read *Maus* periodically, for example, and *Asterios Polyp*, Marjane Satrapi's *Persepolis* and Crumb's work continues to inspire me to no end. Of course, Sacco, Ware, Clowes, Tomine, Seth, Gary Panter, Charles Burns, Chester Brown. You know, "The usual gang of idiots" that have continued to produce really engaging work.

KW: Have you read Mazzucchelli's older work?
PK: At the time, certainly—*Batman Year One, Daredevil*—his storytelling is fantastic. I know that he's a little ashamed of that work and I wish I could wave a wand and tell him that it's really okay. There's a process of distancing yourself from your early work that I can relate to. What I really admire about his work is how much it holds onto the history of comics in lots of different ways—Milton Caniff is in there, for example. I also enjoy the work of the big names in alternative comics, such as Chris Ware. But his work almost makes my brain hurt. It's so complicated, in a wonderful way, such that I sometimes find myself overwhelmed by the material. I often end up focusing on a single page. *Lint* floored me.

I often find myself returning to the work of people of the comic strip greats like McCay, Cliff Sterrett, Herriman, and Lyonel Feininger, but I also read everything that my cohorts at *WW3* are doing like Seth Tobocman, Eric Drooker, Sabrina Jones, Sue Coe, and Kevin Pyle. When it comes to the kind of material that we publish in *World War 3*, I sometimes find that I appreciate it more as time goes by. We published a story by Peter Bagge in the first issue of *WW3* . . . the drawing was pretty atrocious.

KW: Sure.
PK: And the writing was so great that I found myself quoting the piece for years. This is what I emphasize to my students. The drawing in this instance is perfunctory. As a cartoonist, Bagge's in the middle of figuring things out. But the writing is exemplary. He developed his drawing over time.

KW: I assume that every few years *WW3* attracts a new group of young political cartoonists. You must have met, mentored, and evaluated just a stream of cartoonists over the years. It must be hard. You can't publish everyone's work. And rejection can really sting.

PK: What's really difficult is figuring these things out as a group. You might have encouraged a young cartoonist to submit something, and given them feedback on their work. Another member of the editorial group may never have met this person, and might simply respond by saying, "It's not very good." You have to contend with that. That's happened throughout the years.

Speaking for myself, I'm more willing to publish someone who's work is moving in an interesting direction, even if they're not yet quite there, than sending that person away and thereby ensuring that they'll never come back. I obviously admire Art Spiegelman, and Francois Mouly, and what they achieved with *Raw*. But they clearly sent a lot of people away.

KW: Were you ever in *Raw*?

PK: No. I was one of the people who was sent away. I showed Art a piece when I was in art school, and he was teaching at the School of Visual Arts. He absolutely hated it. It was exactly what he didn't like, is how he put it. [laughter] It was a Bernie Krigstein-influenced piece that I thought he'd be sure to love, especially since I'd read his coauthored article about Krigstein's story "Master Race." "Master Race" had always been one of my favorite comics and I loved seeing how Spiegelman, John Benson, and David Kasakove dissected it in their essay in *Squa Tront*. I thought Spiegelman would dig my homage. He didn't.

KW: And yet you forgave him.

PK: The piece wasn't that good! I was still in the process of forming things. But I continued to do my work. I wasn't one of those people who was bowled over by the criticisms. I talk about it in my class but it's not easy to convey—the importance of dealing with failure.

KW: Tenacity.

PK: Yes, soldiering on when faced with failure. The ability to confront failure, which happens all the time, not only in terms of formal rejections from other people but also in terms of something that you might be working on at the moment and your inabilities. I thought about failure every day when I was working on *Ruins*. There were times when I'd put down two strokes and one of them would seem wrong. It was very frustrating. It was a very difficult process. There were lots of times when I wondered, "Who's going to give a shit about this story, and what these characters are doing? Does this have value? Should I be working on this at a time when Rome is burning?" All of these questions kept coming up. "When it finally comes out will it just go thud or will it be of value? Can I afford to do this because a long graphic novel is so much work and the finances just don't work out at all." It's financial suicide to do a book like *Ruins*. "Am I going down rather than up?" All of these questions are plagues on most artists in one way or another. At the same time, every completed page is an occasion for celebration. Whoo-hoo!

Steve Heller was an art director I dealt with . . .

KW: Sure, legendary.

PK: He gave me the first job I had at the *New York Times*. But he was always a little scary to deal with. He had no compunction telling me that something was mediocre, or just plain bad. His highest praise was "It'll do." In those early days I always felt like working with him was a test. You have to be able to take criticism, and in the end I learned a lot from Heller.

KW: My student evaluations improved once I stopped trying to impress them or be their friend.

PK: Indeed. That's a whole process that you have to go through. I've gone from angry babysitter, to scolding parent, to "I don't give a shit, if you want to fail go right ahead," to something in the middle. It all depends on the individual. I might talk to somebody who's full of themselves very differently than I do to someone who might be trembling. I've had students cry in class.

KW: That's hard.

PK: Over a crit. And I'm thinking to myself, "I didn't say anything that harsh, and tears are streaming down your face." What I don't try to do is fill in when there's a distinct lack of enthusiasm on the part of a student. I try not to be the enthusiast for them. That's not my job. One of my rules: I will not spend more time talking about a piece of work than the artist spent on creating it.

KW: Part of your job as a teacher is helping students make connections. Pointing them toward specific artists, books, films, or what have you.

PK: Yes, precisely. Changes in technology have made a difference. One of the things I have at Harvard that I haven't had anywhere else is a teaching assistant. And so while I'm teaching the class, if I refer to an artist, boom, their work will be up on the big screen. If I mention Hitchcock, we'll watch the first few minutes of *Strangers on a Train*. If I talk about the letters between Vincent van Gogh and his brother Theo, we might see a clip from the movie. Or clips from German expressionist films, and of course we can also look at high resolution images by pretty much any artist I can think of.

HUMOR

KW: Humor is an important element in your work. You've done pieces for the Simpsons comics, for example.

PK: *Treehouse of Horror* has been a showcase for alternative cartoonists and I've done a couple of stories for that. I successfully pitched them a couple of other stories that were pretty off—one of them was nominated for an Eisner a few years ago—and I've somehow managed to put a little political content in these stories. The key for me is that I'm not deviating from my own thing.

KW: Do you feel the need to work on some smaller projects now that you've finished *Ruins*?

PK: I actually have another long story in mind that I'd like to work on.

KW: Are you shy about talking about it, in fear that you'll jinx it?

PK: Not particularly. I've never been shy about talking about my work. [laughter] It's funny. I had a conversation with somebody about this recently. My approach in terms of getting a project going is to talk about it—it helps me figure out what's going to work and what won't work. I end up cornering myself because I find that I have to make the thing happen now that the cat's out of the bag. If you don't tell anybody about your ideas, and they don't happen, then nobody's going to realize that something's missing. With *Ruins*, I told some people about it, and I watched as time went by and I hadn't put pen to paper. I heard a talk at the New York Public Library with Robert Crumb and the art critic Robert Hughes. Crumb is quite reticent about talking about future projects, and wouldn't talk about *Genesis*, for example, even though he was right in the middle of it. He said he didn't like to talk about projects he was working on, because he had a friend who had talked for years about writing the great American novel but never did it. I felt jinxed—what if I'm one of those people! [laughter] I started to realize that there was a chance that I wasn't going to get to it. Thankfully, I finally told yet another person about the book and that conversation helped spark a fire and I started to actually work on it.

The idea I'm playing with has to do with robots. It's a kind of Pinocchio story in which a scientist has figured out a way to turn robots into humans. But he's got an evil assistant who sees the potential for using the same technology to turn people into robots, and therefore achieve world domination. I originally pitched the idea to the Cartoon Network, but nothing came of it.

KW: Are you still thinking about this as an animation project?

PK: No. I'm thinking of it as a graphic novel. At one point I wondered if I should try to get someone else to draw it, which I've never done before. I visualize it as having lots of interesting robot details – someone like Dave Cooper would knock it out of the park. But I know if I do ever get to it, I'll do the entire thing myself, *wishing* Dave Cooper was drawing it!

KW: It sounds as if it builds on some of the stories reprinted in your book *Drawn to New York*.

PK: It would definitely have some of the themes I've worked with previously. Like "The Wall," a story I did back in 1990 where in an alternative universe Donald Trump and another real estate mogul, Harry Helmsley, build a wall separating the east side of Manhattan from the west side. Crazy idea—right? And these days, who remembers Donald Trump? I'm not a science fiction guy per se, but it can be a great vehicle for commenting on society while letting you draw a lot of cool junk. There's another layer to the story, in that there are annual software upgrades for the robots, who go to Times Square on New Years' Eve for the dropping of the ball, and when the ball drops they receive a system update. But some of the robots are for various reasons excluded from the reboot, and they constitute a kind of robot underclass that lives at the edges of the city. They're basically unhooked from the system and therefore they know a whole lot more about reality. Anyway, this may be the only place anyone will read about this idea and it will just go back in the drawer with a number of other things...

At this point I really feel that I need to be primarily addressing climate change in my work. Otherwise I'm missing out on something critical. If I can find a way to put that into the robot story then I can see doing it. If I can't, then I'm going to think, "oh, isn't this a clever, fun way to comment on society that's missing a huge element," since climate change trumps everything else. No *Trump* pun intended!

CLIMATE CHANGE

KW: How do you do comics about climate change? I mean, you can present the scientific argument, and that's been done . . .

PK: . . . and that's not going to cut it . . .

KW: It's a little boring. You can also create climate change-themed illustrations for newspaper and magazine articles. But how do you create a *story* about climate change?

PK: If I could tell you then that's the project I'd be working on. I do have a title for it—"How to Talk to Your Parents About Global Warming," which would be a kid's guide to talking to the people who are supposed to be fixing it. Most of the time these kinds of guides are designed to help parents talk to their kids. In this case it's the other way around, since it's the younger generation who are going to be dealing with this nightmare in the coming years. This could provide the basis for a short nonfiction comic. But I'll probably end up working on the semi-robot story and have it reflect how our society is in total denial of the urgent need to address climate change.

KW: There are people who worry that climate change is sucking the air out of environmental issues, such as habitat conservation and biodiversity.

PK: But those are part and parcel. We're in the midst of the "sixth extinction" and it's all one big ball. Inevitably some people are going to focus on certain issues. One of the big things we're going to have to figure out is how to make desalinization more affordable, since we're going to have more and more water problems. A lot of it comes down to various practical issues facing our species in the twenty-first century. Recycling is a modest band-aid, but it's a start. I'm not one of those people who says don't do the little things because they don't solve the problem.

KW: In the seventies and eighties you and Seth, and the folks around *WW3*, were thinking a lot about nuclear war . . .

PK: . . . absolutely . . .

KW: . . . and now climate change is at the forefront of your thinking. It's the cloud over daily life.

PK: "Warm war" has replaced the Cold War.

KW: Do other people around *WW3* feel as strongly as you do about climate change?

PK: Yes. We did one issue that we called "Unnatural Disasters," and the latest issue focuses on youth and climate change. The next issue that we're going to be working on will be focused on environmental issues. It's getting to the point where if every issue of *WW3* doesn't touch on climate change then we're missing something.

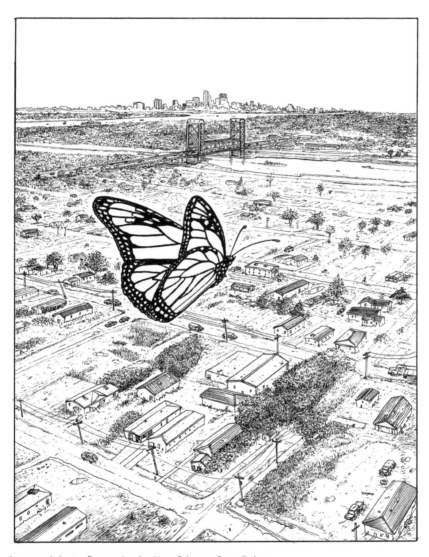

A monarch butterfly passing by New Orleans, from *Ruins*

My fears about nuclear war go back to when I was eight, and watched a movie called *Failsafe* (1964). That's been a drumbeat in the back of my head for my entire life. It's currently overshadowed by what's been happening environmentally. But the nuclear issue hasn't gone away. I'm less worried about an all-out nuclear exchange than by the possibility that a single individual or small group could use a nuclear weapon against a single city, quite possibly New York. I'm also concerned about the possibility of there being a nuclear accident. Some of these weapons are getting old, and there's the question of whether all of the right safeguards are in place. We don't even know. And if there's an accidental launch or detonation then every other nuclear power would go into high alert mode, and that could trigger all sorts of problems.

KW: Does the issue of climate change make you think about your parents? Both of your parents were ardent environmentalists, if I'm not mistaken.

PK: It's folded into it. I was definitely brought up by people who cared about the environment, and who talked about environmental issues at the dinner table. I also grew up at a time when a lot of things were happening in the country at large—in particular, there was the Vietnam War, and the hippie movement, which more or less turned into the environmental movement. I remember going to events in 1971 or 1972 where environmental groups would organize people to go into parks and pick up trash. My father was a college professor, and he certainly knew some of the activists on his campus, which was Case Western Reserve University. Also, we had the news on every night— we would eat together as a family, and watch Walter Cronkite. He was like the father figure of the nation. I was exposed to the horrors of Vietnam, the assassination of both Kennedys and Martin Luther King that was being shown on the nightly news, followed by, "pass the potatoes." All of this had an impact on my brain. In a way, *Mad* magazine helped me deal with the craziness. Humor is a safety valve. Not to get back to religion, but Jewish humor, the flavor I got from *Mad*, is ingrained somewhere in my DNA and the collision of terrible nightly news and dinner reinforced a gallows humor. I don't see humor as a strictly Jewish thing, of course, but certainly things like Harvey Kurtzman and *Mad* and Lenny Bruce and Woody Allen were all things that I revered, and they all made a point of saying . . .

KW: . . . anxiety can be funny.

PK: Exactly.

KW: Let's get back to this image of you watching the news with your family in the late sixties and early seventies. For people from our parents' generation, this period in American history arrives as a complete shock. "What the hell is happening to my country?" and all that. Whereas for kids it was normal—it's what we were used to. What I found hard to come to terms with was the state of things ten years later—1980, say. Student protests, civil rights marches, urban riots; all of things had disappeared. I kind of grew up assuming that the atmosphere that we associate with the late sixties and early seventies would last.

PK: We started *WW3* at that exact moment. Seth and I were both tremendously frustrated by the waves of apathy that we saw all around us. There was also the fact that we had both thought that we would become underground cartoonists. "Here I am," I thought. "I'm old enough to join the movement."

KW: "Put me to work."

PK: Right. And it was all gone, courtesy in part to the government clampdown on head shops in the mid-to-late seventies that destroyed an important part of the underground comix distribution.

KW: Presumably there were some self-inflicted wounds.

PK: And burnout. I certainly experienced some degree of burnout during the Bush years—two wars and economic devastation. And burnout can happen in any movement. You get to a point where any project you're working on needs fresh blood and fresh air. Sometimes things can implode, as a result of endless squabbling. And sometimes success can bring even bigger problems.

KW: Did your parents go too far, or at least your dad, when it came to blaming people in general for the environmental crisis?

PK: Absolutely.

KW: Is that something you argued about or did you consciously avoid the subject?

PK: We sometimes argued about political and environment crisis but he was so committed to the idea that overpopulation was the root cause of every other problem that it didn't seem worth it, especially given the limited amount of time we had once I moved from Cleveland to New York.

At one time he was a prominent figure in the Ohio Sierra Club, but he became increasingly active around zero population growth and the issue of limiting and reducing population numbers practically became the only thing he was interested in. It was instructive in terms of seeing how a strong commitment to a particular set of concerns could take someone off the rails. He ultimately embraced anti-immigrant positions, on the grounds that every person who came to the United States would start using up energy and resources much more intensively and at a level that is not sustainable. His interest in sustainability somehow led him to want to block all forms of immigration. I quickly realized that I was not going to change his views. We simply would have been at loggerheads all of the time. If we had argued about these things we would eventually have stopped speaking to each other altogether.

Our differences became even more sharply posed once I spent time in Mexico and got to meet lots of Mexicans. It reminded me what I already knew; how truly beneficial immigrant labor and culture, from Mexico and elsewhere, has been to our country. Any way you slice it, there's going to be way more immigration in the coming years—that's just the way it is. Millions of people are on the move all over the globe, in some cases courtesy of climate change, resource conflicts, civil war, and so on. Poor people aren't the driving force behind these powerful forces—they're usually the victims.

KW: Do you have a position on population numbers?

PK: It's absolutely the case that the direction we're headed in is unsustainable. It's like a match to the bomb. We're probably already past the point where we could even hope to achieve sustainability. But rather than closing borders we need to encourage education and human development. We need to provide family planning, and in general making things easier rather than harder for people. We could solve a lot of these problems if we simply cut military spending in half. The money is out there. In fact it was recently reported that the Pentagon can't account for 8.5 trillion dollars! The extent to which we lavish money on the military is a crime we rarely discuss. Certainly the media has failed to do much. It's an ungodly amount of money thrown into a hole and little of it ever reaches the common soldiers. They preach security, but this kind of waste is what is screwing our country and the world. It's outrageous that we don't have universal healthcare, and not the gamed version of it in which the insurance companies and pharmaceutical take most of the money. Obamacare is better than nothing but it has a lot of pork barrel built into it.

KW: How often do art directors or magazine editors ask you to create illustrations that address the theme of climate change? Does it come up a lot?

PK: The truth is that since the crash of 2008, and the decline of print-based magazines and newspapers, it's not as common as it once was for me to be approached by art directors and editors at all. But fifty percent of the problem is my doing, since it was my decision to move to Mexico for two years, and to then work on a long graphic novel rather than drumming up illustration jobs. It was my decision to move in that direction. I'm about to try to line up some illustration work, now that *Ruins* is finished. I love doing illustrations, but it's also the case that when I came back from Mexico I was in a stylistic limbo of sorts. I was ready to move beyond the stencil-based approach that I'd been working on for a long time, and I had spent a lot of time in Oaxaca with my sketchbook, using colored pencils. That's what interested me, but I don't want to put that style forward in my illustration work. I don't think that low-key, realistic sketches necessarily work as newspaper illustrations. Newspapers need bold graphics. The sketchbook approach works in the context of *Ruins*, but that's very different. And it can be awkward if you find yourself meeting with an art director, and you are faced with the choice between whether to show this person the work you're currently doing, which isn't a good fit with illustration assignments, or work that's ten years old. I'm still trying to figure out what foot I want to put forward. I might need to create some new images that I can show to these kinds of people.

WORLD WAR 3

KW: You're showing me *WW3* #45, which you edited with Scott Cunningham.
PK: Right. My hand has always been in *WW3* in one respect or another, but so far as actually editing issues goes I've sometimes been involved and sometimes not as involved. Editing the thirty-five-year anthology took a lot of time and energy, of course. Before #45 I was a coeditor on issue #39, which is a relatively big gap. Issue #39 was the "Wordless" issue, which I helped work on when I came back from Mexico. I wanted to create an issue that didn't need translation and that could be handed out to anyone.

Wordless comics have interested me for a long time. In 1990 my wife won a radio contest—the prize was two round-trip tickets to Poland. I was home when the call came, and had no idea that she had even entered the contest. And Poland wasn't on my bucket list. But I had said to Seth a few months earlier, "We are going to go to Europe." I just hadn't said *which* Europe. [laughter]

That turned out to be a really remarkable trip. Betty couldn't go, so Seth and I went. We ended up going to Warsaw, and Auschwitz, but Seth also arranged for us to visit Czechoslovakia. We were in Prague the week that Vaclav Havel became the Czech president. It was right after the Berlin Wall came down, and there was a sense of incredible vibrancy. But we also wanted to say, "Yo, you might not want to embrace capitalism quite so quickly; it's not necessarily what you think it is." All the people we met had nice apartments, and jobs that they didn't have to go to—everything seemed quite relaxed. And I thought,

"This is about to change." When I heard from these people a year or two later, they said they were drowning in tourism and dealing with all of the problems we associate with capitalism. I returned to Prague only two or three years ago, and it was such a dramatic shift. The city was almost unrecognizable. There were lots of neon signs, and Kafka dolls. Prague was a real pearl that had lost some of its shine.

When I returned from that trip I had the notion of putting together some kind of giant anthology of wordless comics that was international in focus. I thought it could reach lots of different kinds of people and start some kind of dialogue. I ended up going to Hungary a few months later, partly in order to promote this idea. Unfortunately it was very hard to get off the ground. I later saw that L'Association, the French publisher, had already created something along these lines, so I stopped pursuing the project. I had had these big ideas about having various publishers co-publish the book in different countries, so the price would be low in places where people couldn't otherwise afford it.

So WW3 #39, which we called "Wordless Worlds," was my tip of the hat to the idea. It fulfilled the idea, but on a smaller scale.

KW: Yet another example of why WW3 has been so valuable over the years.
PK: It's hugely important as a resource and as a home for a whole lot of disparate ideas and projects that might otherwise not find purchase anywhere. It's important to have alternative media for that very reason. At the same time, it's frustrating to reflect on how much work has gone into the magazine and how it is still only a modestly known publication. It's never been particularly embraced by fandom, shall we say. There are a lot of people who might be interested in it, but they might find themselves put off by the more strident aspects and most importantly they might not be able to find a copy.

KW: Is the magazine distributed through Diamond?
PK: Thanks to Top Shelf. Top Shelf has been our foot in that door, but they just recently decided to stop functioning as a distributor, so we're back on our own and will have to find a way to make that work.

KW: If I remember correctly, in the 1980s the same company that distributed *Maximum Rocknroll* was also distributing WW3, so that copies were available at Tower Records.
PK: Yes, Mordam Records distributed us for years. This was one of the things that happened early on with the magazine that proved something that we always believed—that there was an audience for political comics that we weren't

going to reach via specialty stores. Especially back then, most people who spent time in comics stores were superhero readers. Being distributed in music stores meant that we could reach people who were interested in all things "alternative"—including alternative music and alternative art. And it worked really well. We were able to reach a whole new audience, including people like Kevin Pyle, who came across the magazine at a Tower Records in Kansas. He would never have found the magazine otherwise.

KW: Is it fair to say that if you put ten copies of *WW3* in a regular comics store, and ten copies in, say, Tower Records, those copies would sell out quicker in a Tower store?

PK: Absolutely. They would sell better in any record store that sold alternative music. We also hand-delivered magazines to newsstands and other outlets in and around New York City. Again, the people who saw the magazine really ate it up. But getting the magazine distributed has always been difficult, and it remains the case.

KW: Have you ever thought about doing an alternative, radical superhero issue?

PK: No. [laughter] There have probably been individual stories that use superhero imagery, or referenced superheroes in some way, but nothing on a larger scale. It's too inside baseball. We're trying to appeal to people who may never have picked up a superhero comic. I don't want to reinforce the idea that comics equals superheroes.

KW: Has the Top Shelf connection helped significantly with your distribution problem?

PK: Not at all. It's still the case that most comic book stores are focused on superheroes and other kinds of adventure stories. Also, the distribution model used by Diamond means that stores can't return the comics they order. And this means that stores are very reluctant to order anything they can't be confident about. They want an X-Men comic that they can sell one hundred copies of. And so when comic book stores order *WW3* they'll order something like two or three copies. They don't want to risk losing any money. The economics are very difficult. The best place to sell *WW3* is at alternative comics festivals like the MoCCA Festival.

KW: I notice that recent issues are smaller, and come with a spine. I assume this helps with sales?

PK: Yes. It now has a "book" quality that keeps it on the shelf longer. The physical size of the book is smaller but the page count has gone up. The last few issues were 160 pages long. We usually put out an issue every year. Between finances and time that's the best we can do.

KW: I wanted to ask why you chose Bill Ayers to write the foreword to the recently published *WW3* anthology. He's a polarizing figure, even among progressives and leftists. And of course the Weather Underground played a terrible role in the context of the antiwar movement.

PK: I'm a pacifist, and what the Weather Underground did literally blew up in their faces. It's not something I would ever consider doing, or would have subscribed to. But you have to place it in context. Our government was throwing young people into a meat grinder, a war that killed 58,000 Americans, as well as hundreds of thousands or more of Vietnamese. It was horrific. The Vietnam War almost ripped the United States in half. Our country had a nervous breakdown over that stupid war. Yet the government was committed to sending more and more people over there. What's a rational response to an irrational war? You could be a conscientious objector, or leave the country, but neither of those options would actually do anything about stopping the war. People were going up against a giant war machine and trying to figure out a way to stop it. I don't agree with the tactics, but I understand the extreme reaction in the face of the threat of dying in a senseless war.

I'd read Ayer's memoir (*Fugitive Days: Memoirs of an Antiwar Activist*), and admire the work he's done since the sixties, especially in the area of education. I also enjoyed his graphic novel about education. We were on a panel together a few years ago, which is how the connection came about. And *World War 3* tends toward the itchy, so he was a good choice and I love what he wrote. I wanted somebody who would be radical and would provoke a reaction. [laughter] That's fine.

KW: How has *WW3* avoided the trap of endless internal schisms and debates? How have you been able to resist becoming yet another leftwing circular firing squad?

PK: The number one reason we've survived this long, in my opinion, is that we've never made any money. It has always been about commitment to the subjects we are addressing. This isn't a great business model, but it sure as hell removes one of the greatest divisive aspects that usually torpedoes organizations. We have had problems at different points. There have been times when people have become involved in the magazine and experienced personality differences and so on. Hell, Seth and I have somewhat different political approaches and since we've known each other since the age of six, some of our fights are ancient. That's not a question of right versus wrong—I happen to think that we're both right, and that's kept us on track since we actually share the same goal, which is to make the magazine continue.

KW: Are you more inclined to vote for Democrats than he is?
PK: He's probably not as quick to vote for a Democrat as I am. We likely both voted for Nader in 2000.

KW: I know people on Facebook who will never vote for a Democrat, not even Bernie Sanders, now that he's running for President as a Democrat.
PK: Right. I can't speak for Seth, of course, but I'll go out on a limb and say that I would guess that he voted for Obama, as did I. With great trepidation, of course. Seth created a comic at the end of the 2008 election, the moment Obama took office, in which he said, "Okay, now that you're elected what are you actually going to do?" You go into it knowing that you'll be disappointed. But there are sure a lot of lines where, while the Democrats might be disappointing, the Republicans are worse. The most important difference has to do with the Supreme Court. The Republicans appoint people like Scalia and Thomas, and the Democrats' appointments are consistently more liberal.

KW: Have you ever been at a *WW3* meeting and thought to yourself, "this is just a lot of ultra-left nonsense."
PK: I've certainly disagreed with some of the opinions that other people have expressed. That happened quite a bit when we were working on the 9/11 issue. There was some infighting about a piece by someone who actually cheered when the towers collapsed.

KW: Which is for me a classic example of an ultra-left position.
PK: Yeah. That was a piece by a younger cartoonist whose friends initially cheered but who then went down to lower Manhattan to help any way that they could. What happened was later they were harassed by fire department personnel who had seen or heard about the cheering. And this may have been the first response of one or two others around the magazine. It's good to have sharp arguments and disagreements—they can be helpful. And this was especially the case around 9/11, which pressed so many buttons. All of us around the magazine were of course repelled by the drum march to war after 9/11. President Bush didn't become more intelligent on the morning of 9/12. His

administration was horrible, both before 9/11 and after. The wars following 9/11 will ultimately be what has set us on a course to be a second-rate world power.

For what it's worth I don't believe that the official report on 9/11 is correct. I don't know exactly what happened, and I'm not a full-fledged 9/11 conspiracy theorist, but my general tendency is to follow the money. Who benefitted here? Well, Halliburton was given a bottomless budget for reconstruction "in the event of war" a few months before 9/11 took place, and Dick Cheney had been CEO of Halliburton. I look at how 9/11 was handled, how warning memos were ignored like "terrorists could use planes as bombs" and the fact that they cut the budget for counter-terrorism by ten million dollars on *September 10th*! I also look at Building 7 that fell down on the morning of 9/11, and I say, "hmmm." Remind me again what happened to a building that wasn't in fact touched by either airplane? That shouldn't have occurred. It is all pretty murky.

Ultimately I feel like regardless of 9/11, the Bush administration would have found a pretext for a war with Iraq. There was money to be made by going in there and the neocons have been bent on that for ages. Thanks to the Iraq war ISIS has gotten its footing and now we have the military industry's wet-dream—endless war.

KW: Presumably you've met people, on the left and elsewhere, who use conspiracy theories to explain everything that ever happens in the world.

PK: Sure, but no one on the magazine thinks that way. The point of *WW3* is that we give our contributors room to express their opinions. It's a leftwing magazine and that's the perspective that we're operating from. There are, after all, plenty of outlets for people who want a conservative perspective. As Stephen Colbert noted, "Reality has a leftwing bias." The opinions expressed in *WW3* have been pretty diverse. We've certainly published things I don't agree with. All of the editors recognize that it's ok to reevaluate and change your opinion from time-to-time, especially in light of new evidence. That's what intelligent people are supposed to do.

There were times when I felt a little cowed by the magazine's perspective. I've definitely represented a more "centrist" point of view than some people. And I've wanted to publish more humor in the magazine. I get tired of seeing images of fists in the air. There came a time in my life when I got tired of creating those kinds of overly strident images. Though there were certainly times when I would make images and comics just to prove that I was down with the cause. For example, the cover to my book *Speechless* features a screaming face. Over the years I've become a little tired of that type of imagery. I'm kind of

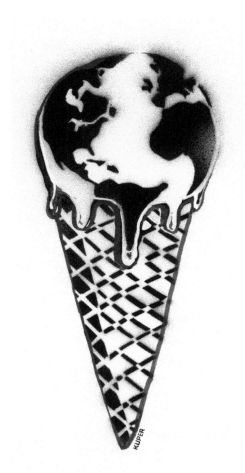

I Scream

sorry that I represented my career with this kind of screaming image, because it's a misrepresentation. It's an aspect of what I have to say, but I'd like to think that I have broader things to say.

KW: What type of image would you select now for the *Speechless* cover?
PK: Probably an image of New York City under water. [laughter] Or something that suggests more than one direction. I don't want to be on a soapbox all the time, playing the part of Mr. Didactic. That's not the way to reach people. Some people have an ability to make great political art that's also straightforward—Seth, Sue Coe, and a handful of others. I want to create work that sneaks up on people; that uses irony and humor to reach them.

KW: Do you tend to avoid re-reading your early work? Do you sometimes pull a book off the shelf and say, "Hmmm, I haven't read this one in a while."

PK: It tends to fall off the shelf, [laughter] although it's also the case that sometimes somebody will ask me to sign something that I haven't looked at in a while at a comic convention. A lot of the time I have trouble looking at old *and* new work. Some of this is because if you spend a lot of time working on something it's hard to really see it for what it is. It's like a musician who spends hours recording a song and by the end they can't even hear it. There always has to be a grace period where you have to let the work go. I haven't arrived at that point with *Ruins*. Sometimes when I look at it, I'm horrified. I see problems with the drawings, or mistakes with the storytelling, things like that. Yet there are other times when I've picked the book up and thought that it was pretty fluid. I want to be able to learn from my work—to be able to look at it more or less objectively to decide what works and what doesn't. But that's not easy to achieve, especially when it comes to assessing a book that runs for 328 pages.

SELF-PUBLISHING

KW: You've done a lot of self-publishing over the years, from teenage fanzines to *World War 3*, but also a couple of books as well. Eye Press is you, right?

PK: Yes.

KW: Do you enjoy self-publishing? Do you do it as a last resort?

PK: It's not so much the last resort. It often makes sense if I want something to come out quickly, without strings attached. The print runs are usually pretty small. One of the books I published was *Topsy Turvy*, a collection of political strips that had originally appeared in the *Daily News*. I wanted something that could be out in time for the 2000 presidential election. I didn't shop it around very much, but the first response I got was, "too of the moment." Though I knew this kind of book doesn't have a long shelf life after the political figures are history, I didn't care. I wanted to get the information, and the work, out there and it was time sensitive, so I printed it myself.

The *Self-Evident* book was a little different. It was a bit of a lark. I didn't think that I would be able to find a publisher a book of 100 different self-portraits for some reason. [laughter] There are always different reasons for doing these kinds of things. I've also done very limited edition artist's books in collaboration with people at Sundog Press at the University of North Dakota.

KW: What does "artist's book" mean in this context?
PK: Well, I've adapted Kafka short stories into the form of an accordion. Have you seen those?

KW: No. Damn, man, how many different kinds of things have you worked on?
PK: I've done about eight of these books. I've done roughly one a year for the past several years in collaboration with a wonderful guy named Kim Fink who teaches in the Department of Art and Design at the University of North Dakota.

KW: These are really limited editions.
PK: Like, twenty-five, tops. Hand made, silk screened, hand pressed.

KW: Does self-publishing work for you in terms of the finances? Is it viable for you in part because you spend so much time tabling at conventions?
PK: To some extent. Happily I've been able to recoup the print costs fairly quickly, usually with the help of convention sales. At some point I hope to do more with my website. It's also nice to have something new to swap comics with people whose work I like. My main concern is that I don't end up losing money; I'm not trying to make a lot of money with these books.

KW: I don't know the precise numbers to use, but let's say that a small publisher prints 1,000 copies of one of your books, and you print 300 copies and sell the book yourself. I assume you would make more money back from the 300 copies than the 1,000 copies.
PK: Absolutely. At the same time, I don't want to have to wear too many hats. But I'm that guy who's always dressed for winter, even on the hottest day. [laughter] Even with the bigger publishers you have to do a lot of the promotional work yourself. The amount of time and energy I've had to pour into promoting my work over the years is daunting and draining. But I generally like doing signings, giving talks, and sometimes even going to conventions, though at any given point I always feel like crying. There's a lot about promoting one's work that just feels like an ant pushing a boulder up a hill.

MOM AND DAD

KW: What did your parents most like about your work? I assume they were supportive in general about your decision to pursue a career as a cartoonist.

PK: Very supportive. The first time that they were genuinely excited about my career was when I was published in the *New York Times*. They were both big readers of the *Times*.

KW: Did they show it off to friends?
PK: Big time. I'm sure there was a little phone tree every time something of mine appeared on the op-ed page. And there was a long period of time when I was doing a lot of work for the *Times*. They also noticed whenever I did something for the *New Yorker, Time, Mother Jones*—places like that. They also liked my adaptation of *The Jungle*. That was my mother's favorite of my books. I thought about them a lot when we were working on what we called the "death" issue of *WW3*. We were all dealing with our parents' mortality. We were aging into doing stories about mortality—not the kind of mortality that comes as a result of bombs and guns but rather old age. That made for some really interesting storytelling.

KW: *The Jungle* was successful, but my impression is that *Metamorphosis* has been even more successful, in terms of sales.
PK: By a long shot.

KW: Is it your most commercially successful work, apart from *Spy vs. Spy*, which is a special case because it had a built-in audience?
PK: Yes. That book also had a built-in audience and has gotten into lots of school curriculums. Kafka's work really translates into comics beautifully. He's such a visual storyteller and *The Metamorphosis* is one of the great works of literature of the twentieth century. I'd started creating short adaptations of his work beginning in 1988, which led to the collection *Give It Up! And other Short Stories* (1995) before getting to *The Metamorphosis* (2003).

At that time hardly anyone had tried to adapt Kafka into comics. I found it very appealing to translate his work in that way. When I found out that Crumb was also working on adapting Kafka I was a little worried that people would think that I was just following in his footsteps, but I was already committed to the project by that point. If I had discovered that Crumb was working in this area before I'd put pen to paper I probably wouldn't have started.

Metamorphosis was the logical follow-up to the Kafka short stories. It's a very adaptable story and it's right up my alley. *The Trial* could be adapted but it wouldn't be the same—it lacks that fantasy element that I really love. *Metamorphosis* gave me the opportunity to create crazy imagery that a different story might not have offered. I'm also grateful that Terry Nantier from

NBM was very enthusiastic about publishing the book. But this was just at that point when mainstream publishers were starting to go, "Hey, we'd like to publish graphic novels." I showed some sample pages I'd done to a friend of mine at Crown just to get his opinion and, unbeknownst to me, he brought up the idea at an editor's meeting the next day. Next thing I know he asked if I wanted Crown to publish it. Unfortunately I had to go to NBM and asked them if they could match Crown's offer. Crown is part of Random House, and they have very good distribution. Between the question of pay and even more importantly, distribution, I had to go with Crown. When you are talking about doing that much work, I really wanted to make sure it would get a wider audience and Random House really has that. I was very tired of putting an enormous amount of work into something only to see it sell a few thousand copies. It took me six months of intense labor to make that book and a year to recover from the intense labor.

KW: What explains the success of your version of *Metamorphosis*?
PK: It's become popular with high school courses, public libraries, and college courses. Some teachers like to teach it alongside the original story, using it as a bridge for their students.

KW: Do you get emails from high school and college students?
PK: I do. There are nine editions of the book—Hebrew, Turkish, Czech, German, French, Spanish, Italian, Portuguese, and of course English.

KW: Is it the most widely translated of your works?
PK: By a long shot. But I'm riding on Kafka's coattails. And of course it's a great opportunity to introduce people to what comics can do. I feel honored that it was well responded to.

KW: Was there a point at which you could speak Hebrew?
PK: Oh yeah. I was fluent when I was ten, when I had lived in Israel for a year. My parents just dropped us into the local schools, which pretty much forced us to learn Hebrew. There was a nine-year gap between that experience and when I went back to work on a kibbutz. I was a banana picker. My Hebrew was almost completely gone. I had let it fall out of use. After two weeks it started coming back, and after two months I was fluent again. Now it's gone again. I've been back to Israel a couple of times since and I'm pretty confident that if I spent some time there I'd regain those skills again. The problem, however, is that almost everyone in Israel speaks very good English, and any Arabs you speak

to don't want to speak Hebrew—they'd rather speak English. Everything is so westernized there. I'd rather focus on keeping my Spanish, which is a language that I can throw around on a daily basis here in New York.

KW: Is Israel a western country? Isn't there a sense in which it's culturally part of the region even as tensions with its neighbors have persisted?
PK: To some extent. There are definitely aspects that are completely unlike anything you'd experience in North America or Western Europe. I'm hoping to go back—I'm working with some people about organizing a show in Tel Aviv, which I'm very excited about. Aside from stirring up these childhood memories, which are really positive, you are stepping through a time portal, especially when you visit Jerusalem. It's a remarkable place. There are ruins everywhere, dating back thousands of years. I had a similar experience when I spent time in Egypt. There are only a handful of places that have such a deep connection to the ancient world.

KW: Were your parents fiercely pro-Zionist?
PK: No. Not at all. They were atheists but they observed certain Jewish traditions, such as Passover. Sometimes we celebrated Hanukkah, sometimes Christmas, and sometimes both. My grandfather, on my father's side, liked to dress up as Santa, while my grandmother on my mother's side was devout and spoke with a heavy Yiddish accent. Cleveland has a large Jewish community, and of course so does New York, so there isn't the pressure to express yourself as a Jew because so much of what is around you is already Jewish. It's just part of the landscape.

When we lived in Mexico it was very different. One of our landlords was Jewish, and she gave us a list of all the Jews of Oaxaca. [laughter] I was like, "I don't want to be on this list—I could get rounded up!" But we ended up celebrating several of Jewish holidays when we were there—probably more than we would have had we stayed in New York.

KW: Does your daughter think of herself as Jewish?
PK: She thinks of herself as a New Yorker, and there's an overlay between being a New Yorker and cultural Judaism. I probably should have promoted religion more heavily so that she would then be able to reject it. One of my fears is that she'll embrace a different religion because there's a gap in her life. Weirdly enough both of my sisters are very Jewish—they put their kids through Jewish schools and organized Bar Mitzvahs and Bat Mitzvahs and all that. We didn't do that with our daughter. One of the joys of being an adult is getting to pick and choose, and not having to sit through long services!

KW: Do you find the issue of Israel personally uncomfortable?
PK: Oh hell yeah.

KW: Do you find yourself torn between people who are 100% pro-Israel, who accept no criticism of Israel, and people who would like to see Israel disappear?
PK: Like lots of people, I'm outraged about what's happened to the Palestinians, and outraged by the policies of the Netanyahu government.

KW: But there are plenty of folks who would take this a lot further, and say that you shouldn't even go to Israel.
PK: Right. Yes. I'm not in that group.

KW: The idea of boycotting Israel makes me uncomfortable.
PK: Likewise. You can boycott certain aspects, absolutely. If there's a corporation that's making money off of Palestinian suffering—by all means boycott that. But I don't lump it all together. People could just as well boycott the United States, given what it has done overseas. In all my travels, I never found anybody who was confused by the distinction between a particular government and individual people. And I really appreciated this, especially during the Bush years when I wanted to apologize all the time for what my country was doing in Iraq, Afghanistan, and elsewhere.

Of course, there's a chunk of society that supports right-wing policies, and that paves the way for the Netanyahu's and the George Bush's. There are definitely people who are part-and-parcel of all that. But I would not lump it together to the point where I'd say that any country should just wither and die. Israel definitely needs new policies. So does the United States.

KW: Do you think you'll be traveling more, now that your daughter is heading to college?
PK: I know I'll be traveling a lot over the next year or two because of *Ruins*. I'm going to Mexico four times, and to France for the Angoulême Festival. I'll also be spending a little time in Columbus, Ohio, and in the fall I'll be traveling to Harvard once a week. At some point I'll be going to Texas, and there are other trips that I'm planning. My wife is probably more tolerant of these upcoming trips just because I'm not placing any extra parenting chores on her shoulders, and I'm less likely to worry about missing some piece of my daughter's childhood.

I can't predict where I'll be invited next—the world of comics keeps expanding. But I'm more inclined than ever before to think hard before I accept each invitation, because of the enormous environmental cost of air travel. We are all confronting the contradictions of our lifestyles and our choices. It's a question of trying to find out where the right line is and what steps we can take to reduce our carbon footprint. We can modify the trouble that's coming. We're going to be reaping the "benefits" of climate change for the foreseeable future. It's going to define the rest of the century and well beyond. Whether we can, or have the will to, modify that impact through our actions is an open question. But we're past the tipping point where the costs of human-induced climate change can be avoided altogether.

PARENTING

KW: How have you managed to avoid putting too many anxieties on the shoulders of your daughter?

PK: There's a difference between being concerned and being freaked out. Part of what helps is that we were able to offer her a happy home. After all, I only have to walk a couple of blocks and I'm at my studio. I get to live in Manhattan, so just walking out the door makes me want to jump for joy. And creating comics gives me great satisfaction. My daughter gets to see her parents as two genuinely contented people who have managed to figure out how to stay together over a period of thirty years. I took her to the climate change march, and to the big protests against the Iraq war, but we shielded her from the news right in the weeks and months after 9/11. She was only five at the time. When she was younger we shielded her from movies that had too much violence in them. Sometimes when we're at the beach, and I see a cloud that I note reminds me of a mushroom cloud, she'll say, "Thanks for that, dad. Thanks for bumming me out." [laughter] We joke a lot. We're not glum. It's not exclusively Jewish, but Jewish humor has a lot in common with gallows humor. I'm always joking with her about very serious topics.

KW: Presumably you wouldn't have worked on *Theo and the Blue Note* (2006) if you hadn't been a father.

PK: Presumably.

KW: Were you disappointed with the book's overall sales?

PK: I was disappointed because I had other ideas for children's books. I was living in Mexico when it came out and wasn't able to promote it in the way that I would have liked. Every time I showed it to kids I got a great response.

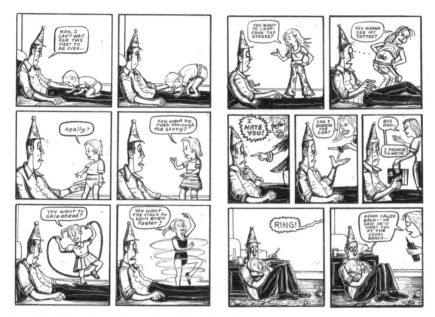

From *Stop Forgetting to Remember*, life on fast forward

As every author knows, you have no control over a book once it goes to the publisher. And you don't know how it will be received over the long term. It was recently published in Spanish, so it's still alive. I was recently reading about a book from the seventies called *Oreo* that was only just rediscovered—a lost classic. But when it first came out it went "thud." There's no telling how much work is out there that will also get rediscovered. It's an aspect of doing the work. All you have going for you is an audience of one, which is yourself. You have to love what you're doing. There is absolutely no guarantee that the work you are doing will reach out and touch anybody. But if you are pouring your heart and soul into it then the work can seep out into the world and make connections. You never can quite tell how things will turn out.

For example, I was invited a couple of years ago to Sydney, Australia, along with Jim Woodring and Scott McCloud, to perform one of my stories at the Sydney Opera House, with a live orchestra, and a large screen projecting my comics. Somebody at the Opera House had seen one of my wordless comics in *Heavy Metal* in the late 1980s, and never forgot about it. When he was in a position to make something happen, he did it. That's a perfect example of . . .

KW: . . . history's unexpected twists and turns.

PK: You have no control over that. And at the same time, something could hit really big that's actually quite mediocre. The thing that might attract the biggest notice is your weakest work.

KW: Pet rocks.

PK: Something that will appear in your obit. "Really? That?" [laughter] I run on what is appealing to me at a given time and what I feel is urgent. And then I hope that I can bring along an audience for the ride.

KW: Is there anything you can point to, apart from *Theo and the Blue Note*, and say that you did this because you were a dad?

PK: Gosh. In certain ways *Sticks and Stones* (2004) is that. It's an allegory that hopefully works for different audiences, age-wise. It was marketed as an adult graphic novel but perhaps it could have been marketed more as a children's book that could also appeal to grown-ups. I kept hearing from people that their kids were really eating it up. There's a Portuguese edition that's coming out in March next year.

KW: And you handle all of these foreign rights issues by yourself.

PK: Since I travel a lot, I try to use those trips to make connections with publishers in various parts of the world. If I'm in Brazil, I might meet a publisher and encourage them to get in touch with someone at Random House, say. I'm steadily doing whatever I can to bring different parties together. *The System* came out last year in Mexico. I'd already gotten back the rights from Vertigo and went to my Mexico publisher and made it happen.

KW: Was it hard to get the rights back from Vertigo?

PK: No, it wasn't. They were very kind about it. It went out of print, and that was that. I try to always make certain that when I sign a contract it includes a clause that says that I will get the rights once it goes out of print, so that the publisher doesn't just sit on it. *Sticks and Stones* just went out of print and I'm in the middle of reclaiming my rights.

KW: In a given week, what percentage of the time are you working on contracts, business deals, answering email, and the like, versus the time you get to make comics?

PK: Well, if I'm working on a project like *Ruins* then I'll be drawing most of the time I'm at my studio. When I was working on *Ruins* I would get into the studio around 9:30, work until the early evening, go home for dinner, and then come back to the studio for another few hours of work, finally getting to bed around midnight or even later. This was for a period of five or six months. Now I can barely pick up a pencil, and most of my time I'm promoting *Ruins* and things like that.

KW: How much work was involved in creating the watches that feature images from *Ruins*?

PK: Hardly any work at all. The watch company approached me, and I presented them with a handful of designs. They make them on-demand, I'm assuming. All I'll do is let people know that they're available. There are some people in the comics world who are particularly adept at using social media. I'm a few steps into it. You basically have to have an incredible ability to juggle the business end of things along with the creative things. At various points I've had an assistant to help me with things like dealing with the Post Office, working on InDesign, and periodically more artistic work—some have been former or current students.

I'm fortunate in that I don't mind working on promotion. I don't mind giving talks, signing books, tabling at conventions, and so on. I especially enjoy promoting things in Mexico. The press there is very enthusiastic and they don't feel as if they have to be aloof. If I'm dealing with someone at the *New York Times* they aren't going to tell me how much they enjoy my work. In Mexico they're bubbling with enthusiasm. They also have no compunctions about publishing multiple interviews with the same artist in mainstream newspapers and magazines that come out at the same time. I might do ten interviews back-to-back, and they'll come out in the same week, and no one seems to mind. You don't get that in the United States.

KW: Is it fair to say that Mexico has an unusually well-developed tradition of narrative art, through such things as murals, posters, and so on?

PK: There's something to that. In my case, the journalists and critics I met seemed to appreciate that I was willing to spend a lot of time in Mexico, and to write and draw about the country with a great deal of enthusiasm.

KW: Do you have strong feelings about Jessica Abel's *La Perdida*?

PK: Strong feelings? No. I have great respect for Jessica's work; I thought it was an engaging book. If I had a complaint it would be that since it was in black-and-white it missed out on something really essential, which are the colors of Mexico. This played up the more documentary quality in a good way, but made

Mexico seems like mostly a dangerous place, which misses a bigger picture. I knew I had to do a full-color work if I was going to create a graphic novel set in Mexico. I should add that I lived in Oaxaca, which is a small place. She lived in Mexico City, which has over twenty-two million people. It's a very different place. It's a mega-city. She was probably true to her experiences.

KW: I can't think of many other examples of U.S. cartoonists writing and drawing about their experiences in Mexico.
PK: Right. You could also point to *Love and Rockets*, which is about Latin culture on both sides of the border. They've been at that for a long time. I focused on a particular town at a particular moment in time.

KW: Is Oaxaca known for being an unusually political part of the country?
PK: Yes. It's a place known for very leftwing, activist politics. So, yes, it is.

KW: Did you move there because of the politics?
PK: No. We had already visited the area and were under the impression that it was an extremely quiet and pastoral place. It certainly didn't turn out that way! I would have had a much less interesting time if it had been as quiet as I had thought. When the political disturbance began most gringos fled the area. We were some of the only outsiders who stayed in Oaxaca. This meant that we had much greater contact with the locals than we would have otherwise. It's a popular tourist destination, and normally every restaurant is packed to the gills. This wasn't the case once the protests started. There were lots of times when we'd be the only people in a restaurant, and the owner would come over and hang out and talk. When we went back two years later these places were packed again, although sometimes people recognized us and gave us a table right away. If you live in a place like Oaxaca for two years you can get to know a lot of people. I couldn't walk down the street without running into people I knew. It was the opposite of being anonymous.

KW: "Closely-knit"?
PK: Closely-knit. It reminded me of why I'm not a small town person—gossip traveled very fast in Oaxaca. Whatever troubles anyone is having, everyone knows about it. There's not a lot of privacy, although there are people who lived in remote areas nearby who are pretty much living off the grid.

FREELANCE WORK

KW: Was there ever a point at which a magazine or newspaper used one of your illustrations to accompany a piece that you really didn't agree with?

PK: There were definitely times when I turned down freelance assignments because I didn't want my work to accompany a terrible piece that they were about to publish. When I first started doing work for the *Times* they were using my pieces in the Book Review section, which was really nice. Then I started getting offers from the Business section, and I didn't have as much of a rudder as I do now and I was of course excited to get work that paid real money. I started to do work for *Business Week* and all sorts of other business magazines.

KW: *Business Week* sometimes publishes good articles.
PK: Definitely.

KW: More often than those bastards at *Forbes*. [laughter]
PK: Right. And I even worked for *Forbes* a few times. I came up with a piece for *Forbes* that also ran in *WW3*, and was used as a banner in Italy as part of a protest against gentrification. A somewhat different question is whether to do illustrations for work that I have no opinion about, that I neither like nor hate. I used to take all kinds of assignments because I needed the money, even if I felt indifferent about the subject matter. But I got to the point where I couldn't compartmentalize things any more, and only wanted to work on things that I could really get behind.

I was asked a couple of times to provide illustrations for pieces by Charles Krauthammer. He's vociferously rightwing, but he was writing articles for *Time*, which I had been working for. In these cases I tried to come up with images that provided an opposing point of view. But he wrote a piece right after 9/11 that was about why we should go and bomb everybody. I had had a couple of drinks and told the art director that there was absolutely no angle that I could take that would make this work. So I passed on the assignment, and thought, "oh well, I just burned that bridge." When the piece came out it was accompanied by a photo of people waving flags. It seems that they couldn't find any cartoonist who was willing to illustrate Krauthammer's piece of shit. [laughter] I got a call from the same art director two weeks later and I ended up creating illustrations for pieces by Garrison Keillor, and various antiwar essays, and I got a lot more work. Sometimes that happens.

KW: Are you saying that you don't have to *fuck people over to survive*?

PK: That is correct! And, appropriately, the title of Seth's first book.

I would occasionally get panic attacks when I did work for people I didn't agree with. I had a job for a while of illustrating columns by William Safire, a right-leaning journalist, for the *New York Times Magazine*. When they offered me the job I told them right away that I didn't agree with Safire about anything, but the editors were remarkably enthusiastic about having me do it. Safire hated what I did and pressured them to fire me. Basically I would do a counter-point to almost everything he wrote. The editors took some kind of glee in it. At one point I wanted to take a trip somewhere, and told the editors that I needed to take a break. Their response was that I could only take a break when Safire takes a break. [laughter] The idea that I would tie my schedule to William Safire's was not going to happen. I said, "No, I'm going to take a break now." I was replaced right away of course.

KW: Safire's one of those people who mattered for a long time and now he's pretty much forgotten.

PK: "Nattering nabobs of negativism." He wrote lots of speeches for Spiro Agnew, but his legacy didn't last very long. After he died his publisher asked if I would allow them to include one of my illustrations in a book of his essays. I wrote back and said, "You know he hated my work, right?" I can't remember if they used the piece or if my response ended the conversation.

KW: Were your parents and Seth's parents friends?

PK: Oh yeah. Seth's mom helped out my mom when our family first moved to Cleveland in 1964. My sister and Seth's sister were the same age and were and still are close friends. Our families were totally interlocked. Seth's dad taught at Case Western Reserve and my dad also taught at Case Western. Seth's dad was fairly rightwing . . .

KW: Is he still alive?

PK: Just barely. When he was at Case Western he was working on wave technology that was being used on submarines. He was a very bright guy, very thoughtful, and Seth would argue his head off with him. [laughter] But they didn't stifle Seth's opinions. He was encouraged to be a thinker, and a reader. And he was that. Seth's parents even drove us to our very first comics convention, in 1970, when we were eleven. They were our chaperones, and they would drive us to places that we otherwise couldn't have gotten to. It was through Seth's dad that we got a printer for our first fanzine, and he printed it for free.

ART WORLD

KW: Are you interested in having more to do with the art world? Are you sorry that a major gallery doesn't represent your work?

PK: Galleries are as treacherous as anything. The image that always comes to mind is of an incredibly wealthy person who doesn't know anything about the work but who's interested in whether the piece will fit in the front hallway of their summer home. It's one of those situations where you have to always say the right thing—in the art world there's always a running line of bullshit that you have to be on top of. People like Jeff Koons and Damien Hirst are somehow able to convince incredibly wealthy people that their work is of value. It's for the bourgeoisie and all that. I'm more than happy to get paid for what I do, and if somebody genuinely likes my work and they have money I'm thrilled to sell them original work. You want to own a piece of my work and put it on your wall, great! You want to encase it in plastic and put it in a climate-controlled room, because you think it'll gain in value? Not great.

Galleries automatically take fifty per cent of the money—you have to therefore sell your work at a price that puts it into the stratosphere, rendering it unaffordable for precisely those people who are most likely to enjoy my work. And of course the fact that I do things like illustrations for magazines and newspapers makes it more difficult for my work to be accepted in the art world. And for years, comics were like the kiss of death in the gallery world. This has changed dramatically in the past couple of years but this is another reason why I'm irritated by the gallery scene. "Oh, now I'm ok. I see. Oh, right. Now we're full-fledged human beings. Thank you for that." That condescending attitude absolutely permeates the art world. The value of things is totally arbitrary. It's like a random finger that points to things and says, "This is valuable, but that's not." Things that I tend to value are very often undervalued by the art world. Once in a while the finger points at someone like Robert Crumb, and what they've done over the years suddenly gains in value. Fortunately he's alive to enjoy it. Jules Feiffer should get top dollar for the cartoons he does—he makes beautiful images and he's also important in terms of American history.

That said, I would be more than happy to have one foot in the art world, just as I straddle other worlds. And I'm going to have a show at the Scott Eder Gallery in Brooklyn, and I have a show coming up at a gallery in Milan. So I'm going to sometimes do these kinds of things. But I'm reticent about selling my work in places where I have to give the gallery half the money.

KW: Is there somebody whose work you collect yourself?

PK: Unfortunately, most of what I like is further and further out of reach, like Winsor McCay. I got a few things by him years ago. Also, Crumb. I got lucky. I met him when I was very young—twelve or thirteen —and traded him art for 78 rpm records that he was interested in. I met him through Harvey Pekar, and Seth and I got to interview Crumb for our zine. And I really enjoy trading work with other artists. Jules Feiffer gave me a drawing he did for my fiftieth birthday. Things like that, that come out of being in the field. I'd rather get a piece of work from the artist than from a gallery, that's for sure. I recently traded some *Spy vs. Spy* pages for a piece by Jim Woodring. He's definitely one of the miraculous cartoonists.

Interview with Robert Crumb

PETER KUPER AND SETH TOBOCMAN / 1971

From *G.A.S. Lite* 1.1. Copy of original interview pages follow.

[Handwritten note at the top of the interview by Harvey Pekar: "Bob—the kids I told you about wanted you to answer the questions on this list, which they gave me to send to you. They want to publish an interview article on you in their fanzine. They're serious science fiction-fantasy comic fans!"]

Peter Kuper & Seth Tobocman: How old are you?
Robert Crumb: 27—born August 30, 1943.

PK&ST: What was your first professional art job?
RC: Mmmm . . . I remember . . . My father got me a job with Latex Corporation where he worked. I did visual aids and safety posters for a dollar an hour. I worked there in the summers of '58 and '59 when I was 14 and 15. This was in Dover, Del.

PK&ST: Do you consider "underground" comix a highly profitable industry?
RC: I make a good living at it, but only recently has it started paying off, and that's only because I've got a dozen comics out on the stands . . . I'd say in general, no, it isn't a highly profitably industry . . .

PK&ST: What was the first underground comic book?
RC: The first underground comic books were done by Joel Beck in 1965 . . ."Lenny of Laredo" was one, I think, and "Marching Marvin" . . . No, wait . . . There was one earlier than that . . . Jack Jaxon's "God Nose" done in Texas in 1963 . . .

PK&ST: What would you say is the main difference between underground comics and regular comics.

RC: There are a lot of differences but the main one is that the cartoonists in the underground except no limits on their freedom of expression, whereas the straight cartoonists work within the limits set up by the businessmen who run the publishing companies. Also, our distribution is much smaller and underground comics are not really "periodicals" like the straight comics.

PK&ST: What kind of people do you think read underground comix.
RC: The kind of people who read underground comics are the same kind of people who go to hippie stores and your liberal-type bookstores . . . The same kind of people who smoke marijuana . . . Some hippies, some intellectuals . . . I dunno . . .

PK&ST: Some people would say underground comix contain too much sex and violence, what is your response to this?
RC: These people are correct.

PK&ST: Who is your favorite comic artist?
RC: Me.

PK&ST: Who is your favorite writer.
RC: Me.

PK&ST: What artists influenced you the most?
RC: I'd say the "influence" on me is collective . . . No one guy influenced me the most . . . There are some many . . . Thousands of 'em . . . I am just part of a stream of culture . . . you dig?

PK&ST: Of all the characters you have invented, who is your favorite?
RC: I guess my favorite is "Yeti, the Abominable Snow-Girl" . . . She's my dream-girl . . .

PK&ST: What are you working on now?
RC: A story for *Bijou Funnies* no. 6 . . .

PK&ST: Do you try to tell anything to your readers through your comics? If so, what?
RC: No, I don't "try" to tell my readers anything . . . It doesn't work that way . . . It's tricky . . . Y'hafta walk that razor's edge . . . Y'know what I mean?

"The Dance of Life" ~ circa 1972 by R. Crumb

G.A.S. Lite, volume two, number ten, edited by Kuper and Tobocman, with cover art by R. Crumb

PK&ST: Have you ever done any non-humorous comics?
RC: That's a matter of opinion . . . haha . . .

PK&ST: Why did you become an underground artist?
RC: Mainly because I got sick and tired of being a lackey for a bunch of domi-
neering ass-hole businessmen . . . I'd rather be a bum than take orders from
those shmucks anymore . . . The straight comics have gotten too restricted
. . . Who th'hell wants to work for DC or th'fuckin' newspaper syndicates . . .
They're all shits . . .

PK&ST: What are your hobbies.
RC: Drawing cartoons, fucking . . . listening to music, taking drugs, eating . . .

PK&ST: What were or are your goals in life?
RC: To draw as many comics as I possibly can without getting in a rut, and to
fuck a lot of women and girls, and to listen to a lot of good music, and take a
lot of drugs and eat a lot . . . Eventually I hope to die . . . But not right away . . .

PK&ST: Has your style changed since you started underground comix?
RC: Yes . . . It changed quite radically during the time I was taking a lot of LSD
. . . Through acid I became more immersed in the collective subconscious and
less attached to my own ego—which improved my drawing and gave it a richness it lacked before that . . . In fact, I think I'm about due for another trip . . .

PK&ST: Are there any hack underground artists?
RC: Oh . . . I dunno . . . It's hard to be a hack in th'underground . . . Not enough
money in it . . . You have to love it to want to do it 'cause you sure as hell ain't
gonna get rich off it . . . A coupla punks thought it looked like easy money an'
tried t'hack it, but they didn't last long . . .

PK&ST: What comics do you by regularly?
RC: None . . . I don't buy th'straight comics hardly ever, unless there's some
particularly good art by [Wally] Wood in one, or I dig on an exceptionally
twisted romance comic . . . And I get all th'underground comics for free . . .

PK&ST: What do you think of the comics of, say, 20 or 30 years ago compared
to today's?
RC: Well, in a lot of ways, us new guys could never touch what they did back
then . . . it was a whole different thing . . . A class difference . . . They were lower

class cartoonists mostly, and their work had a lot of muscle . . . The drawing styles were powerful . . . The EC came along sort of in between . . . Trying to make th'comics hi-class . . . Now, with th'underground comics, you have a range of styles that mostly tend to be more primitive in a sense, but also more cerebral or something, I dunno . . . I can't talk about it . . .

PK&ST: What do you think of the less humorous underground comics such as *Quagmire*, and *Moondog*.
RC: They're ok . . . I got nothin' against 'em . . .

PK&ST: Do you take pleasure in making underground comix?
RC: Ohh . . . Some of it is pleasurable, some of it ain't . . . I mean, anything you do has a certain amount of just plain hard work involved in it, y'know? Tedious, boring, aggravating hard work. Discipline, y'dig? But I'm always glad when it's done that I saw it through . . . Let's put it this way, it ain't easy . . . But I'd rather draw comics than work at Republic Steel . . .

PK&ST: There are those who say that, while a few years ago underground comix were full of innovative new Ideas, they now are simply rehashing the same old things they did before. How do you react to this?
RC: Oh yeah? Who are these people? Where do they live? Point them out to me . . . What do they want? Blood? A three-ring circus?

Sigh . . . Perhaps they are right . . . I worry about my comics becoming boring and repetitious sometimes . . . I think maybe I should quit while I'm ahead . . . But . . . I just can't seem to stop drawin' them comics . . . Oh well, hope they don't become boring . . .

PK&ST: Do you agree with the statement of Ted White (editor of *Fantastic Stories*) that the future of graphic art lies with the underground comics?
RC: Did he say that? Far-fuckin' out . . .

PK&ST: Do you think comics should always have a message?
RC: Oh absolutely . . . Not only that, but the message should always be "By the way, how's your mom, Ed?" or something similar . . .

PK&ST: What do you think of the Comics Code Authority?
RC: I think it's a fine thing . . . The comics code has done its part in helping cartoonists to liberate themselves from the strangle-hold of business-men by forcing us to go "underground" . . .

PK&ST: Could you give us a brief rundown of the history of underground comics?
RC: No . . .

PK&ST: Are underground comix distributed outside the U.S.?
RC: Yeh, some people in Europe are distributing them over there . . . Also some European cartoonists have started poppin' up who are pretty good, boy . . .

PK&ST: What do you think the future holds for comics, underground or otherwise?
RC: God only knows, and he ain't tellin!

PK&ST: Is there anything in particular you would like to say to finish of this interview?
RC: Well, in conclusion, I would just like to say that I don't think you guys oughta take comic books so seriously . . . I mean, after all, they're just comic-books . . . They're not meant to be taken so seriously . . . I mean, dig on 'em, look at 'em, swap 'em, trade 'em, collect 'em, but don't take 'em so GODDAMN SERIOUSLY . . . Comic and sci-fi fans of the world, get laid!!!

Bob — the kids I told you about wanted you to answer the questions on this list, which they gave me to send to you. They want to publish an interview article on you in their fanzine [...]

How old are you? 27- BORN AUGUST 30TH 1943

What was your first professional art job? HMMM..., I REMEMBER...
... MY FATHER GOT ME A JOB WITH LATEY CORPORATION WHERE HE WORKED. I DID VISUAL AIDS AND SAFETY POSTERS FOR A DOLLAR AN HOUR. I WORKED THERE IN THE SUMMERS OF '58 AND '59 WHEN I WAS 14 AND 15. THIS WAS IN DOVER, DEL.

Do you consider "Underground" comix a highly profitable industry?
I MAKE A GOOD LIVING AT IT, BUT ONLY RECENTLY HAS IT STARTED PAYING OFF, AND THAT'S ONLY BECAUSE I'VE GOT A DOZEN COMICS OUT ON THE STANDS... I'D SAY IN GENERAL, NO, IT ISNT A HIGHLY PROFITABLE INDUSTRY...

What was the first underground comicbook?
THE FIRST UNDERGROUND COMIC BOOKS WERE DONE BY JOEL BECK IN 1965... LENNY OF LAREDO" WAS ONE, I THINK, AND "MARCHING MARVIN"... NO, WAIT... THERE WAS ONE EARLIER THAN THAT... JACK JAXON'S "GOD NOSE" DONE IN TEXAS IN 1963...

What would you say is the main difference betwun between Underground comics and regular comics.
THERE ARE ALOT OF DIFFERENCES BUT THE MAIN ONE IS THAT THE CARTOONISTS IN THE UNDERGROUND EXCEPT NO LIMITS ON THEIR FREEDOM OF EXPRESSION, WHERE AS THE STRAIGHT CARTOONISTS WORK WITHIN THE LIMITS SET UP BY THE BUSINESS MEN WHO RUN THE PUBLISHING COMPANIES. ALSO, OUR DISTRIBUTION IS MUCH SMALLER AND UNDER-GROUND COMICS ARE NOT REALLY "PERIODICALS" LIKE THE STRAIGHT COMICS.

What kind of people do you think read underground comix.
THE KIND OF PEOPLE WHO READ UNDERGROUND COMICS ARE THE SAME KIND OF PEOPLE WHO GO TO HIPPIE STORES AND YOUR LIBERAL-TYPE BOOK STORES... THE SAME KIND OF PEOPLE WHO SMOKE MARIJUANA.., SOME HIPPIES, SOME INTELLECTUALS.., I DUNNO...

Some people would say that underground comix contain too much sex and violence, what is your response to this?
THESE PEOPLE ARE CORRECT.

Who is your favorite comic artist? ME.

Who is your favorite writer. ME.

What artists influenced you the most? I'D SAY THE "INFLUENCE" ON ME IS COLLECTIVE..., NO ONE GUY INFLUENCED ME THE MOST... THERE ARE SOME MANY..., THOUSANDS OF 'EM... I AM JUST PART OF A STREAM OF CULTURE... YOU DIG?

Of all the characters you have invented, who is your favorite?
I GUESS MY FAVORITE IS "YETI, THE ABOMINABLE SNOW-GIRL"... SHE'S MY DREAM-GIRL...

Robert Crumb's handwritten responses to Kuper and Tobocman's questions; reprinted with the permission of R. Crumb

What are you working on now?
A STORY FOR BIJOU FUNNIES NO. 6...

Do you try to tell anything to your readers
through your comics? If so, what? NO, I DONT "TRY" TO TELL
MY READERS ANYTHING... IT DOESNT WORK THAT WAY... IT'S TRICKY,...
Y' HAFTA WALK THAT RAZOR'S EDGE..., Y' KNOW WHAT I MEAN?

Have you ever done any non humorous writing comics?
THAT'S A MATTER OF OPINION... HA HA ,..

Why did you become an underground artist?
MAINLY BECAUSE I GOT SICK AND TIRED OF BEING A LACKEY FOR A BUNCH
OF DOMINEERING ASS-HOLE BUSINESSMEN .., I'D RATHER BE A BUM THAN TAKE
ORDERS FROM THOSE SHMUCKS ANYMORE..., THE STRAIGHT COMICS HAVE GOTTEN TOO
RESTRICTED... WHO TH' HELL WANTS TO WORK FOR DC OR TH' FUCKIN' NEWSPAPER
SYNDICATES... THEY'RE ALL SHITS...
What are your hobbies.
DRAWING CARTOONS, FUCKING,..., LISTENING TO MUSIC, TAKING
DRUGS, EATING...

What were or are your goals in life?
TO DRAW AS MANY COMICS AS I POSSIBLY CAN WITHOUT GETTING IN A
RUT, AND TO FUCK A LOT OF WOMEN AND GIRLS, AND TO LISTEN TO ALOT
OF GOOD MUSIC, AND TAKE A LOT OF DRUGS AND EAT ALOT,.. EVENTUALLY
I HOPE TO DIE... BUT NOT RIGHT AWAY...
Has your stile changed since you started underground comix?
YES... IT CHANGED QUITE RADICALLY DURING THE TIME I WAS TAKING ALOT
OF LSD... THROUGH ACID, I BECAME MORE IMMERSED IN THE COLLECTIVE SUB-
CONSCIOUS AND LESS ATTACHED TO MY OWN EGO, ———— WHICH IMPROVED MY
DRAWING AND GAVE IT A RICHNESS IT LACKED BEFORE THAT... IN FACT, I THINK
I'M ABOUT DUE FOR ANOTHER TRIP~~~
Are there any hack underground artists?
OH,.., I DUNNO... IT'S HARD TO BE A HACK IN TH' UNDERGROUND... NOT
ENOUGH MONEY IN IT... YOU HAVE TO LOVE IT TO WANT TO DO IT 'CAUSE YOU
SURE AS HELL AINT GONNA GET RICH OFF IT... A COUPLA PUNKS THOUGHT IT
LOOKED LIKE EASY MONEY AN' TRIED T' HACK IT, BUT THEY DIDNT LAST LONG,...
What comics do you by regularly?
NONE... I DONT BUY TH' STRAIGHT COMICS HARDLY EVER, UNLESS THERE'S
SOME PARTICULARLY GOOD ART BY WOOD IN ONE, OR I DIG ON AN EXCEPTIONALLY
TWISTED ROMANCE COMIC.... AND I GET ALL TH' UNDERGROUND COMICS FOR FREE...

What do you think of the comics of, say, 20 or 30
years ago compared to todays.
WELL, IN A LOT OF WAYS, US NEW GUYS COULD NEVER TOUCH WHAT THEY DID
BACK THEN... IT WAS A WHOLE DIFFERENT THING... A CLASS DIFFERENCE... THEY WERE
LOWER CLASS CARTOONISTS MOSTLY, AND THEIR WORK HAD ALOT OF MUSCLE... THE
DRAWING STYLES WERE POWERFUL... THEN EC CAME ALONG SORT OF IN BETWEEN...,
TRYING TO MAKE TH' COMICS HI-CLASS... NOW, WITH TH' UNDERGROUND COMICS, YOU
HAVE A RANGE OF STYLES THAT MOSTLY TEND TO BE MORE PRIMITIVE IN A SENSE,
BUT ALSO MORE CEREBRAL OR SOMETHING, I DUNNO ... I CANT TALK ABOUT
IT ...

What do you think of the less humorous underground
comics such as Quagmire, and Moondog.

THEY'RE O.K.... I GOT NOTHIN' AGAINST 'EM...

Do you take pleasure in making Underground Comix?

OHH...SOME OF IT IS PLEASURABLE, SOME OF IT AINT...I MEAN,
ANYTHING YOU DO HAS A CERTAIN AMOUNT OF JUST PLAIN HARD WORK
INVOLVED IN IT, Y'KNOW?   TEDIOUS, BORING, AGGRAVATING HARD WORK..
DISCIPLINE, Y'DIG?   BUT I'M ALWAYS GLAD WHEN IT'S DONE THAT
I SAW IT THROUGH.... LET'S PUT IT THIS WAY, IT AINT EASY.... BUT I'D
RATHER DRAW COMICS THAN WORK AT REPUBLIC STEEL...

There are those who say that, while a few years
ago underground comix were full of inovative new Ideas
, they ~~hxxxxlnst~~ now are simply rehashing the same old
things they did bifore. How do you react to this?

OH YEAH? WHO ARE THESE PEOPLE? WHERE DO THEY LIVE?
POINT THEM OUT TO ME.... WHAT DO THEY WANT? BLOOD? A THREE-
RING CIRCUS?

SIGH.... PERHAPS THEY ARE RIGHT...I WORRY ABOUT MY COMICS
BECOMING BORING AND REPETITIOUS SOMETHINGS... I THINK MAYBE I SHOULD
QUIT WHILE I'M AHEAD...BUT...I JUST CANT SEEM TO STOP DRAWIN' THEM
COMICS... OH WELL, HOPE THEY DONT BECOME BORING...

Do you agree with the statment of Ted White (editor of
Fantastic Stories) that the future of graphic art lies
with the underground comics?

DID HE SAY THAT? FAR-FUCKIN' OUT...

Do you think comics should ~~bx~~ always have a message?

OH ABSOLUTELY... NOT ONLY THAT, BUT THE MESSAGE SHOULD
ALWAYS BE " BY THE WAY, HOW'S YOUR MOM, ED?" OR SOMETHING
SIMILAR...

What do you think of the comics code athority?

I THINK IT'S A FINE THING... THE COMICS CODE HAS DONE IT'S PART
IN HELPING CARTOONISTS TO LIBERATE THEMSELVES FROM THE STRANGLE-HOLD OF
BUSINESS-MEN BY FORCING US TO GO "UNDERGROUND"...

Could you give us a brief rundown on the history
of underground comics?

NO....

Are Underground comix distributed outsid the U.S.?

YEH, SOME PEOPLE IN EUROPE ARE DISTRIBUTING THEM OVER THERE...
ALSO, SOME EUROPEAN UNDERGROUND CARTOONISTS HAVING STARTED POPPIN' UP WHO
ARE PRETTY GOOD, BOY...

What do you think the future holds for comics, underground
or otherwise?

GOD ONLY KNOWS, AND HE AINT TELLIN!....

Is there anything in particular you would like to
say to finish of this interveiw?

WELL, IN CONCLUSION, I WOULD JUST LIKE TO SAY THAT I
DONT THINK YOU GUYS OUGHTA TAKE COMIC BOOKS SO SERIOUSLY....
I MEAN, AFTER ALL, THEY'RE JUST COMIC-BOOKS... THEY'RE NOT MENT
TO BE TAKEN SO SERIOUSLY... I MEAN, DIG ON 'EM, LOOK AT 'EM,
SWAP 'EM, TRADE 'EM, COLLECT 'EM, BUT DONT TAKE 'EM SO
GODDAMN SERIOUSLY...
COMIC AND SCI-FI FANS OF THE WORLD,
GET LAID !!!

Vaughn Bodē Interview

PETER KUPER AND SETH TOBOCMAN / 1972

From *G.A.S. Lite* 2.10. Reprinted by permission.

Peter Kuper and Seth Tobocman: Could you give us a rundown on your career?

Vaughn Bodē: Well, I started out in commercial art after I got out of the Army. In 1958 and '59 I was in the Army. I was a technical illustrator in the Army and a military policeman. But I was AWOL most of the time. But then, of course, I was a highly trained specialist in knowing what to do, being a policeman. Then I started working in various commercial jobs and working in commercial illustration. And then worked myself to positions in Hollywood. I worked as an art director for a manufacturing company. And then eventually I started into working back here in the East and got into more technical illustration and, of course, I didn't like that. But then I went into college and then from college I started into the cartooning.

I had been using the cartooning media to express my schizophrenic involvement with reality. Which is really where it's all at for me. I never designed myself as a professional. My style comes from just a personal involvement with my work. And so you hear, for instance, that I can do this show. I can do this show because I was there. I was on all these planets, I did all these things, just like I was gone for years. That's why I can stand up there; I know what they talk like because that's the way I talked when I was there. So I went into illustrating science fiction covers and then I went out of illustration getting very fed up with it, and went into the underground. Working in the underground I finished college and just was generally interested in the underground, and then the *Cavalier* magazine had me come up out of the underground and work for them. They saw me in the *East Village Other* and they asked me if I would do some stuff for them and I said, "Yes I will, if I retain all the rights and if you don't bug me. Don't even ask to see the pencils." Which they don't.

PK&ST: Do they bug you about deadlines?

VB: Yes they do. I'm supposed to be working right now. On Monday I'm supposed to be turning in my latest set. But I told them I wouldn't be able to get finished until Friday. So I'm going back to work like a mad man in my studio up on a mountain in Woodstock.

So I just started and I continue working in the underground. Now the underground artists, a lot of them, are in San Francisco. My brother just came up and he says, "Listen, Vaughn, these guys think you're a hack." My contemporaries think I'm a hack because I'm coming out with no new material. I'm coming out with *Junkwaffel* but they misunderstood. *Junkwaffel* was sold as a collection of old work that I had done, in a series of books. Because nobody has ever really seen them. Like who saw [*Wash*] *Tubbs*? Nobody! Maybe a hundred and fifty people, or two hundred. And *The Man* for instance was not seen by anybody. It was only seen by a few colleges and things. So it was just my idea to get my work out as far as I could. But now I'm going to be going into performing and lecturing at universities.

PK&ST: Have you ever thought of making a motion picture?

VB: I have two motion pictures already outlined. They were negotiating with me before *Fritz the Cat* (1972).

PK&ST: Why didn't yours come out first?

VB: Well, Ralph Bakshi, who directed *Fritz the Cat*, was a friend of mine and he wanted to do my movie and then they decided that they'd do my movie second and I didn't want to sign up second. I just realized that if I signed my material over to them they might hold it forever.

PK&ST: We hear that Crumb was not too satisfied with *Fritz the Cat*.

VB: Furious! He said he'd give up the character. He'd even change his style.

PK&ST: Does it worry you that they might do something to your film?

VB: After *Fritz the Cat*, I'll just make sure that I have right of refusal on scenes and things like that. I've got an agent in New York, Henry Morrison, who's a really good agent. He's [Robert] Silverberg's agent and [Roger] Zelazny's and he's really going to be selling the movie.

PK&ST: What is the *Deadbone Platoon*?

VB: A United States Captain wrote to me during the high point of the [Vietnam] war and said that his platoon now call themselves the Deadbone Platoon.

And he sent pictures of the men standing around their helicopters, the pilots and the gunners. And he says, "We fly combat." And he says, "As a matter of fact, the North Vietnamese know about your series, too." Cause he said, "They tried to misdirect us by calling us in scramble. You know, by coming on saying 'Deadbone Platoon, your coordinates for your targets have changed.'" And they'd try to foul them up and they'd come on in English sometimes and say it. So this Captain and everybody else, they've got this thing called "The Bode Bible" in which they collect all the Bode work and everything else. The National Cartoonist Society said that they would send me over to meet the platoon if I wanted. But I'd have to go over with the National Cartoonists Society tour and I couldn't afford the time. It was a six-week tour.

They asked if I would sign something for them and I designed a patch. I don't know what happened. I think that they used it on the helicopter. They definitely used it on their helmets and they made it into patches for their tunics. It's the Hundred and First Air Mobile Squad.

PK&ST: How would you feel about people making patches and other such items to capitalize on your work like they have done to Crumb?
VB: I had an offer to have my work done in jigsaw puzzles. I turned that down because that's just crass commercialism. I want tasteful commercialism. My work is being translated next year into seven languages: Danish, Swedish, German, French, Italian, Spanish, and Japanese.

PK&ST: What about all the dialect stuff in your work?
VB: Well, this is going to be one of our translating problems, to make sure that the people who are translating it put it into their dialogue. For instance, "ball" here in this country means fuck and not over in Europe. It doesn't mean that. They have their own colloquialisms so what we're going to have to do is be very careful that they translate to their slang.

PK&ST: If you had an animated movie would you have someone else do the drawings for you?
VB: They better! I would do the storyboard and the major part of the script. And probably would do the voices of the characters myself. I don't think that I would get involved in the actual animation. I don't want to. Ralph Bakshi was courting me for a long time to do a series for him and to do movies so he showed me the *Fritz the Cat* thing that was being done. And told me all about the animation and things like that. And he would guarantee in my contract

that they would keep my style; they would keep motion and dialogue and everything else the way my characters are.

PK&ST: Do you think that comics should carry a message?
VB: Of course. That's why I'm not working for Stan Lee or DC.

PK&ST: What about Warren Publishing?
VB: Warren? Well, no, I won't say that because like [publisher James] Warren really wanted me very much to work for him knowing that everything I do I try to aim at some relevance because I consider myself a satirist. Originally I really considered myself a writer, but then I realized that writers are artists and we are all artists, so I stopped doing that kind of definition trip. And so let's say I'm a social satirist, a sexual satirist of late. And I'm always trying to deal with problems. When I'm working on "Sunpot," for instance, I'm working to bring it all together, the narration parts, to show very obviously that this thing was a personal system of satire, really. We are, each of us, the Sunpot system. It's like a somewhat fucked up system sometimes, sometimes a very effective, powerful system.

I've gotta say that the first job is to entertain. And it's always the first job; that's what I try to do. I'm not up there on a heavy trip to make people bored. So you try and entertain and you try to weave things in, if you can. If you're sensitive enough, it automatically happens. You weave things and opinions and feelings into various levels and depths. So that's really relevance. Relevance comes by the artist.

PK&ST: Why did you become an underground artist?
VB: Because I wanted my freedom.

PK&ST: Well, in the undergrounds, do they just say, "Do whatever you want and we'll take it?" Is there any editorial policy at all?
VB: The only editorial policy, for instance, from these companies are they have an editorial philosophy and you can do anything you damn well please on that particular thing. One company says, "Look, we like things on drugs." See, and anything about drugs is fine. But they wouldn't take *The Man*, because that's not part of their policy. But they'd take something that is like a real *Zap* comic. There is no editorial censorship. And with *Cavalier* magazine, the only reason I've stayed with them for four years is because they have only censored me like four times in all that time. They just don't like a few words. Like, they are worried about getting pulled off the stands by the Army.

PK&ST: How did you get into the underground comics?

VB: Well, as a matter of fact, when I go out to California in January, I'm taking out a number of artists' work. They have given me work and Last Gasp Comix was very interested in having me be the director for Last Gasp Pure in the East Coast. The whole thing of their distribution and generally getting together new comics groups out here. I'm not going to do that. But I'm going to introduce some artists to them. So it's simply, send the work in. It's very easy. And if they like the work or they dig what you like to say, then you've got yourself into comix.

PK&ST: Is there any character by someone else that you'd like to draw?

VB: Yes, sure! When it's a really fine piece of work.

PK&ST: For instance?

VB: Crumb's stuff. I really like so much of what he does. As a matter of fact, he's such a genius, you know. He does it in pencil. He draws directly the way he draws. He just draws. Him and Dave Sheridan. He's an underground cartoonist. I'd really like to be able to draw his way, his characters, of course to paint like Bob McGinnis. He's a cover painter. But as characters go, yeah, I guess it's those guys.

PK&ST: What do you think of comics from, say, twenty or thirty years ago compared to today's?

VB: Betty Boop, you mean?

PK&ST: Whatever you think of when you think of comics from those times.

VB: Well, I liked a lot of them very much. Of course, we're all caught up in nostalgia and I guess that's what I like about them. I was just looking at some of them downstairs [at the convention]. Some of them that I didn't even remember had a big influence on me. You know, Captain Atom? Boy, I really forgot about that until I saw it. And I realized, "Wow! That was one of the things that started me drawing machines!" It was their awful machines. I think a lot of it is lousy, but a lot of it is really fantastic. I like Captain Marvel about the best, really.

PK&ST: What are you working on now?

VB: I'm preparing my lecture tours and continuing to work for *Cavalier*. The Playboy organization is considering a series by me as a matter of fact. It's considering "Cheech Wizard" for one of their magazines, so I'm just kinda waiting for that, but that's what I'm doing. That's enough.

PK&ST: You speak of your work as satire but some of it seems a little too serious to be called satire, don't you think? Like "Machines," for instance?
VB: Oh, sure! That is satire. Very serious. Satire is simply, I supposed, just a personal exposure of an attitude or of a condition, like war. A lot of people called me very violent, for instance, for "Cobalt 60." I designed "Cobalt 60"; most of the characters had never been seen by anybody. I've got like a hundred characters.

PK&ST: What are your goals in life?
VB: Well, they're pretty heavy. Mostly, they're spiritual. And I'll be moving further and further and further from the work that I'm doing now. And my whole trip is a very, very heavy one. And that's where I've been for a while. Ever since I was like with this boy guru. Really far out!

PK&ST: In a lot of your work, you've had to write a lot of introductory material before you started the real story. Like that robot catalogue bit at the beginning of "Machines." Does it ever bother you to have to do that much?
VB: No. You see, I approach these things as realities, and I've got like, you wouldn't believe how much unpublished stuff. I've got something that I'm going to be coming out with next year. It's called "Kluger Putch," which has listed in it like a hundred and thirty-five moons. And that's never been published and that's for a character group that I haven't even worked with yet.

PK&ST: There's a group of artists consisting of [Jeffrey Catherine] Jones, [Michael William] Kaluta, [Bernie] Wrightson and a few others, where they've sort of influenced each other to the point where you could almost call them a school of art. Do you consider yourself part of that?
VB: Gee, that's hard to say. I guess so in certain ways. I don't know. I can't really answer that because we're developing so fast.

PK&ST: Have you had any formal training in your field?
VB: I have a Bachelor of Arts degree from Syracuse University. And I've had, of course, an awful lot of work.

PK&ST: What would your advice be to someone trying to get into undergrounds?

VB: Well, in the undergrounds like I guess if they really wanna say something, then they should go in that direction. But my advice would be to do it, and not to stop, and not to give themselves those kind of goals, limit themselves.

PK&ST: Is there anything you would like to say to finish off the interview?
VB: Keep on trucking!

G.A.S. *Lite* Presents a Bill Gaines Interview!

PETER KUPER AND SETH TOBOCMAN / 1972

From *G.A.S. Lite* 2.10. Reprinted by permission.

Peter Kuper and Seth Tobocman: How did you get the idea for *Mad*?
Bill Gaines: Well, we were publishing crime comics and war comics and horror comics and we wanted something funny. So, I knew that Harvey Kurtzman had done humor, so I asked him to come up with a new humor magazine, and it was *Mad*.

PK&ST: How did you become publisher of EC Comics?
BG: My father had started E.C. after he left D.C. and he was killed in an accident in 1947, and that's how I got into the comic book business.

PK&ST: How did you acquire so many good artists?
BG: Somebody like [Wally] Wood we got before he was famous. Woody developed with us and helped make us famous. [Frank] Frazetta came along a little later. But E.C. was the kind of place that artists like to work because they had artistic freedom to a large extent. So some of the best artists ended up coming to us. We didn't really go after them; they came after us.

PK&ST: What do you think of the [Comics] Code?
BG: Not very much.

PK&ST: There was a code set up previous to the present one. What did you think of that one?
BG: Well, that code wasn't so much a code as it was the opinion of this particular lawyer whose name was [Henry E.] Schultz, whether what we were doing was permissible or not. Generally it was much easier to work under that code than under the present code. However, *because* it was so easy to work under

that code, we got into a lot of trouble [laughs]. That's what led to the present code.

PK&ST: Why did you switch over entirely to *Mad*?
BG: Because after the code came along and we dropped all the horror and crime books and put out the New Direction books they all lost so much money that I had to stop them. And the only one that still was making money by then was *Mad*. The reason for that was because we had changed *Mad* from a comic to a 25-cent black-and-white, as it is now, and we didn't go through the code. So, we were fortunate in that one book was left, which was all we had.

PK&ST: Where did Alfred E. Newman come from?
BG: Harvey Kurtzman first used Alfred E. Newman on the *Mad* reader in 1954. It was a paperback; the first paperback book, Ballantine.

PK&ST: Is that out of print?
BG: Oh, no. It's still around, but it has a new cover. Alfred E. Newman had been around for about eighty years and he was on postcards and pictures and Harvey just got a postcard and liked it and started to use him.

PK&ST: Who brought this character up in the beginning?
BG: No one knows for sure. We've been trying for eighty years to find out exactly where it came from and nobody knows.

PK&ST: What do you think of the movie *Tales from the Crypt* (1972)?
BG: Well, I wasn't too happy with it. It could have been better.

PK&ST: Did it follow your stories closely?
BG: It followed some of them pretty closely—some of them not so closely.

PK&ST: Specifically . . . ?
BG: It followed "Poetic Justice" pretty closely.

PK&ST: Were there any new stories in the film?
BG: They were all old E.C. stories.

PK&ST: Why did you go over to DC?
BG: I didn't go over to DC I'm over there helping Carmine [Infantino] with the business end a little bit, that's all. I'm still at *Mad* mostly.

PK&ST: What do you think of the horror books of the '60s and '70s as compared to E.C.?

BG: Well of course, the color stuff goes through the code, so it's much tamer. The black-and-white stuff—the art generally is beautiful. I think the script sometimes is weak, but they got a lot of fine art in there.

PK&ST: Have you read any Warren books lately?

BG: Not for a long time.

PK&ST: How many years have you been publisher of E.C.?

BG: Twenty-six.

PK&ST: Who's your newest artist?

BG: Paul Peter Porges, who's an old-timer in the art trade. He started doing work for us in the last couple of years. He's about the newest artist we have. We rarely take on a new artist. Once in a while we'll run a job by an artist—maybe just one time. I can't think of anyone who's been a regular. Torres—Angelo Torres—who we took on when Mort Drucker couldn't handle two stories an issue.

PK&ST: He's been copying Mort Drucker?

BG: Well, we want him to.

PK&ST: Why was there such a change between old and new *Mad*?

BG: Well, of course, Harvey Kurtzman was the editor then and Al Feldstein was the editor since 1956, so the first four years are going to be different than the last sixteen.

PK&ST: Is it true that Eerie Publications is getting sued for taking something from an E.C.?

BG: There was somebody recently. We've sued somebody twice in the last three or four years in the black-and-white field and maybe that's the one you're talking about. I don't too clearly remember who it was, but probably that is who you mean. They recently stole a Wood story, I think, and we nailed them on that one and we got a few bucks out of it.

PK&ST: Has Wood been doing much for you lately?

BG: Only one Woody job in ten years, I think, and that was something on the Catholic Church.

PK&ST: Would you have wanted to stay with the science fiction books?

BG: Oh, we loved them. They weren't making money, but we enjoyed them. Moneywise, everything that happened turned out to be for the best. We made much more money with *Mad* at a quarter than we made with the whole line of comics at a dime. But if I had been given the choice at the time, not knowing that, I would have stuck with what I had.

PK&ST: Are you grateful then for the circumstances that brought you into this situation?

BG: Well, in a sense, yes. If a guy takes a baseball bat and tries to hit you over the head with it and instead of hitting you he misses and breaks open a piece of furniture that has a million dollars in it, and it's yours, you can be grateful that the guy tried to hit you. But it doesn't mean you're going to love him for it. He wasn't trying to do it. As such you can say that the Comic Code made me a rich man. You know, I'm not happy with them because of it.

PK&ST: At D.C. are you simply giving advice, or do you have a say in what's going on?

BG: Well, Carmine and I get along very well, and there are not any arguments. I'm only up there one day every week, and now and then I'm up there every *two* weeks. Today is the day to be there. Today's a holiday so I won't be there this week.

PK&ST: Have you ever thought of bringing back those old E.C.'s? Because you're making so much money on *Mad* you can really afford to.

BG: No, not in the format we edited it. You have to understand that all this stuff, much as you like it, doesn't necessarily mean that it's commercially feasible. Comic books today must be printed at no less than a quarter of a million, and to put it out as a comic book, it wouldn't sell. I don't think there's a quarter of a million people interested in the old E.C.'s. A few thousand; a quarter of a million is an awful lot of people.

PK&ST: At this convention, I, myself, just bought $13 worth of E.C.'s.

BG: Yeah, I know, but this is just pretzels. This whole convention, with all the people who came and went, there's only about 3,500 people. A quarter of a million! That's two hundred and fifty thousand —unbelievable numbers. It's hard to conceive what a quarter of a million is. You can *say* it, but you can't really conceive what a quarter of a million is.

PK&ST: Were there any science fiction writers particularly influenced by the E.C. SF stuff?
BG: You mean other writers?

PK&ST: Mostly from outside the comics field.
BG: Oh, yes! Particularly Ray Bradbury.

PK&ST: Can DC reprint E.C. material since both are under Kinney?
BG: Now, let's get this straight. Kinney owns *Mad*, but Kinney does not own the rights to any of the other E.C. books. I only sold *Mad*, so D.C. has no claim to anything in the old E.C. line.

PK&ST: Do you have anything planned in the future besides *Mad*?
BG: No.

PK&ST: Do you think that there will be any changes in *Mad* in the foreseeable future?
BG: Not that I know of.

PK&ST: Do you have anything to say to finish up the interview?
BG: Only that I'm very impressed with the way you guys interview.

. . . And on that unlikely note, our Bill Gaines interview comes to

the end.

Jack Kirby Interview

PETER KUPER AND SETH TOBOCMAN / 1972

From *G.A.S. Lite* 2.10. Reprinted by permission.

Peter Kuper and Seth Tobocman: Could you repeat for the readers the symbolism of the Hulk?
Jack Kirby: The Hulk—when he is the Hulk—is the epitome of ignorance and therefore unstoppable, because ignorance combined with power is unstoppable. He represents everything that is primitive and that's why he is the way he is, and is so hard to contend with. A cave man endowed with superhero powers is unstoppable and becomes overwhelming. When he is Dr. Banner he's entirely different. He is a disciplined man, well-educated and under control.

PK&ST: And without much power?
JK: Well, he's got power in his knowledge. That's symbolic of all of us, because when we're out of control we're all capable of doing as much damage as the Hulk.

PK&ST: Could you give us a brief rundown on your career in comics?
JK: I began probably with the kind of stuff that needed improvement and over the years it got improvement because I worked at it and, of course, today I still see avenues where my art can either be changed or improved.

PK&ST: What single character is your favorite?
JK: All of them, because when I work on a character, each character is important to me. I try to make them as dimensional as possible. It's not an ego trip; it's just my responsibility to see that I don't give the reader caricatures.

PK&ST: Where does most of the influence come from in your art . . . such as style?

JK: The style is your own to begin with if you have no formal schooling in art. You know, you swipe and you cannibalize and you take the best of a lot of the other artists and they become your school—they become your influence; but the style that develops is your own.

PK&ST: Was there anyone who influenced your writing?
JK: There wasn't a certain writer—just my experience of writers—all sorts of writers. I combined whatever I learned from them with my own sense of drama. Each person has his own sense of drama. It could be passionate drama or sometimes it could be very cool drama. I feel that extreme drama will make a larger impact on the reader.

PK&ST: What do you have planned for the future?
JK: Anything that's assigned to me by D.C.

PK&ST: Are there any new concepts that you will be bringing up, or new characters, such as . . .
JK: I'm not going to give you "such as" because I would be giving away my ideas. I can only say that I am entertaining a variety of ideas that I will submit to the proper people and see what they think of them.

PK&ST: What, if any, is the symbolism of Galactus and the Silver Surfer?
JK: Galactus is an overwhelming force; an energetic, overwhelming force that I believe we all have to contend with from time to time; a force we can't control. He represents a force as strong as a hurricane or a natural disaster of some kind, like a landslide or a cyclone. Those are forces that we can't predict or control. They just come and if we're in their path we can get hurt and if we're not in their path we can only watch them and just wonder at the bigness of them. Galactus represents that kind of thing. In the instance of the Fantastic Four, the Fantastic Four represented the challenged to Man to stand against those forces, like Galactus.

PK&ST: Do you have a favorite inker?
JK: No, they are all my favorites, because they represent a variety of styles that I like to see on my work.

PK&ST: Do you pick up most of the comics that come out on the stands?
JK: Not really. No. Being a pro, I receive comics from time to time. I haven't got time to go out and browse through the newsstands, so I collect what comics are sent to me and I keep those.

PK&ST: What do you think of Steve Ditko's Mr. A?
JK: I like anything Steve does. Steve is a very creative person and I respect him as an individual and I expect anything good from Steve.

PK&ST: Do you intend to have in "The Demon" any of the regular other D.C. characters like you had in the "New Gods"?
JK: Anything can happen in a comic strip and we can bring in any kind of a character if we think that it would make a commercially good story, so characters can come from any corner. They can come from the Gods, they can come from adventure characters, or certainly from traditional D.C. characters.

PK&ST: What exactly is Big Barda? Is there any symbolism behind it?
JK: Well, I think Big Barda represents a woman to me . . . all women. And, of course, I was raised among women like Big Barda, large women, warm women. And despite the bigness of their size, they're very feminine, and a man can regard them with respect, which I do.

PK&ST: It has been said that you like drawing buildings and rocks and huge cities and structures.
JK: It's not the main thing I enjoy doing, but it represents something I know very well, and that's the city.

PK&ST: Where did you pick up this technique of the super buildings?
JK: I'm basically a city boy and have lived in the city all my life, and certainly the first thing I know about is a building, because it's one of the first things I saw when I hit the street as a child. I'm quite sure that if you had to draw a building, you'd do it very well if you were a city boy.

PK&ST: What do you think of Neal Adams' artwork?
JK: I think Neal is a fine artist. He is an artist in an illustrative sense—a fine illustrator.

PK&ST: What do you think of Denny O'Neil's relevance in Green Lantern and Green Arrow?
JK: Gee, I think Denny O'Neil is a good writer and he can handle a subject well.

PK&ST: What do you have to say about the new young group of artists coming into comics now?

JK: New artists coming in or who really want to get in should be encouraged and given avenues of opportunity where they can make some headway in comics. I think what comics need is a variety of new writing styles, new drawing styles, new thinking styles, and anybody who wants to do comics I think should be able to do them.

PK&ST: How many pages do you do a day?
JK: I do three comfortably.

PK&ST: Alex Toth has said that the publishers are putting too many restrictions on the artists and writers. Do you think this is true?
JK: I wouldn't like to make a comment about organizational structure because I believe that this kind of thing should be thrashed out among the professionals themselves and certainly not discussed with the fans, so if there are any areas of conflict I believe it's between whoever is really involved professionally.

PK&ST: What do you think of the Comics Code?
JK: I think it is very flexible and very fair and certainly more reasonable these days.

PK&ST: Have you ever had trouble with it in your earlier days or now?
JK: I think everybody did, because when you first devise something in response to a reaction, it gets severe and then begins to lessen.

PK&ST: Could you repeat what you said yesterday about your Gods?
JK: To put it short, the Gods are giant reflections of ourselves. They are ourselves as we think we should be or we think we might be. They are idealistic and dramatic versions. They make a lot more noise than we do and therefore attract a lot more attention than we do. We feel that we've been fulfilled in some way if our own images act out the fantasies that we entertain.

PK&ST: Is it true that Jim Steranko and Mr. Miracle are one and the same?
JK: Let me say that some of Jim Steranko is in Mr. Miracle, but not all because Mr. Miracle has a mystic tie-up that has nothing to do with real people. Jim Steranko was a good escape artist before he became an artist. He is certainly a fine entertainer and what he says is true. I did discuss that I had an idea that was similar to what he had done and certainly Jim Steranko being part of my experience was a part of the idea.

PK&ST: How many years have you been in comics?
JK: Probably close to thirty-five.

PK&ST: What is the symbolism behind Orion?
JK: Orion is you. Orion is people who are not good, who are not evil, but have the potential for both and when they exercise both they get a reaction and have to take the risks for what they do or say. Orion does, too. He is tormented by his own potential for savagery, by his own potential for goodness.

PK&ST: Is there anything you would like to say to finish off this interview?
JK: I thank you guys for your interest. And if you represent a group or club, I thank them for their interest. I'd like to say hello to anyone who reads what we had to say here, and I hope their interest in comics keeps up. I'd like them to know that every professional who works in comics is only trying to do his best to entertain them and give them their twenty cents worth (or whatever a comic costs). That's all.

Thank You Jack!

ADDITIONAL RESOURCES

Ahrens, Lois, ed. *The Real Cost of Prisons Comix*. Oakland, CA: PM Press, 2008.

Beauchamp, Monte, ed. *Master Marks: Cartoonists Who Changed the World*. New York: Simon & Schuster, 2014.

Beronä, David. *Wordless Books: The Original Graphic Novels*. New York: Harry N. Abrams, 2008.

Brodner, Steve, ed. *Artists Against the War*. New York: Underwood Books, 2011.

Buhle, Paul. *Jews and American Comics: An Illustrated History of an American Art Form*. New York: New Press, 2008.

_____, ed. *Students for a Democratic Society*: A Graphic History. New York: Hill and Wang, 2008.

_____. "Toward the Understanding of the Visual Vernacular: Radicalism in Comics and Cartoons," *Rethinking Marxism* 18.3 (2006): 367–381.

Buhle, Paul, and David Berger, eds. *Bohemians: A Graphic History*. New York: Verso, 2014.

Buhle, Paul, and Nicole Schulman, eds. *Wobblies!: A Graphic History of the Industrial Workers of the World*. New York: Verso, 2005.

Folbre, Nancy, and Randy Albelda. *The War on the Poor: A Defense Manual*. New York: New Press, 1996.

Hatfield, Charles. *Alternative Comics: An Emerging Literature*. Jackson, MS: University Press of Mississippi, 2005.

Heller, Steven, and Michael Dooley, eds. *Education of a Comic Artist*. New York: Allworth Press, 2005.

Irving, Christopher, and Seth Kushner. *Leaping Tall Buildings: The Origins of American Comic Books*. New York: Powerhouse Books, 2012.

Jacobs, Karrie, and Steve Heller, eds. *Angry Graphics: Protest Posters of the Reagan/Bush Era*. Salt Lake City: Peregrine Smith Books, 1992.

Jones, Sabrina. *Isadora Duncan: A Graphic Biography*. New York: Hill and Wang, 2008.

Jones, Sabrina, and Marc Mauer. *Race to Incarcerate: A Graphic Retelling*. New York: New Press, 2013.

Katz, Harry, ed. *Cartoon America: Comic Art in the Library of Congress*. New York: Harry N. Abrams, 2006.

Lovell, Jarret. "This is Not a Comic Book: Jarret Lovell Interviews Graphic Artist Peter Kuper," *Crime, Media, Culture: An International Journal* 2.1 (April 2006): 75–83.

Patri, Giacomo. *White Collar: A Novel in Linocuts*. Mineola, NY: Dover Graphic Novels, 2016.

Pekar, Harvey, and Paul Buhle, eds. *The Beats: A Graphic History*. New York: Hill and Wang, 2010.

_____, eds. *Yiddishkeit: Jewish Vernacular and the New Land.* New York: Harry N. Abrams, 2011.

Pyle, Kevin. *Blindspot: A Graphic Novel.* New York: Henry Holt, 2007.

_____. *Katman.* New York: Henry Holt, 2009.

_____. *Lab U.S.A.: Illuminated Documents.* Oakland, CA: Autonomedia, 2001.

_____. *Take What You Can Carry.* Square Fish: New York: 2012.

Pyle, Kevin, and Scott Cunningham. *Bad For You: Exposing the War on Fun!* New York: Henry Holt, 2014.

Rall, Ted, ed. *Attitude: The New Subversive Political Cartoonists.* New York: NBM, 2002.

Stromberg, Fredrik. *Comic Art Propaganda: A Graphic History.* New York: St. Martin's, 2010.

Szutz, Szegedi. *My War.* Mineola, NY: Dover Graphic Novels, 2015.

Tobocman, Seth. *Disaster and Resistance: Comics and Landscapes for the Twenty-First Century.* Oakland, CA: AK Press, 2009.

_____. *War in the Neighborhood: A Graphic Novel.* New York: Autonomedia, 2000.

_____. *You Don't Have to Fuck People Over to Survive.* Oakland, CA: AK Press, 2009.

Worcester, Kent. "Journalistic Comics," in Frank Bramlett, Roy T. Cook, and Aaron Meskin, eds. *The Routledge Companion to Comics and Graphic Novels.* New York: Routledge, 2016.

_____. "New York City, 9/11 and Comics," *Radical History Review* 111 (Fall 2011): 139–154.

_____. "Waxing Politic With Seth Tobocman," *The Comics Journal* 233 (May 2001): 78–102.

Yoe, Craig, ed. *The Great Antiwar Cartoons.* Seattle: Fantagraphics, 2009.

INDEX

CPSIA information can be obtained
at www.ICGtesting.com
Printed in the USA
LVHW01s0406070918
589366LV00001B/60/P

9 781496 818454